China: The Bankable State

Bhabani Shankar Nayak
Editor

China: The Bankable State

 Springer

Editor
Bhabani Shankar Nayak
Business School for the Creative Industries
University for the Creative Arts
Epsom, UK

ISBN 978-981-16-5251-6   ISBN 978-981-16-5252-3   (eBook)
https://doi.org/10.1007/978-981-16-5252-3

This Springer imprint is published by the registered company Springer Nature Singapore Pte Ltd.
The registered company address is: 152 Beach Road, #21-01/04 Gateway East, Singapore 189721,
Singapore

This book is dedicated to the Chinese working classes.

Preface

The ugly head of racism is out in open air amidst the COVID-19 pandemic. The racism against Chinese people and propaganda against the achievements of the Chinese Revolution spreads like coronavirus. The anti-Chinese media coverage also replicates the history of anti-communist propaganda and campaign against the Soviet Union from the days of its inception to fall. The anti-Soviet propaganda continues to appear in the front pages of mainstream media even after three decades of its demise. The ruling and non-ruling capitalist class, their well-paid right wing and liberal think tanks and intellectuals continue to argue that *there is no alternative* to capitalist world order after the collapse of the Soviet Union. This means socialism is a utopia and it can never be an alternative to capitalism. The objectives of such ideological propaganda are to distort the truth and hide incredible revolutionary achievements of the Soviet Union. Many anti-Soviet books, articles, newspapers, editorials, posters, advertisements, magazines, films, stories and documentaries were produced to sustain the narratives that uphold the interests of the bourgeoisies. The communists, socialists and workers parties were depicted like demons strangling the capitalist gods and goddesses of individual prosperity, liberty, democracy and freedom. The socialist alternative to capitalism is portrayed as apocalyptic culture of death.

History is witness to the failed experiments and achievements of socialism in states spanning from the Soviet Union to ones in Asia, Africa and Latin America. Our living experiences of capitalism in the twenty-first century document the inhuman stories of death, destitution, inequalities, hunger, homelessness, environmental catastrophises and war. Capitalism destroys our planet and all human values of our society based on peace, prosperity and solidarity. Throughout world history, anti-communist and anti-socialist propaganda led by the capitalist system has served the forces of tyranny. Dictatorships, authoritarian regimes, fascism, Nazism, xenophobia, growth of terrorism and reactionary right-wing forces are products of capitalism. The capitalist system is not a friend of democracy, freedom, human rights and human emancipation from illness, poverty and inequalities. In spite of all its powers and propaganda, capitalism failed as a system.

Deaths and destitution due to pandemics are not new in human history. COVID-19 is not the first pandemic and is not going to be the last one. But for the first time, there are attempts to delegitimise the state and government of China in the eyes of its people when human beings in general and working-class people in particular are facing annihilating economic crisis again amidst the COVID-19 pandemic. The crisis is accelerated by racism and anti-Chinese propaganda. The specific objective is to defeat the achievements of Chinese people and their revolution that uplifted millions from hunger, homelessness, illness, illiteracy and unemployment. The general objective is to defeat all available experiences of alternatives to capitalism. The western capitalist media plays a major role in achieving these twin objectives. Therefore, capitalist media is spreading stereotypes on food habits of Chinese people and propagating a negative image of Chinese society, state and its government during this pandemic. The successful containment and reversal of COVID-19 is an achievement of the Chinese state and government. The capitalist states and governments in Europe and America have failed their citizens during this pandemic.

The incredible achievements of China show that the alternative to capitalist healthcare system is possible and inevitable. The Chinese medical aid to Italy, Spain and many other countries in the world shows that solidarity during a pandemic is only possible under non-capitalist healthcare systems. Therefore, it is imperative for working-class people all over the world to defend socialist experiences and achievements of Chinese people and stand against racial slurs against Chinese population outside China. It is not Chinese virus but COVID-19 which is a pandemic. It can only be defeated if we can reverse the business of illness spread by pharmaceutical corporations, private hospitals and health insurance companies under capitalism. The failure to learn the lessons of history from the anti-Soviet propaganda then and anti-Chinese propaganda now will be an unimaginable defeat of working-class people all over the world. The pandemic of capitalism will continue to produce death and destitution for its own profit. Human lives, animals and the environment are disposable under capitalism. It is time to debunk the capitalist myths and celebrate socialist achievements even during this pandemic.

The first chapter deals with the role of state in the rise and success of commercial banks in China. The second chapter argues that state plays a significant role in the risk management of Chinese commercial banks by regulating capital in the interests of people. The third chapter offers alternative strategies of credit risk management within regional and local context in China. Chapter 4 deals with strategies and transformations of the Chinese banking industry by looking at HSBC China Ltd. Chapter 5 is maps the financial development and economic growth in China. The sixth chapter analyses the Beijing praxis of establishing the relationship between financial development and national economic growth in China. The seventh chapter depicts the role of state in promoting science and technology in agriculture for poverty alleviation. The eighth chapter locates the growth strategies of the Chinese wine industry. Chapter 9, which is the final chapter, outlines challenges and perspectives on China as a bankable state for its people.

From agriculture and banking to wine production, the Chinese state is playing a significant role in the transformation of the Chinese economy and society. The people of China and the Chinese state have made enormous contribution in shaping alternative politics, economics and culture within all its limitations. It is important to make meaningful criticisms and contributions to sharpen and widen the available alternatives to empower people within and outside China.

Epsom, UK   Bhabani Shankar Nayak

About the Book

China: The Bankable State rejects neoliberal consensus and focuses on crucial contributions of the Chinese state in shaping Chinese economy. It makes crucial theoretical contributions to the study of local political economy of China. It engages with Chinese state responses to challenges China faces in the processes of reform, transition and development of both commercial and non-commercial banks. It explores Chinese economic growth and development policy processes and their uniqueness in the wider world economy. The book examines Chinese financial policy praxis and offers an insightful account of its successes for the wider resurgence of alternative political economy of local development.

Contents

About the Editor

Bhabani Shankar Nayak is a political economist working as Professor of Business Management and Director of MBA, University for the Creative Arts, UK. He has worked in the universities in Sussex, Glasgow, Manchester, York and Coventry the last eighteen years. His research interests consist of four closely interrelated and mutually guiding programmes: (i) political economy of sustainable development and gender and environment in South Asia; (ii) market, microfinance, religion and social business; (iii) faith, freedom, globalisation and governance; and (iv) Hindu religion and capitalism. The regional focus of his research is on the impacts of neoliberalism on social, cultural and economic transition of indigenous and rural communities in South Asia. He is the author of books like *Nationalising Crisis: The Political Economy of Public Policy in India*, *Hindu Fundamentalism and Spirit of Capitalism in India* and *Disenchanted India and Beyond: Musings on the Lockdown Alternatives*.

Contributors

Hao Chen Adam Smith Business School, University of Glasgow, Glasgow, UK

Yilin Gao Adam Smith Business School, University of Glasgow, Glasgow, UK

Huaihua Lai University of Glasgow, Glasgow, UK

Jiapeng Li Adam Smith Business School, University of Glasgow, Glasgow, UK

Bhabani Shankar Nayak Business School for the Creative Industries, University for the Creative Arts, Epsom, UK

Xinying Wang Coventry Business School, Coventry University, Coventry, UK

Jia Xu Anhui Rende Chuanghe Investment Management Co. Ltd, Anhui, China

Zhong Yingnan Adam Business School, University of Glasgow, Glasgow, UK

Chapter 1
Role of State in the Evolution and Success of Commercial Banks in China

Bhabani Shankar Nayak and Yilin Gao

Introduction

The chapter outlines the role of state in the evolution of commercial banks in China. It looks at different stages of its development process. The chapter engages with the deepening of state led financial reforms which led to the competitive advantage of China's commercial banking industry. The state-owned commercial banks, large joint-stock commercial banks, and small private commercial banks keep increasing their strengths due to regulations and monitoring by the Chinese state. Therefore, the chapter argues that state-owned commercial banks have relatively large market share and dominate in commercial banking sector due to the state.

There was a mono-bank system prior to the 1978 reform in China. From 1948 to 1978, China implemented a planned economic system with advanced tactics for production materials and products. In the period when material data flow was limited, banks were not yet been able to carry out independent economic business. They were merely completing tasks the state and government money processing agencies distributing. At this stage, the People's Bank of China controls the monetary funds in China as a whole (Berger et al., 2004). All financial businesses are also operated and managed by the People's Bank of China, and there are few contacts with international financial institutions such as the International Monetary Fund and the Asian Development Bank. The aim of banks, which were part of the administration was ensuring the national production plans to be fulfilled. As a result, banks had no incentive to improve themselves to win the competition when competing with others (Jin & Zhang, 2009).

B. S. Nayak (✉)
Business School for the Creative Industries, University for the Creative Arts, Epsom, UK
e-mail: Bhabani.nayak@uca.ac.uk

Y. Gao
Adam Smith Business School, University of Glasgow, Glasgow, UK

In December 1978, the People's Bank of China began to transform into the Central Bank of China, and gradually established a multi-level banking system such as a city commercial bank, a nationwide joint-stock bank, and a state-owned large-scale commercial bank, which were supervised and managed by the China Banking Regulatory Commission (CBRC, 2011). In October 1992, to further deepen reform and promote economic development, the state emphasised the gradual entry into the stage of the socialist market economy. At the end of 1993, the state promulgated relevant policies and regulations aimed at creating a unique professional commercial bank in China. Since then, China Development Bank, China Agricultural Development Bank and China Export-Import Bank have been established and listed. The establishment of the three major policy banks marks the formal separation of commercial banks from Chinese policies. Many joint-stock commercial banks immediately emerged including Hua Xia Bank, Pudong Bank, and Everbright Bank in China, when China carried out the transformation of the internal operating mechanisms of the four major state-owned commercial banks. The emergence of this batch of banks brought a new competitive landscape to commercial banks at that time, namely eliminating monopoly and promoting competition.

Following China's accession to the WTO in 2001, the financial industry faced the coexistence of opportunities and challenges in joining WTO development. In February 2002, the highest-level financial conference was convened. The meeting proposed to accelerate the comprehensive reform of state-owned commercial banks including abolishing the credit ceiling for deposits and loans, handling non-performing loans of state-owned commercial banks, and recapitalising state-owned commercial banks (Gao and Li, 2011). Banks are also encouraged to seek the listing on stock exchanges, introduce management incentives, and introduce foreign strategic investors. In addition, the meeting indicated that it is necessary to activate the National Commercial Bank, and under the premise of adequate supervision, appropriately reduce the control over commercial banks and encourage and assist competent commercial banks in reforming the modern enterprise system (Tong, 2005).

Since 2005, the China Banking Regulatory Commission has begun to convert state-owned banks to joint-stock companies by introducing overseas strategic investors and listing on stock exchanges. During the of recapitalisation, banks have achieved diversified ownership and are now operating as profitable commercial banks with less government intervention. Specifically, the market share of the five largest state-owned banks fell in the last decade, while the market share of other types of commercial banks like CCB, which have less state intervention and may have better corporate governance than state-owned banks, increased steadily (Ferry, 2009). By the end of December 2006, China has removed all geographical and customer restrictions on foreign banks according to the terms of the accession agreement. Foreign banks are no longer treated differently when competing with domestic banks, and there were 42 locally licensed foreign banks allowed to engage in local and foreign currency businesses with all types of customers at the end of 2013. By attracting foreign capital, foreign banks intensify competition in China's banking industry and introduce advanced management techniques and expertise to promote the efficiency of Chinese banks (Luo et al., 2015).

The state-owned large-scale commercial banks are the pillar of China's economy. They have become real commercial banks in response to banking reforms, and have gradually become modern enterprises. The services of these banks are mainly provided for large-scale business units, which are significantly affected by the national policies. Joint-stock commercial banks, which play increasingly important roles in the market-oriented reform of China's commercial banks and in deepening the improvement of the financial system are mainly to assist the development of the entire commercial bank. The business of them is primarily to provide financial services for Sino-foreign joint ventures, private enterprises, individual smallholder economy. Moreover, domestic joint-stock commercial banks are also indispensable, which have a proper governance structure; also, the scale of joint-stock business is between large state-owned commercial banks and other commercial banks. Their customer orientation is mainly medium-sized enterprises, which can be penetrated by both sides, and there is an expansion capacity for future development (Yuan, 2014). As a representative of a different commercial bank, China City Commercial Bank as an integral part of China's commercial bank was developed based on a cooperative city bank, and mainly supplements the development of the entire commercial bank. Guo and Liu highlighted that city commercial banks obeying the basic principles of commercial banks mainly serve private enterprises and promote the rapid development of local economies.

The sustainable development of city commercial banks therefore plays a vital role in supporting the reform of the financial system, the simplicity and convenience of SME loans, and the resolution of a regional financial crisis. Besides city commercial banks, joint-stock banks, and domestic large-scale commercial banks, there also exists other financial institutions including rural credit cooperatives, rural commercial banks, policy banks, foreign banks and so on (Wu, 2017). Other financial institutions have improved China's financial organisational system and played an increasingly important role in advancing China's economic transformation, technological transformation, optimising industrial structure, and increasing the added value of the industrial chain.

Lineages of State-Owned Commercial Banks in China

Following the establishment of the People's Bank of China from the financial sector in 1978, three state-owned professional banks, the Agricultural Bank of China, the Bank of China, and the Construction Bank of China, were separated from the Ministry of Finance and People's Bank of China in 1979 (Chen & Zhen, 2011). Following the start of the urban reform, the People's Bank of China gradually withdrew from the market for commercial currency transactions and established a bank specialised in dealing with commercial currency transactions - the Industrial and Commercial Bank of China (Shang, 2000). The establishment of the Industrial and Commercial Bank of China has dramatically promoted the flow of social currency funds after the reform. Aiming at alleviating financial burdens and facilitating a rapid change of the stock market, the state once again divested the bad assets of the four major state-owned banks which are sold through market bidding to asset management companies. The introduction of overseas strategic investors has become a strategic choice for the reform of state-owned commercial stocks due to longer-term considerations. This not only changed management mechanism of state-owned commercial banks but enhanced their competitiveness (Lei, 2014).

After joining the WTO, the Chinese banking industry has also been fully open to foreign investment. At the end of 2003, the government proposed that the state encouraged and supported competent commercial banks to carry out recent enterprise reforms and create conditions for listing as soon as possible while improving the business level. At the same time, the CBRC introduced five principles for the introduction of foreign investors (Liu, 2014). However, for CCB, BOC, and ICBC, the work involved in entering foreign capital is exceptionally challenging when considering price, risk and low transparency of these banks.

In 2005, CCB successfully introduced two investors from Bank of America and Temasek Holdings Co., Ltd. In the same year, BOC introduced RBS, Temasek, UBS and Asian Development Bank as investors. In 2006, ICBC received foreign exchange capital injections from American Express and Germany Allianz; in the following year, the Bank of Communications became a member of the state-owned banks and formed the current "five major state-owned commercial banks" (Li, 2013). The completion of the financial restructuring, the introduction of overseas strategic investors, and the establishment of joint-stock limited companies, to some extent, solved the institutional problems which restricted the development of banks. To further adapt to the needs of China's domestic market economy, promote the reform of modern enterprises, and supervise the holding of shareholders of enterprises, it is necessary to reform the shares further and introduce non-state-owned capital (Ferry, 2009). The listing of state-owned commercial banks is the best way to achieve this goal. Bank of Communications among five state-owned commercial banks raising more than two billion dollars through the IPO in Hong Kong in 2005 is the first bank listed in stock exchange while CCB, BOC and ICBC issued their IPOs respectively in 2005 and 2006. With the listing of ABC in 2010 in Shanghai and Hong Kong Stock Exchanges, all the state-owned commercial banks finished their IPOs (Tan, 2014).

Competitiveness of State-Owned Commercial Banks in China

Although China's state-owned commercial banks are commercially viable, they are still severely constrained when compared with commercial banks in foreign countries, mainly due to historical reasons and policy interventions. State-owned commercial banks are still supervised by the government whose financial flows are mostly distributed according to geographical and sectoral formulas, and they have little control over the cost base.

The state-owned commercial banks which still play the role of "financial supervisors" of state-owned enterprises and the large state-owned industrial sector are inextricably linked to maintaining the stability of national output, especially employment (Xu et al., 2013). Therefore, the Chinese government is always ready to rescue any failed state-owned commercial banks by capital injection and taking over bad assets. Based on this evidence, Chinese state-owned commercial banks are unique among the commercial bank industry. However, state-owned commercial banks have a relatively large market share and are therefore the dominance in the development of commercial banks (Fu, 2007).

There are several significant competitive advantages of China's state-owned commercial banks: firstly, they have relatively large assets; then their management fees are lower than those of foreign banks because of government control; thirdly, Chinese state-owned commercial banks have many branches based on substantially fixed customer base (Wang, 2010). Although the five major state-owned commercial banks are listed, the government still holds the major shares of these banks. As a consequence, Chinese people generally think that state-owned commercial banks are the most reliable (Qian, 2016).

Recently, China's state-owned commercial banks have been working harder to improve their competitiveness with the emergence of other stock-joint commercial banks and foreign banks by paying more attention to intermediary business than to traditional companies. The state-owned commercial banks are facing more and more customer groups whose basic needs are getting higher and higher. Kong found that the traditional product types and management models of state-owned commercial banks can no longer meet the needs of the general customers which require state-owned commercial banks to carry out reforms and innovations. Due to the small number of intermediate businesses of state-owned commercial banks in China, there is still a significant gap compared with foreign advanced state-owned commercial banks. At present, there are more than 3000 intermediary services issued by the World Bank, and there are only about 300 kinds of intermediary business in China. According to the survey, the proportion of the intermediary business income of major state-owned commercial banks in the developed western economies led by the United States is around 50%.

In contrast, the proportion of the non-interest income of state-owned commercial banks in China is relatively small although it has been dramatically improved. To be specific, by the end of 2016, Bank of China had the highest non-interest income share of 36.72% while Agricultural Bank of China only accounted for 21.33% of non-interest income which was lowest among five state-owned commercial banks. Among them, the proportion of the non-interest income of the Bank of Communications has improved the fastest from 18.47% to 30.17%. However, the operating revenues of the five state-owned commercial banks in the past 5 years are still dominated by interest income, and the proportion of non-interest income to operating revenue is not high comparing with foreign commercial banks.

It is necessary to change the unfavorable situation such as a single profit model and narrow investment channels as soon as possible before the interest rate market are fully opened.

In comparison with foreign banks, China's state-owned commercial banks still have insufficient competitiveness (Yang, 2009). Although the financial indicators of Chinese state-owned commercial banks have gradually approached to international level and been improved more than before, financial indicators do not adequately reflect the current state of competition. In contrast, some survival factors like competition strategy, marketing ability and customer demand which are rarely involved in ranking do determine the long-term competitiveness of commercial banks. For example, service quality problems including poor service attitude, lack of business expansion capacity and inefficient working process do exist in China's state-owned commercial bank causing them less competitive than foreign commercial banks.

According to the result of "Research report of Chinese and foreign commercial banks competitiveness in Beijing" which based on five indicators: external environment, operation condition, business development capacity, product innovation and organizational management, the indicators of all foreign banks rank higher than China's commercial banks. This result surmises that the competitiveness of China's state-owned commercial banks is not as optimistic as one might think. China's state-owned commercial banks do have some problems with service quality and inefficient workflow processes. Although the customer base of China's state-owned commercial banks is relatively stable, if financial innovation and service quality are not improved, existing and potential customers might be transferred to foreign banks. Additionally, the financial products of state-owned commercial banks have not established a right brand image, and the brand image of them remains in the memory of history. For example, when people talk about China Construction Bank, they first think that their financial products are related to construction investment.

Although joint-stock banks and foreign-funded banks are thought to be more efficient than the state-owned banks in some aspect, state-owned commercial banks still dominate the market under the protection of the Chinese government and gain monopoly profits (Huang et al., 2014). Moreover, Yao et al. (2008) found that the efficiency of the state-owned banks is not necessarily lower than that of joint-stock banks. There is substantial evidence that Bank of China is one of the best performing commercial banks in China. Besides, the Bank of China and Industrial and Commercial Bank of China as the representatives of state-owned commercial banks have dominated the market with high-tech efficiency and profitability (Hao, 2006).

Conclusion

The market structure of China's commercial banking industry is monopolistic competitive market structure. According to the basic principles of western economic theories, monopolistic enterprises should have monopolistic profits. Specifically, companies that are in a monopolistic position will generate higher earnings than those competing in the general competitive structure of the entire market (Andrijauskas et al., 2014).

However, the market power of state-owned banks, which occupies a large market share and institutional network advantage, does not have the benefit of the monopoly, even worse its performance is generally worse than that of general joint-stock commercial banks. The reason why state-owned commercial banks have market monopoly power without monopoly performance is that China has come from the planned economy to the market economy reform. Before 1993, China's state-owned commercial banks operated not according to the laws of the market economy but governed the construction of social funds under the leadership of governments at all levels. This resulted in a considerable amount of non-quantity assets that affected the competitiveness of state-owned commercial banks (Qian, 2016).

After the financial restructuring and shareholding system reform, the major state-owned banks have undergone vast changes in corporate governance and business philosophy. A qualitative leap has taken place in the areas of capital strength, risk management, and profitable business structure. The gap with the top ten international banks is gradually narrowing, and some indicators have even surpassed. The major state-owned banks have primarily withstood the test of the financial crisis in the past 2 years, their international influence has been significantly enhanced, and their international status and global competitiveness have increased rapidly.

Qualitative trends in the improvement of the overall competitiveness of the state-owned banks in China can be obtained based on existing theories. However, it cannot quantitatively reflect the specific competitiveness of them. Hence, a further quantitative empirical analysis is needed to explore the detailed changes in the overall level of competitiveness.

References

Andrijauskas, R., Jasienė, M., & Staroselskaja, J. (2014). Increasing the competitiveness of commercial banks on the basis of innovation. *Management Theory and Studies for Rural Business and Infrastructure Development, 36*(4), 730–745.

Berger, A., Demirguc-Kunt, A., Haubrich, J., & Levine, R. (2004). Introduction: Bank concentration and competition: An evolution in the making. *Journal of Money, Credit, and Banking, 36* (3), 433–453.

CBRC. (2011). *Annual Report.* China Banking Regulatory Commission (CBRC).

Chen, G., & Zhen, S. (2011). Incorporating covariates into integrated factor analysis of multi-view data. *Biometrics, 73*(4), 1433–1442.

Fu, C. (2007). *The analysis of the factors of profitability and its influence of state-owned commercial banks in China* (pp. 19–22). Shandong University.

Hao, C. (2006). Development of financial intermediation and economic growth: The Chinese experience. *China Economic Review, 17*(4), 340–367.

Huang, C., Li, Y., & Zhao, H. (2014). The competitiveness of China's commercial banks based on factor analysis. *China Journal of Enterprise Operations Research, 9*(1), 134–137.

Jin, X., & Zhang, L. (2009). *A comparative research on the international competitive power of Chinese large-scale commercial banks-An empirical study based on the factor analysis* (pp. 23–29). Capital University of Finance and Economics.

Lei, C. (2014). The reform of state-owned commercial banks in China: A political economy perspective. *Economic and Political Studies, 2*(2), 67–88.

Li, Z. (2013). *A study on the International competitiveness of China's large commercial banks* (pp. 33–159). Southwestern University of Finance and Economics.

Liu, M. (2014). *The research of competitiveness evaluation on commercial bank in our country* (pp. 59–98). University of Tianjin.

Luo, F., Dong, J., Armitage, Y., & Hou, M. X. (2015). China's financial system: Opportunities and challenges. In P. H. F. Joseph & M. Randall (Eds.), *Capitalizing China* (pp. 59–138). US.

Qian, R. (2016). *The state-owned commercial bank competitiveness analysis*. North China Electric Power University.

Shang, Q. (2000). An indexation system for assessing emerging Chinese Bank competitiveness: The case of Huaxia Bank. *Acta Oeconomica, 65*(s2), 55–69.

Tan, Y. (2014). Competition and profitability in the Chinese Banking Industry: New evidence from different banking markets. *The Journal of Developing Areas, 48*(3), 312–316.

Tong, R. (2005). *The study on competitiveness of Chinese commercial bank; Empirical research based on factor analysis*. Southwestern University of Finance and Economics.

Wang, C. (2010). *Research of comprehensive assessment system for listed banks' competitiveness*. Beijing Jiaotong University.

Wu, J. (2017). *Analysis of the competitiveness of Chinese commercial banks based on factor analysis method. Postgraduate*. Jilin University.

Xu, J., Gan, C., & Hu, B. (2013). An empirical analysis of China's Big four state- owned banks' performance: A data envelopment analysis. *Journal of Banking Regulation, 16*(1), 1–21.

Yang, X. (2009). Banking reforms and monetary policy in the People's Republic of China: Is the Chinese central banking system ready for joining the WTO? (review). *China Review International, 10*(2), 399–403.

Yao, S. J., Han, Z. W., & Feng, G. F. (2008). Ownership reform, foreign competition and efficiency of Chinese commercial banks: A non-parametric approach. *The World Economy, 31*(10), 1315–1324.

Yuan, Z. (2014). Government ownership and exposure to political uncertainty: Evidence from China. *Journal of Banking & Finance, 84*, 152–165.

Chapter 2
Historical Trends and Transitions in Credit Risk Management of Chinese Commercial Banks

Bhabani Shankar Nayak and Jia Xu

Introduction

This chapter outlines different trends and transitions in the history of credit risk management of Chinese commercial banks. By critically reviewing different stages of credit management and its historical evolution, it helps in understanding the nature of subjective challenges faced by Chinese commercial banks to manage credit risks. It reviews post reform policies in particularly after 1978 to locate the policy transitions and trajectories of credit risk management of commercial banks in China. It helps to understand the problems and prospects of effective credit management of risks by Chinese commercial banks. It argues that Chinese commercial banks are facing greater challenges in managing risk after the entry of foreign banks to China. Therefore, it is important for the commercial banks in China to develop its own credit management mechanisms within the context of Chinese banking environment.

Banking operations have two aspects: issuing loans and taking deposits from the public. The lending and borrowing process contains a great deal of uncertainty. It is difficult to avoid risk in the traditional lending activity of banks because it is impossible to forecast the future solvency of lenders (Freixas & Rochet, 2008). Alman (2012) divided the financial risks which occur in financial institutions into three types: credit risk, market risk and liquidity risk. One of the most important risks which banks encounter is the credit risk, which is defined as the potential that a borrower will fail to meet repayment liability according to the agreed terms (Crouhy et al., 2014). Theoretically, there are three types of credit risk: the first is credit default risk arising from a borrower being unable to pay the loan obligations in full or

B. Shankar Nayak (✉)
Business School for the Creative Industries, University for the Creative Arts, Epsom, UK
e-mail: Bhabani.nayak@uca.ac.uk

J. Xu
Anhui Rende Chuanghe Investment Management Co. Ltd, Anhui, China

the loan obligations go 90 days past the agreed date of payment. The second is concentration risk which is linked to the exposure to an individual or group with the possibility of producing losses large enough to threaten a bank's core operations. The third is country risk originating from when a sovereign state stops foreign currency payment or a sovereign state defaults on its loan obligations (Grundke, 2010). With the development of modern finance, Research into credit risk has changed from the traditional qualitative analysis into quantitative credit risk management models (Tsai et al., 2016). The management of credit risk is mainly reflected in the process of lending, which contains a range of requirements on pre-loan investigation, lending principle, approval of loan and after-loan management (Hilscher & Wilson, 2016).

With regard to the Asian crisis in the late 1990s and the 2008 global financial crisis, the lax standards of loan business managers in monitoring the loans were the main cause and a more efficient credit risk management was seen as the solution (Deventer et al., 2005). Similarly, credit risk has often been the main reason for many difficult banking crises in developing countries (Blanchard et al., 2010). Because of the high competition in the banking sector of developing economies, banks made loans without analysing the borrowers' credibility which resulted in a large amount of non-performing loans (Hasan et al., 2009).

It is hard not to mention the predomination of China in the rise of developing countries. Its Gross Domestic product (GDP) of $ 11 trillion in 2016 signals China as the second most prosperous economy only just behind the USA. During the last 5 years, the GDP growth rate has regularly been higher than 6.7% according to the National Bureau of Statistics of China (2017). This fast-growing economy has led to a remarkable development in commercial banking. In 2016, the China Banking Regulatory Commission (CBRC) reported that the total amount of domestic and foreign currency assets in Chinese banking sector was 232 trillion and 250 billion yuan while the non-performing loan ratio of commercial banks was 1.74% (Data. worldbank.org, 2017). However, the real level of bad debt in China is ten times the official amount according to the rating agency Fitch. Compared to the international non-performing loan ratios which were all below 5% from 2011 to 2015, there has been a large gap in credit risk management between Chinese commercial banks and international commercial banks (Edwin, 2017).

Historical Evolution of Credit Management of Commercial Banks in China

Although banking can be traced back to the temples of Babylon where money exchange took place in 2000 B.C., it is generally believed that banks actually appeared in Venice, Italy, in 1580, and modern banks began in 1694 when the Bank of England was founded. In the late Ming Dynasty, there were three kinds of financial institutions that controlled the loan business of the country: Piaohao,

Qianzhuang and foreign banks. Customers of Piaohao and Qianzhuang were different. Owners of large companies and governors preferred Piaohao, but owners of small firms and local citizens tended to use Qianzhuang. After the Opium War, some foreign banks entered the financial business in China and made huge profits with their privileges. The first foreign bank was the Bank of England who entered into China in 1845. In 1897, the Chinese Commercial Bank started as the first domestic bank (Wilson & Yang, 2016).

In the 1930s, the old Chinese ruling Kuomintang regime established the financial system including four banks, two bureaus and one coffer (the Central Bank, China Bank, Bank of Communications, Farmers' Bank, Chinese Central Trust Bureau, Postal Remittance Bureau and the Central Cooperative Coffer). This system also included provincial, city, county and government-private joint banks (Hsiao-yi, 1982). In addition, there was a group of private banks and Qianzhuang founded by national capitalists in China, about one third of which were concentrated in Shanghai, but most of them were not large and speculative and played a very limited role in the loan business (Wilson & Yang, 2016).

With the end of the Second World War and the victory of Chinese People's Liberation War, the new Chinese government established the People's Bank of China and began issuing Renminbi in 1948. Meanwhile, all foreign banks in China were abolished and foreign currencies were forbidden. Since then, China under the planned economy system has formed the universal banking system by the People's Bank of China while other banks were components of it. The People's Bank of China has become a commercial bank that handles deposits, loans and exchange transactions, and also served as the central bank (Li, 1995). However, during the "Cultural Revolution", under the guidance of the "left" ideology, the independence of banks gradually disappeared. For example, the People's Bank of China became an affiliate of the Ministry of Finance. Many leaders confused financial funds with credit funds and carried out a lot of actions against the economic laws (Chen, 2016).

In 1978, the Communist Party of China comprehensively corrected the 'Cultural Revolution' and its previous 'left' ideological mistakes in the third Plenary Session of the 11th Central Committee, which led to a new period of reform and 'opening up'. Under the guidance of Deng Xiaoping, the credit risk management of Chinese banking industry gradually went through the following four stages (Mohanty, 1998).

Credit Risk Management Under Early Reform Period from 1978 to 1983

In 1978, although the People's Bank of China restored its status as an independent ministerial unit, its dual functions of commercial banks and central banks did not change. Under the guidance of the policy of reform and 'opening up' in 1979, several state-owned specialized banks were separated from the People's Bank of

China. To be specific, the Agricultural Bank of China was in charge of rural financial business and the Bank of China was responsible for foreign trade credit and foreign exchange. The China Construction Bank is responsible for long-term investment and loan business (Wang, 2003). In 1983, the Industrial and Commercial Bank of China took over the services of credit and savings from the People's Bank of China. China had basically formed a banking system consisting of the Central Bank as the leader and four major national specialized banks as the backbone.

During this period, China's economy was running and developing in accordance with the typical product-related economic system. This is a highly centralized, administrative based, capital supply oriented system. Under the traditional product economy system, credit risk is assumed by the state. In addition to the fight against corruption and the misappropriation of financial funds, credit risk management mainly relies on the allocation of mandatory loan plans. As long as enterprises are not bankrupt, banks can make loans as planned. Therefore, the risk concept of both society and banks is weak (Long & Zhang, 2001).

Credit Risk Management Under the Planned Economy in China from 1984 to 1993

Since 1984, China's banking system has expanded rapidly in order to promote the transformation from planned economy to market economy. The Central Bank has introduced a policy – 'the four national banks can choose enterprises as clients and enterprises can choose banks for loan applications'. This encouraged competition between the four national banks, thus breaking the traditional pattern of the unified collection of bank funds and unified expenditure. The four state-owned banks began to extend their business to the countryside, providing loans for the booming township enterprises (Zhang et al., 2016).

In 1986, Deng Xiaoping called for greater steps in financial reform to make banks become the real commercial banks. So, what did this mean? In the initial stages of reform and 'opening up', the four national specialized banks were engaged in both government-led credit business and market-driven credit business. Then, the National Development Bank, the Export-Import Bank of China, and the Agricultural Development Bank of China were set up to deal with the entire government-led loan business, which separated the government-led loan business from the market-driven credit business (Fleisher & Renard, 2011). It provided legal guarantees for the four national specialized banks to become the real commercial banks and to provide market-driven credit business.

In 1984, the Central Committee of the Communist Party of China made it clear that China's socialist economy was a planned commodity economy based on public ownership. Under this system, the banking industry not only increased its vitality but also increased the pressure. On one hand, the credit business developed rapidly - expanding the scope of loans, setting up fixed assets, providing more households loans, issuing more loans for science and technology development. On the other hand, the credit risk of banks was gradually exposed and intensified. Preventing and defusing credit risks have become a top priority for banks. Therefore, Chinese regulators have established the deposit reserve system, bad debt reserve system, deposit system, credit card system and the asset liability management system. These systems constitute the cornerstone of future banking credit risk management (Okazaki, 2017).

Market Economy and Credit Risk Management in China from 1994 to 2000

After nearly 20 years of reform and development, China had formed a socialist market economy system with the four-major state-owned commercial banks working as the backbone of the banking industry. However, as a result of the unsolved problems from the previous planned commodity economy period, it was hard to push forward reform during the early stages of socialist market economy. Meanwhile, the East Asian financial crisis sounded a warning to China's financial industry in 1997 (Lin et al., 2009). The four-major state-owned commercial banks played a major role during this stage. Their main characteristics were as follows.

First, credit financing was still organised by the government, especially after conducting the 'funds to loans policy for state-owned enterprises'. This indicates the transfer from that the Ministry of Finance subsidies to state-owned enterprises to where banks that can grant loans to state-owned enterprises. On one hand, financial subsidies for state-owned enterprises were on the decline. On the other hand, potential subsidies for state-owned enterprises from bank loans were increasing. Of all the subsidies received by state-owned enterprises in 1985, only 24.2% came from banks, but this data increased to 43.6% in 1994. At the same time, because of the low profitability and high debt ratio of many state-owned enterprises, they became highly dependent on banks for financing, but it was difficult for them to repay the principal and interest on time. This resulted in a large number of non-performing loans (NPLs) to banks (Chan, 2010).

Secondly, the government had greater intervention with bank operations. Sometimes the government intervened directly in the management of the banks, by means of administrative orders to force banks to lend to firms on the verge of bankruptcy, to make arrangements for laid-off workers, to pay taxes, and even to make up deficits. In some provinces, local governments even ordered banks to lend to firms at the end of year to help firms pay taxes in order to achieve their fiscal revenue targets (Okazaki, 2017).

Thirdly, bank managers started with their own interests to maximize banks' size and costs. On one hand, they were keen to expand the institutions. On the other hand, they were keen to increase the costs of banks, especially the construction of luxury office buildings and training centres which can result in bank profits declining.

According to reports from the State Statistical Bureau between 1989 and 1998, the balance of credit assets of the four-major state-owned commercial banks were 11 times higher. However, the total profits grew by only 26%, while the management fees were 8.9 times higher (Umar & Sun, 2016).

Fourthly, the internal management of banks was weak, and there was no effective risk prevention measure. In the banking business, it was common to borrow new loans to repay the old, to charge interests for both credits and loans and to apply for loan extensions. In the non-credit assets, there were problems such as discrepancies between book value and actual value and indiscriminate use of loans. In the off-balance sheet business, there were some phenomena such as granting excessive credit (International Monetary Fund, 2014).

In 1992, commercial banks participated in the real estate industry and securities market speculation which led to a chaotic situation in the financial industry. Therefore, the Chinese regulators promulgated the Law of the People's Bank of China and the Law of Chinese Commercial Banks in 1995. The law of commercial banks clearly stipulated that Chinese commercial banks should not engage in the securities market, trusts or insurance industries. For the first time, a systematic legal system was set up for the supervision of commercial banks in china (Wong, 2005).

In 1998, the Chinese commercial banks learned the experience from national commercial banks and loan assets were divided into five categories: normal, concern, secondary, doubt, and loss according to their risk degree. According to the financial status and changes in cash flow of enterprises, banks can now dynamically grasp the changes of credit risk (Chi & Li, 2017).

WTO and Credit Risk Management Tendencies in China During 2001

After 15 years of long and arduous negotiations, China gained the entry into the World Trade Organization (WTO) in 2001. China has promised to cancel all geographical restrictions within 5 years. It gradually cancelled its clients' restrictions on Renminbi business and allowed foreign banks to provide services to all Chinese customers. It now allows foreign banks to set up outlets in cities and their examination and approval conditions are the same as those for the Chinese banks. China also cancelled all existing non-approval policies for foreign banks in terms of the ownership, establishing head offices and setting up branches. Meanwhile, foreign banks and financial institutions were allowed to provide loans to motors and enjoyed the same supervision as Chinese financial institutions. In addition, foreign banks were allowed to provide personal consumption loans to Chinese residents (Ji & Thomas, 2002).

Challenges of Chinese Commercial Banks in Managing Risks

After the entry of foreign banks, the credit risk management of Chinese commercial banks faced severe challenges. First, the competitiveness of Chinese commercial banks, especially state-owned banks, was poor because most of them were state-owned and protected by the government under the old planned economy and had not already finished the transformation to face the fierce competition under the current market economy. According to the reports of Hang Seng Bank of Hong Kong in 2001, its costs only accounted for 24.4% of total income, while the costs in state-owned banks were around 90%. The pre-tax earnings per capita of Hang Seng Bank was one million 570 thousand Hong Kong dollars, ten times higher than that of the state-owned banks. At the same time, Hang Seng Bank's one-year deposit interest rates ranged from 1.7% to 2.2%, compared with 3.6% for state-owned banks. The higher the deposit interest rates range, the lower attractiveness the banks (Cui, 2012).

Second, the capital adequacy ratio was low. In the early 1980s, the Chinese government suspended capital investment in state-owned banks. After the financial crisis in South-east Asia in 1997, the Chinese government issued 270 billion yuan of special treasury bonds to supplement the capital of the four-major state-owned commercial banks, but did not establish a normal capital supply channel for them. For a long time, the capital adequacy ratio of the four state-owned commercial banks did not reach 8% of the regulatory requirements. At the same time, a large gap existed in the extraction of the reserve for bad debts (Chen, 2003). In 2003, the government permitted commercial banks to issue subordinated bonds to increase their subsidiary capital. In the same year, the Government Council decided to inject $45 billion to the Bank of China and China Construction Bank to supplement their capital. In addition, the total capital adequacy ratio of 113 Chinese urban commercial banks was only 1.36% at the end of 2004 (The Economist, 2004).

Thirdly, the non-performing loan ratio was high. By the end of 2002, the balance of non-performing loans of banking financial institutions was 25,980 billion yuan. This figure did not include a one-time transfer by the government of 1 trillion and 400 billion yuan to commercial banks to deal with non-performing loans between 1999 and 2000. At the end of 2003, the non-performing loan balance of the banking financial institutions was 24,406 billion yuan and the non-performing loan (NPL) ratio was 15.19%. The average non-performing loan ratio of the four-major state-owned commercial banks was 19.74%, while the NPL ratio of the top 100 international banks was only about 5% (Shih, 2004).

The large number of non-performing loans of Chinese commercial banks was mostly caused by continuous losses in state-owned enterprises and the lack of a united credit rating system shared by banking industry. Loan applications from the state-owned enterprises were usually approved even if they were on the verge of insolvency. Chinese commercial banks would also try to extend loans to state-owned enterprises (Guo, 2012).

To provide healthy financial system and reduce the high non-performing loans, the Chinese government organised four asset management companies handing for the non-performing loans problem. To be specific, China Cinda Asset Management Company was the first asset management company. It was established in 1999 and reformed as a joint-stock company in 2010. China Cinda aimed to reduce the non-performing loans of commercial banks in China, especially for the non-performing loans with the China Construction Bank (Pierce & Yee, 2001). The other three asset management companies including the Chellona Orient Asset Management Company which received bad assets of the Bank of China; the China Huarong Asset Management Company correspondingly received the bad loans of the Industrial and Commercial Bank of China; and the China Great Wall Asset Management Company correspondingly received the non-performing assets of the Agricultural Bank of China (Ma & Fung, 2002).

Meanwhile, the ideal of developing a centralized credit scoring system attracted the Chinese government's attention. In 2002, at the Sixteenth National Congress of the Chinese Communist Party, this initiative was broadly discussed and resulted in formal legal documents to establish a unified credit rating system. The People's Bank of China played a leading role in this operation (Hornby, 2017).

In addition, in order to establish internationally recognized credit risk regulatory standards, the Chinese commercial banks adjusted the structure of credit assets and improved credit quality in accordance with the Basel III agreement on capital adequacy standards. The Basel III requires that the core capital adequacy ratio of commercial banks be raised from 4% to 6%, while 2.5% of protection buffer capital and 2.5% of countercyclical reserve capital were also required, so the minimum requirement of the entire core capital adequacy ratio is 8.5%. Chinese commercial banks also were to regularly report to the People's Bank of China, shareholders, and creditors on the operation and risk status of their credit assets. This increased the transparency of credit assets (Long & Zhang, 2001).

Since China began to implement stock market reform and the listing of the state-owned commercial banks, related studies about the credit risk of commercial banks have attracted academic attention and different problems in this field have achieved fruitful solutions. However, the fundamental problems are that a large amount of research was limited in the theoretical field while the research on the practical level of commercial banks' risk measurement has been relatively weak (Isanzu, 2017).

Problems in the Credit Risk Management of Chinese Commercial Banks

Most research on credit risk management of Chinese commercial banks has focused on analysing the existing problems, causes, and countermeasures. Peng et al. (2001) recognised some problems by comparing Chinese commercial banks with those in the Western developed countries in terms of credit risk controlling systems. Compared to the Western commercial banks who separate the loan approval department and the loan business department, the division of responsibilities and powers of these two departments in Chinese commercial banks is not clear. This implies that the internal control system is imperfect. For example, the loan business department pays more attention on profitability than the quality of pre-loan investigation reports. When the loan is overdue, the loan business department will shift the responsibility to the loan approval department, which means the necessary dual regulation becomes a single regulation. In addition, leaders in the loan business department have greater decision-making power than the leaders in the credit approval department. Therefore, the measurement of credit risk is actually subjective and unclear. In terms of credit file management, archives, especially those containing some important information, are incomplete.

Chen (2010) outlined the causes of loan default for Chinese commercial banks. The financial system in China is imperfect and the business credit rating is deteriorating. The efficiency of capital use, such as the conversion rate of savings to credit, is still low. The banking industry cannot share enterprise credit rating information. Similar to the situation which often happens in the UK, some Chinese companies have discovered the supervision loopholes and fled their debtor identities by forming new companies. After China joined the WTO, foreign banks try to grab top quality clients in China, which brings tremendous changes in the borrowers' credit situation for domestic commercial banks. For instance, the advantages of Standard Chartered Bank and Citibank in personal consumption loans have attracted a large number of high-quality white-collar workers in provinces and made many local banks unable to compete with them.

Yan (2004) provided effective suggestions for mitigating the credit risk faced by Chinese commercial banks. Although the customer rating and five level classification of loans have been established, there is still a lack of effective information collection and feedback channels. Therefore, the establishment of effective information collection and processing system is the first step in good credit risk management. Compared with the international commercial banks, the internal rating method of Chinese commercial banks is too simple. An effective internal rating method should be established by banks through referring to the mature international rating models and combining these models with the industry and regional characteristics of Chinses enterprises. In order to better implement these suggestions, Chinese commercial banks need to pay attention to the relevant techniques as follows.

Techniques in the Credit Risk Management of Chinese Commercial Banks

Chinese academics do not pay much attention to research and development of techniques of credit risk management and its applications which are based on the achievements of other countries. Dou and Xi (2008) demonstrated the practical application of the four most typical credit risk measure models, namely the Credit Metrics Model, Credit Portfolio Model, KMV Model and the Credit Risk Plus

Model, in South-east Asia such as South Korea and Hong Kong. For example, based on the Credit Metrics Model, commercial banks can separate the core parameters of credit data into several available variables in their actual operation such as the loan threshold interest rate, default recovery rate and the Value at Risk (VaR). Then, they use these parameters to calculate the default distribution of loans in South-east Asia. Liu and Wang (2006) focused their attention on the techniques in the Credit Risk Plus Model. There are three core aspects which should be paid attention to in practical application. This model only need to consider two statuses of loans - whether default or not. Meanwhile, default variables obey Poisson distribution so different loans are independent of each other. In addition, this model considers three kinds of uncertainty: the volatility of the default rate around the average default rate, the scale of loss after loan default and the uncertainty of the average default rate over time.

Thereafter, Cheng et al. (2009) highlighted the related problems when using different estimation techniques to get the possibility of default, the risk exposure and the probability of credit loss. These estimation techniques include the loss distribution simulation method, Monte Carlo simulation and Credit Risk Plus simulation approach. They concluded that these techniques require certain assumptions and complete data. If the assumptions are not met or the data are not comprehensive and true, then the Value at Risk (VaR) obtained by these techniques is not true. In reality, the construction of the internal rating system of Chinese banking industry has just begun, so the data-base for implementing these technologies is poor.

Applicability of Foreign Credit Risk Measurement Models in Chinese Commercial Banks

The analysis of whether foreign credit risk measurement models can be used in Chinese commercial banks not only provides options for practical operations but also makes the possibility of creating new credit risk controlling models (Ma et al., 2006).

Cao and He (2006) considered these credit risk measurement models are based on the background of the foreign market, which is not consistent with the specific situation in China and cannot be used directly. Meanwhile, they argued that these models provide some reference for quantitative analysis of credit risk in China. With the development of credit risk quantification and maturity of various application conditions, the application of credit risk measurement models in Chinese commercial banks is an inevitable trend. In order to realize the feasibility of various credit risk measurement models, Wang (2007) offered some suggestions on the reform of the capital market with an increasing number of listed companies; the upgrade of macro and industry databases (e.g. GDP growth rate, unemployment rate, and exchange rate); and the cooperation between banks' internal rating system and external rating agencies.

Conclusion

In summary, the relevant research in developed countries can be very important reference point for the credit risk assessment of Chinese commercial banks, but this kind of reference should not be copied without question. (Wang et al., 2017). Meanwhile, in response to the revision of foreign risk measurement models, Wu et al., (2010) suggested that the banks should consider data adoption, credit rating and market environment and human resources. In terms of data adoption, five indicators have a decisive impact on forecasting default results: the current asset turnover, net asset turnover, asset net interest rate, rate of return on net assets and the total assets growth rate. Banks should pay more attention to these indicators before a firm's loan is issued. In terms of firms' credit rating, the empirical evidence showed that the accuracy of the financial position of firms in the previous year was the highest. Therefore, banks should grasp the latest financial situation of enterprises to improve the prediction accuracy. When using the credit risk measurement models, loan approvers need to understand the limitations of models and use several methods at the same to reduce error.

The entry of foreign commercial banks increased the potential credit risk for the Chinese commercial banks. But it is an opportunity for the commercial banks in China to develop its own credit management mechanisms within the context of Chinese banking environment. It is better for the Chinese commercial banks to understand both global and local banking environment to understand credit risk management within historical context and current Chinese situations. Any attempt to follow the model driven credit management system developed by the American or European situation can have disastrous consequences.

References

Alman, M. (2012). Shari'ah supervisory board composition effects on Islamic banks' risk-taking behavior. *SSRN Electronic Journal*, August Issue. https://doi.org/10.2139/ssrn.2140042.

Blanchard, O., Dell'Ariccia, G., & Mauro, P. (2010). Rethinking macroeconomic policy, Rethinking Macroeconomic Policy, *10*(3), 2–19.

Cao, D. S., & He, M. S. (2006). Comparison and reference of commercial bank credit risk model. *Finance Research, 2006*(10), 90–97.

Chan, M. (2010). Financial markets of China: Issues and perspectives. *Chinese Economy, 43*(6), 4–7.

Chen, J. (2003). Capital adequacy of Chinese banks: Evaluation and enhancement. *Journal of Banking Regulation, 4*(4), 320–327.

Chen, W. (2010). Countermeasures to improve the level of credit risk management of commercial banks in China. *Financial Economy: Theoretical Edition, 2010*(3), 10–12.

Chen, J. (2016). Out of the shadows and back to the future: CPC and law in China, Asia. *Pacific Law Review, 24*(2), 176–201.

Cheng, K., Chu, Z. D., & Mi, Y. (2009). Research on VaR estimation technology for credit risk of commercial bank credit portfolio. *Shanghai Economic Research, 2009*(2), 103–111.

Chi, Q., & Li, W. (2017). Economic policy uncertainty, credit risks and banks' lending decisions: Evidence from Chinese commercial banks. *China Journal of Accounting Research, 10*(1), 33–50.

Crouhy, M., Galai, D., & Mark, R. (2014). *The essentials of risk management.* McGraw-Hill Education.

Cui, Y. (2012). Empirical test on building up competitiveness appraisal system of joint stock commercial banks in China. *International Journal of Economics and Finance, 4*(9).

Deventer, D., Imai, K., & Mesler, M. (2005). *Advanced financial risk management.* Wiley.

Dou, W. Z., & Xi, L. (2008). Evaluating credit risk of bank credit based on credit metrics model. *Reform and Strategy, 24*(10), 81–84.

Edwin, V. M. (2017). *Singapore jails ex-traders.* Royal Bank of Canada fined by South Korean court. [Online] Available at: https://www.snl.com/interactivex/article.aspx?id=39574515&Printable=1&KPLT=7. Last accessed 27 July 2017.

Fleisher, B., & Renard, M. (2011). Symposium: Thirty years of reforms: What about capitalism in China? *China Economic Review, 22*(4), 627.

Freixas, X., & Rochet, J. C. (2008). *Microeconomics of banking* (2nd ed.). MIT Press.

Grundke, P. (2010). Top-down approaches for integrated risk management: How accurate are they? *European Journal of Operational Research, 203*(3), 662–672.

Guo, Y. A. (2012). *Research on the measurement and control of credit risk of commercial banks in China.* PhD thesis, Shandong University.

Hasan, I., Wachtel, P., & Zhou, M. (2009). Institutional development, financial deepening and economic growth: Evidence from China. *Journal of Banking & Finance, 33*(1), 157–170.

Hilscher, J. & Wilson, M. (2016). Credit ratings and credit risk: Is one measure enough?. *Management Science, 63*(10).

Hornby, L. (2017). *China changes tack on 'social credit' scheme plan.* [Online] Available at: https://www.ft.com/content/f772a9ce-60c4-11e7-91a7-502f7ee26895. Accessed on 18th of July, 2017.

Hsiao-yi, C. (1982). An introduction to the historical Commission of the Kuomintang. *Chinese Studies in History, 15*(3), 46–60.

International Monetary Fund. (2014). People's Republic of China-Hong Kong Special Administrative Region: Financial Sector Assessment Program-Basel Core Principles for Effective Banking Supervision-Detailed Assessment of Observance. *IMF Staff Country Reports, 14* (207), 1.

Isanzu, S. J. (2017). The impact of credit risk on the financial performance of Chinese banks. *Journal of International Business Research and Marketing, 2*(3), 14–17.

Ji, C., & Thomas, S. (2002). WTO and China's financial services sector. *Journal of Contemporary China, 11*(33), 673–682.

Li, K. (1995). *A glossary of political terms of the People's Republic of China.* The Chinese University Press.

Lin, H., Tsao, C., & Yang, C. (2009). Bank reforms, competition and efficiency in China's banking system: Are Small City Bank entrants more efficient? *China & World Economy, 17*(5), 69–87.

Liu, H. C., & Wang, L. (2006). Credit risk plus model application in credit risk management of commercial banks. *Journal of Yunnan University of Finance and Economics, 22*(5), 20–25.

Long, H. M., & Zhang, W. (2001). Credit risk management of commercial banks: Historical changes and development. *The Theory and Practice of Finance and Economics, 22*(111), 40–43.

Ma, G. N., & Fung, B. S. C. (2002). China's asset management corporations. *Bank for International Settlements, 2002*(115), 1020–0959.

Ma, C. Q., Ding, Y., & Zhang, H. (2006). Study on commercial bank credit risk and its measurement model. *Modern Management Science, 2006*(10), 5–6.

Mohanty, M. (1998). The new ideological banner: Deng Xiaoping theory. *China Report, 34*(1), 101–105.

Okazaki, K. (2017). Banking system reform in China: The challenges to improving its efficiency in serving the real economy. *Asian Economic Policy Review, 12*(2), 303–320.

Peng, J. G., Mo, W. G., & Peng, J. (2001). The characteristics of the modern western commercial bank credit risk management in China and the reference. *Clothing Herald, 13*(3), 26–30.

Pierce, D., & Yee, L. (2001, July). China's bank asset management companies: Gold in them Thar Hills? *Topics in Chinese Law*. O'Melveny & Myers LLP.

Shih, V. (2004). Dealing with non-performing loans: Political constraints and financial policies in China. *The China Quarterly, 180*, 922–944.

The Economist. (2004). *A $45 billion shot in the arm* [online]. Available at: http://www.economist.com/node/2328008 Last accessed 18 July, 2017.

Tsai, S., Li, G., Wu, C., Zheng, Y., & Wang, J. (2016). An empirical research on evaluating banks' credit assessment of corporate customers. *Springerplus, 5*(1).

Umar, M., & Sun, G. (2016). Non-performing loans (NPLs), liquidity creation, and moral hazard: Case of Chinese banks. *China Finance and Economic Review, 4*(1).

Wang, X. (2003). Banking reforms and monetary policy in the People's Republic of China: Is the Chinese central banking system ready for joining the WTO? (review). *China Review International, 10*(2), 399–403.

Wang, B. X. (2007). Credit risk management models of commercial banks in China compared with the international ones. *China Finance and Economic Review, 29*(3), 65–70.

Wang, Y., Wang, W., & Wang, J. (2017). Credit risk management framework for rural commercial banks in China. *Journal of Financial Risk Management, 06*(01), 48–65.

Wilson, C., & Yang, F. (2016). Shanxi Piaohao and Shanghai Qianzhuang: A comparison of the two main banking systems of nineteenth-century China. *Business History, 58*(3), 433–452.

Wong, K. (2005). Law of assembly in China: People's Republic of China vs. Republic of China. *International Journal of the Sociology of Law, 33*(4), 215–245.

Wu, X. N., Liu, K. M., & Huang, A. D. (2010). The dilemma of financial early-warning model and the identification and prevention of bank credit risk. *Financial Reform, 2010*(1), 43–46.

Yan, Q. M. (2004). Empirical analysis of credit risk VaR of commercial banks in China. *Financial Research, 2004*(10), 40–47.

Zhang, D., Cai, J., Dickinson, D., & Kutan, A. (2016). Non-performing loans, moral hazard and regulation of the Chinese commercial banking system. *Journal of Banking & Finance, 63*, 48–60.

Chapter 3
Alternative Strategies of Credit Risk Management in the Guangdong Nanyue Bank in China

Bhabani Shankar Nayak and Jia Xu

Introduction

The Guangdong Nanyue Bank (GNB) shows the alternative strategies of credit risk management which led to its growth. It was formed out of local government finances and enterprise shares but spread its base to six cities and ranked as one of the top ten banks in the country. Since its establishment, the bank has been adhering to its market positioning: serving small and medium-sized enterprises, serving local citizens and serving trade financing. In order to better regulate the credit approval procedures and improve the credit level of decision-making, GNB has developed a set of applicable measures for the management of credit risk, set up corresponding departments and allocated professional staff for credit risk control before approval of loan, during the loan, and after the loan. The chapter looks at the alternative strategies followed by GNB to manage credit risk and grow successfully within the banking industries in China.

Guangdong Nanyue Bank (GNB) was founded in January 1998 and registered in Zhanjiang city in Guangdong province which is the southernmost coastal city of China. As a local commercial bank, it was formed out of local government finances and enterprise shares. It has a registered capital of 4 billion 620 million yuan and employs 2000 people. Its main branches are located in the six cities: Guangzhou, Shenzhen, Chongqing, Changsha, Foshan and Dongguan. It has a subsidiary called Zhongshan Ancient Town Nanyue Village Bank. Among 130 city commercial banks in China, the current asset size of GNB is ranked within the top ten banks (GNB, 2017).

B. S. Nayak (✉)
Business School for the Creative Industries, University for the Creative Arts, Epsom, UK
e-mail: Bhabani.nayak@uca.ac.uk

J. Xu
Anhui Rende Chuanghe Investment Management Co. Ltd, Anhui, China

Since its establishment, the bank has been adhering to its market positioning: serving small and medium-sized enterprises, serving local citizens and serving trade financing. After 19 years of development, GNB has achieved a leap from being a local commercial bank to a regional joint-stock commercial bank. With continuous improvement in its operation and management level, it achieved good ratings from the China Banking Regulatory Commission (CBRC). It has been rated second in the past 4 years. In 2011, it was rated '2B' which is the highest rating of Chinese city commercial banks (GNB, 2017).

In order to better regulate the credit approval procedures and improve the credit level of decision-making, GNB has developed a set of applicable measures for the management of credit risk, set up corresponding departments and allocated professional staff for credit risk control before approval of loan, during the loan, and after the loan (Ye, 2017).

Systemic Credit Risk Management in the GNB

According to the expected loss of credit assets, the China Banking Regulatory Commission (CBRC) usually divides loans into five categories: Normal, Special mention, Sub-standard, Doubt and Loss. In order to measure credit risk more accurately, GNB divides the credit assets into ten categories based on the five categories. In Table 3.1, the smaller the number, the higher the security of credit assets. The risk level of credit assets is determined by the level of credit risk of the borrower and the guarantor (Cai, 2015). The GNB has classified different levels of loan in following terms which guides its operations of credit risk management.

In the framework of credit risk management, GNB studied the experience of the Western commercial banks. The loan business is divided into three lines – marketing line, risk line and operations line. The marketing line includes corporate finance, personal finance, financial markets, investment banking, small and micro- businesses and branches at all levels. The operations line includes the operation management department, science and technology department, network bank, audit department, manpower department, comprehensive department and the finance department. The risk line includes the Head Office risk management department and branch risk management departments. The Head Office risk management department is responsible for the credit risk management of the whole bank. The head office risk management department evaluates the performance of leaders in all branch risk management departments without any influence of the marketing line and operations line (Yang, 2015).

The credit risk management process in GNB is divided into three parts: before a loan, during the loan, and after the loan. Before a loan, the management of credit risk usually includes three aspects: the examination of credit application materials before credit is approved and the evaluation of customer credit rating. During the loan, the principle of separating the loan business department from the loan approval department must be strictly adhered to in order to avoid the situation that blindly pursuing

Table 3.1 From five to ten different levels of classification of loans

Five level classification	Definition	Ten level classification	Definition
Normal	The borrower is able to execute the contract, there is no reason to doubt that the principal and interest of the credit assets cannot be repaid in full and on time.	Normal 1	The borrower's ability to repay and the willingness to repay is very strong, and there is very ample evidence that credit assets can be repaid on time.
		Normal 2	Borrowers have a very strong repayment ability and willingness to repay, and there is sufficient evidence that credit assets can be repaid on time.
		Normal 3	Borrowers have a strong willingness to repay and repayment ability, there is no reason to doubt that credit assets cannot be repaid on time.
		Normal 4	Borrowers have a strong willingness to repay and repayment ability, there is no sufficient reason to doubt that credit assets cannot be repaid on time.
		Normal 5	Borrowers have a willingness to repay and repayment ability, there is no sufficient reason to doubt that credit assets cannot be repaid on time.
Special mention	Although borrowers currently have the ability to repay principal and interest and other obligations, they will still have default risk.	Special mention 1	Although there are factors that adversely affect the repayment, the risk mitigation effect is good and the expected credit assets can be recovered for a period of time after maturity.
		Special mention 2	Although there are factors that have a major adverse impact on repayment, there is still evidence that appropriate measures can be taken to recover credit assets within a short period of time after maturity.
Substandard	The debtor's solvency is clearly a problem. They are unable to repay the loan principal and interest in full.	Substandard	
Doubt	If the debtor fails to repay the principal and interest of the loan in full, he will suffer greater	Doubt	

(continued)

Table 3.1 (continued)

Five level classification	Definition	Ten level classification	Definition
	losses even if he has executed the guarantee.		
Loss	After all measures are taken, principal and interest cannot be recovered or only a small part can be recovered.	Loss	

Source: GNB Annual Report 2011–2016, http://www.gdnybank.com/tzzgx/index.html#mao_c. Access date: 18/06/2018

the profits and ignoring the huge defaults (Kong, 2014). After the loan, the local branches need to inspect the use of loans, revisit customers monthly and classify credit assets regularly. When a risk associated with credit assets arises, the local branches need to take measures for disposing of non-performing loans and report the real condition to the Head Office (Liu, 2014).

Operation and Quality of Credit Assets

In 2016, Chinese regulators required banks to continue to strengthen their internal control and risk management in terms of their loans to local governments, companies, real estate industry and off-balance sheet business. Under this regulatory background, GNB realized that the transition from passive to active risk control and made the main risk indicators meet regulatory requirements (Wang, 2013).

By following empirical evidences from the above indicators in the Table 3.2, Yang (2016) argued that the credit operation of GNB was in good condition with no major risk vulnerabilities between 2011 and 2016. This is because the rate of non-performing loans was effectively controlled. Despite the rate of non-performing loan was only 1.08% in 2011, the non-performing loan ratios for the rest of the years were relatively stable at around 1.56%. In 2016, there was a slight increase in the non-performing loan ratio relative to that in 2015. Meanwhile, the credit concentration degree decreased significantly. The credit concentration of a single group customer and the maximum single group customer loan concentration are all important indicators of credit risk supervision. Since 2011, GNB has taken effective measures and customer concentration and loan concentration have decreased significantly. The entire correlation degree has also obviously reduced. The whole correlation degree is the ratio of the total amount of credit of all related parties to net capital. The bigger the indicator, the greater the credit risk faced by the banks. In 2013, GNB shifted from risk control to active risk management and after that the whole correlation degree went into sharp decline, down by 6.51%. However, the fluctuations of the whole correlation degree were large, reaching its lowest level

Table 3.2 The core indicators of credit risk supervision of the GNB from 2011 to 2016

Risk index	Standard value	December 2011	December 2012	December 2013	December 2014	December 2015	December 2016
Non-Performing Loan(NPL) ratio (%)	≤5	1.08	1.48	1.43	1.26	1.76	1.87
Credit concentration degree of a single customer (%)	≤15	13.21	10.24	7.15	6.22	6.52	5.35
Loan concentration of a single group customer (%)	≤10	10.10	6.51	4.51	6.22	9.41	10.30
Credit concentration of the largest ten group customers (%)	≤100	60.20	56.67	57.77	—	—	—
Total correlation (%)	≤50	—	19.52	12.99	3.94	14.67	15.23

Source: GNB Annual Report 2011–2016, http://www.gdnybank.com/tzzgx/index.html#mao_c. Access date: 18/06/2018

Table 3.3 The main business of the GNB in 2015 and 2016. Unit: Thousand yuan

Item	December 2016	December 2015	Year-on-year change(%)
Loans	81,181,983	70,514,411	15.13
Corporate loans	62,740,090	56,468,456	11.11
Individual loans	12,549,365	9,701,882	29.35
Discount	5,892,528	4,344,073	35.65
Deposits	127,316,189	110,813,115	14.89
Corporate deposits	83,316,291	80,617,379	3.35
Individual deposits	14,426,516	12,987,872	11.08
Others	29,573,382	17,207,864	71.86

Source: GNB annual report 2016, (Zhanjiang: Guangdong Nanyue Bank Press, 2016), p. 15

Table 3.4 The capital adequacy ratios of the GNB in 2015 and 2016

Item	December 2016	December 2015	Year-on-year change (%)
Capital adequacy ratio	11.82%	10.95%	↑
Tier one capital adequacy ratio	9.63%	8.83%	↑
Core tier one capital adequacy ratio	9.63%	8.82%	↑
Leverage ratio	5.62%	5.13%	↑

Source: GNB Annual Report 2016, (Zhanjiang: Guangdong Nanyue Bank Press, 2016), p. 15

Table 3.5 The liquidity coverage of the GNB in 2016

Item	December 2016
Liquidity coverage	118.37%
Qualified high-quality liquid assets(10,000 yuan)	2,073,985
Net cash outflows over the next 30 days (10,000 yuan)	1,752,095

Source: GNB Annual Report 2016, (Zhanjiang: Guangdong Nanyue Bank Press, 2016), p. 15

in 2014 by 3.94%, and rising to 15.23% again by 2016. Overall, this indicator meets the regulatory requirement (GNB, 2016).

Tables 3.3 and 3.4 show that the GNB is expanding. The entire loan and deposit business developed strongly from 2015 to 2016. The total amount of loans was 81,182 million yuan by the end of 2016 while the non-performing loans' total was 1518 million yuan, which was an increase of 277 million yuan comparing to the non-performing loans at the end of 2015 (GNB, 2016).

Meanwhile, the China Banking Regulatory Commission required the bank's capital adequacy ratio and core capital adequacy ratio to be 10.5% and 8.5% respectively. GNB achieved 11.82% and 9.63%, which just met the regulatory targets (Liu, 2014). It is encouraging that the GNB coordinated the relationship between explosive operations and potential liquidity crises as seen in Table 3.5. Its qualified high-quality liquid assets can cover the net cash outflows over the next 30 days in 2016 if needed (GNB, 2016).

Latest Credit Operations and Forecasts

2016 was the first year of China's implementation of the thirteenth five-year plan, which was a crucial period for the upgrading of industrial structure and financial reform. At the same time, this year was also GNB's key period to perform credit system reform during which the credit risk presented new features.

As Chart 3.1 shows, as of April 2017, the non-performing loan ratio of GNB was 1.36%, which exceeded the budget by 0.02%. There were two reasons for this: first, the decline in the scale of loans was the main reason for the non-performing loan rate over budget. The planned size of the whole loan amount was 47 billion 600 million yuan but the actual amount was 44 billion 900 million yuan, and then the loan scale budget gap was 2 billion 700 million yuan. This led to a 0.07% rise in non-performing loan ratio. Secondly, the total amount of non-performing loans (612 million yuan) is 24 million yuan lower than the budget, which led to a 0.05% reduction in the non-performing loan ratio. In summary, the non-performing loan ratio exceeded the budget by 0.02%. Although the total amount of non-performing loans was controlled within the scope of the budget, the loan scale did not complete the budget and the gap reached 2 billion 700 million yuan by April 2017, resulting in bad loan rates over budget indicators. Therefore, in controlling the bad loan balance, the bank will strive for a greater balance of loans (GNB, 2016).

In Chart 3.2, the non-performing loan rate of mortgage business has always been higher than the budget by 0.2–0.5 percentage points since 2017. The main reason is that the loan balance is 37 billion 700 million yuan, which is less than the budget amount of 1 billion 800 million. The deeper reason is that the real estate industry has not yet warmed up as the government has yet to relax the regulation of the real estate industry while the demand side is in a wait-and-see state. A number of data show that the volume of commercial housing transactions declined significantly. On one hand, this has resulted in fewer loans for individuals and a decline in the amount of bank loans. On the other hand, the real estate business cannot sell houses and cannot gain

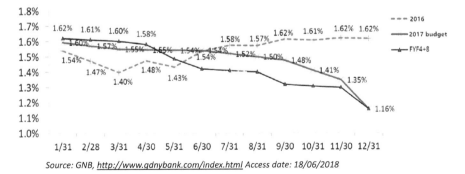

Source: GNB, http://www.gdnybank.com/index.html Access date: 18/06/2018

Chart 3.1 GNB's non-performing loan ratios in 2017 budget
Source: GNB, http://www.gdnybank.com/index.html. Access date: 18/06/2018

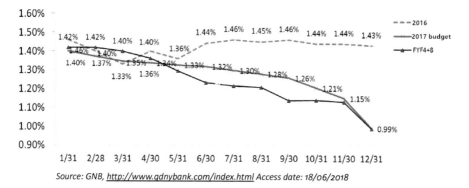

Chart 3.2 The non-performing loan ratios of the mortgage in the GNB in 2017 budget
Source: GNB, http://www.gdnybank.com/index.html. Access date: 18/06/2018

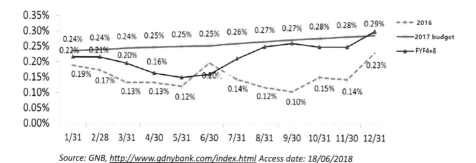

Chart 3.3 The non-performing loan ratios of the Small and Medium-sized Enterprises (SEMs) in the GNB in 2017 budget
Source: GNB, http://www.gdnybank.com/index.html. Access date: 18/06/2018

profits. Therefore, they cannot repay loans resulting in increased non-performing loans for the bank (Ye, 2017).

As shown in Chart 3.3, the small and medium-sized enterprise loan business of GNB amounted to 3 billion 869 million yuan by the end of April 2016, which showed a year-on-year growth of 2 billion 93 million yuan (an increase of 117.85%). The rate of non-performing loans for small and medium enterprises continued to decline and the below budget scale became larger. By the end of April 2017, the non-performing loan ratio of small and medium enterprises had achieved a good result of being below the budget by 0.09% (GNB, 2016). It can be seen that the GNB deserves recognition in the efforts of small and medium firm loan business.

From all these core indicators of credit risk supervision, GNB does meet the approved standard. However, in order to meet the supervision requirements of credit risk management set by the People's Bank of China, Chinese commercial banks have formed a set of methods to reduce the actual non-performing loans. In GNB, the average value of the reported monthly non-performing loan ratios is lower than the annul non-performing loan ratio in reality. Meanwhile, the reported annual non-performing loan ratios of both mortgage business and small and medium-sized enterprise loan business are smaller than the real ones. This means that the GNB's actual rate of non-performing loans is higher than the disclosure value. This indicates potential risks of the bank and credit risk management issues are becoming increasingly apparent (Liu, 2014).

Problems in Credit Risk Management in the GNB

According to the latest data on credit assets in GNB's annual reports, the bank has the following problems in credit risk management. Han (2016) argued that the credit scale of GNB has expanded rapidly but the level of credit risk management needs improvement. In 2006, the bank had just completed its reorganization of assets with total assets of only 8 billion 131 million yuan and deposits totalling 7 billion 397 million yuan. In 2011, the total assets reached 83 billion 241 million yuan and the total deposits amounted to 30 billion 392 million yuan, which showed that the assets increased by ten times and deposits increased by four times. By the end of 2016, the total assets of the bank reached 203 billion 860 million yuan. In just 5 years, the total assets of the bank again increased by 2.5 times. With such a rapid expansion rate, some serious credit risk management problems were gradually emerging, such as non-performing loans increasing year by year and default risk of loans associated with each other. In 2009, the total amount of loans to GNB's seven largest customers was 1 billion 71 million yuan while the total investment of the seven shareholders was only 1 billion 34 million yuan. This means using the loan as equity capital. In 2011, the loan concentration of a single group customer was more than the regulatory standard ($\leq 10\%$), reaching 10.1%. After 5 years of adjustment, the data remained above the regulatory standard, reaching 10.30% in 2016 (GNB Annual Report, 2011–2016).

The internal control system of GNB is not perfect. The supervision and evaluation of credit management is not properly in place. This leads to a lot of indiscriminate investment, indiscriminate loans, and disorderly guarantees. For example, the loan approvers did not pay enough attention to one loan only because the customer was an old customer or was an acquaintance of a superior. Some loan business managers even helped customers to apply to extend the duration of loan contracts and change the important terms without the prior written consent of the guarantor, which resulted in partial or total invalidity of the contract (Wang & Xie, 2015).

For trade credit and cross-regional credit, the loan approval of GNB has not been prudent enough. For example, for a customer who did not meet the entry criteria, the bank relaxed the access threshold and adopted the customer in the form of trade financing. After the loan was issued, it was confirmed that the customer was nominally a stainless-steel company but was actually a financing platform. By engaging in large transactions frequently associated with subordinate trading companies, the customer invented a flow of business transactions to obtain bank credit funds. Meanwhile, effective means in dealing with unexpected defaults is lacking.

For instance, the bank is difficult to obtain the support of the local police and government when a loan is overdue and the bank needs to take back the buildings of the firm. The regional protectionism from local government also makes it relatively difficult for the bank to deal with loan business with cross-regional collaterals (Han, 2016).

Counter-Measures for Strengthening the Credit Risk Management in the GNB

The future development goal of GNB is to become a new national bank of influence and to be a distinctive regional bank with a competitive advantage. By understanding the whole strategy, the following measures could help to solve the problems above and strengthen the management of the Bank who is now under the booming period.

The first method is the introduction of advanced credit risk management techniques. Basel III uses a large number of models to measure the credit risk and the quantitative method is more scientific to adapt to the development tendency of managing credit risks compared to the qualitative method. Therefore, GNB should combine the international quantitative credit risk management models with the special situation of the bank. For example, in the customer relationship management system, the key point is to track the risk and profit of each customer. Citibank used specialised software in this area and achieved good results, which is worth noting (Huang, 2013).

At the same time, the credit approval process of GNB went through the following three steps: the pre-loan investigation, examination and approval and the post-loan evaluation. Only when these steps are linked together effectively and organically can any breach of procedure and administrative interference be effectively eliminated (Han, 2016). Professionals in risk management, finance and law should form an investigation team to provide an independent report before loan. The members of the examination and approval should have higher qualifications than the investigation team, and should have more than 5 years of relevant professional experience and Bachelor's degree or above. Post evaluation should focus on the change of quality of borrowers' credit assets and preparation of an early repayment of loans (Han, 2013a, 2013b).

The second strategy is to increase the training of credit staff. Risk management personnel in different positions should have different trainings. The staff, who have more than 2 years' experience in credit work and have further training potential, should be trained to gradually become the business and technical backbone. The training of newly recruited college students and new entrants from other banks will enable them to become familiar with the bank's regulations and business processes. In addition, a professional skill training mechanism should be established for each month. The head of credit risk management department and external experts would conduct business training and communicate with loan approvers and loan business managers each month (Han, 2016).

With regards to the cross regional credit business, the Bank has been advised to prudently carry out the loan business with cross-regional small and medium-sized enterprises. For regions with higher risk levels and over-capacity industries, there will be no increase in off-site cargo mortgage credit. Although the loans are guaranteed by trade, the borrower's credit status and the first source of repayment should still be the first concern of the bank. The bank cannot reduce the borrower's access standards only because the loan is secured by trade (Liu, 2014).

Finally, GNB's existing pledge business is mostly carried out around commodities such as raw materials. Meanwhile, the Chinese over-capacity issues are outstanding currently, commodity prices are falling sharply and the accounts receivable turnover rates of some enterprises are falling sharply. This has resulted in a huge increase in the probability of corporate capital failures and defaults. In order to cope with the dilemma, the Head Office and the branches of the bank should strengthen ties with each other and build a more comprehensive credit information sharing system (Han, 2016).

Suggestions for Strengthening Credit Risk Management of Chinese Commercial Banks Similar to the GNB

The target for contemporary emerging commercial banks in China should refer to GNB's experience when conducting their small and medium-sized enterprise (SME) loan business, which is 'making the bank become the best services provider to SMEs and making SMEs become the major contributor of profits to the bank' (GNB Financial Report, 2016).

Banks should collect related data in target customer industries and establish a customer database shared by the whole banking industry to reduce the default risk of small and micro-enterprise credit business. At the same time, GNB selects the cultural industry, energy industry, and the environmental protection industry as the long-term target for loan business. The bank also cooperates with an Internet financial services platform. This helps the bank to make full use of the third party funds to reduce costs and transfer risks. The design of a range of online loan products, such as the vegetables industry loans and shipping industry loans, has been showed to be very popular in Zhanjiang city in Guangdong Province (Liu, 2014).

The idea of building a credit factory also can be promoted among commercial banks in Guangdong province. The credit factory idea means the pipe-lined division of labour within the credit risk management department of a bank which imitates the assembly line concept of manufacturing plants. This helps to separate the loan business department from the loan approval department clearly and improves efficiency. In order to build the credit factory, GNB took on board the more mature credit factory operations from the Pingan Bank (another commercial bank in Guangdong province) and have already achieved encouraging improvements (Shen, 2015).

Conclusion

This case study focuses on the credit risk management of the GNB from 2011 to 2016. It shows the successful strategies of the GNB that mitigates credit risk. Therefore, the suggestions on credit risk management for this bank provide inspirations for other Chinese commercial banks. It analysed the current situation and problems of the GNB in controlling credit risk by using economic data in several sectors from 2011 to 2016. The empirical details in charts and tables demonstrates how GNB strenuously managed the relationship between profits and defaults in the last 5 years of its operations.

The GNB is able to take the lead in Guangdong province because it firstly seized the personal consumption loan market and the small and medium-sized enterprise loan business where the defaults are relatively low and profits are relatively high. At the same time, the deeper reason is that this bank is adept at choosing exactly where to develop for loan business at the long run such as the environmental protection industry. Therefore, GNB can enlighten other Chinese commercial banks in credit risk management. It can also be adopted by other commercial banks around the globe.

There are limitations in this case study. Although this case study has put forward the concept of combining the Credit Risk Plus Model with China's actual condition, it has not provided a specific model. Moreover, Basel III requires banks to link credit risk with market risk and operational risk aiming to introduce a comprehensive risk management model. However, this work still lacks an overall grasp and relevant consideration of various risks. Finally, financial risks include banking risk, insurance risk and securities risk. This work has only analysed one part of the total financial risk management – commercial banks' credit risk. Only if this risk builds an organic unity with other kinds of financial risks, it is possible to achieve the goal of the Chinese commercial banks – Security, Liquidity and Profitability. Despite these limitations, the GNB case study provides valuable insights for bank managers and policy makers. The Chinese commercial banking can take GNB's strategic experiences into consideration and make plans for better credit risk management.

References

Cai, J. L. (2015). *The research and analysis of the credit management system of Huizhou branch in Guangdong Nanyue Bank*. Ph.D. thesis, Yunnan University.
GNB. (2011). *Guangdong Nanyue Bank 2011 Financial Report*. Guangdong Nanyue Bank.
GNB. (2012). *Guangdong Nanyue Bank 2012 financial report*. Guangdong Nanyue Bank.

GNB. (2013). *Guangdong Nanyue Bank 2013 Financial Report*. Guangdong Nanyue Bank.

GNB. (2014). *Guangdong Nanyue Bank 2014 Financial Report*. Guangdong Nanyue Bank.

GNB. (2015). *Guangdong Nanyue Bank 2015 Financial Report*. Guangdong Nanyue Bank.

GNB. (2016). *Guangdong Nanyue Bank 2016 Financial Report*. Guangdong Nanyue Bank.

GNB. (2017). *General situation of the Guangdong Nanyue Bank*. [online] Available at: http://www.gdnybank.com/abstract/index.html Last accessed 18 July, 2017.

Han, C. J. (2013a). The development of city commercial banks like Guangdong Nanyue Bank. *Contemporary Economy, 2013*(24), 9–11.

Han, C. J. (2013b). The eight key words for deciding the future of small and medium banks like Guangdong Nanyue Bank. *Banker, 2013*(11), 38–40.

Han, C. J. (2016). Financial innovation is the source of the vitality of supply side reform. *China's Banking Industry, 2016*(3), 1–2.

Huang, H. (2013). Construction of the core value of Guangdong Nanyue Bank. *Chinese Management Information, 2013*(20), 38–39.

Kong, L. (2014). *The design and implementation of human resource management system in Guangdong Nanyue Bank*. Ph.D. thesis, Chongqing University.

Liu, B. (2014). *Research on the core competitiveness of Guangdong Nanyue Bank*. Ph.D. thesis, South China University of Technology.

Shen, R. H. (2015). Credit plants for small and micro enterprise credit: Financial model and technological platform innovation to lead the service to entity economy. *Financial computerization, 2015*(7), 42–43.

Wang, X. Y. (2013). Guangdong Nanyue Bank: A rising star: An interview with the chief information officer of Guangdong Nanyue Bank – Mai Zhiwen. *Financial Times of science and Technology, 2013*(6), 22–22.

Wang, L., & Xie, X. (2015). Study on the efficiency of medium and long term incentive mechanism of urban commercial banks. *Chinese and foreign enterprisers, 2013*(1), 38–41.

Yang, Z. Y. (2015). *The research on small and medium enterprise credit risk management of Guangdong Nanyue Bank*. Ph.D. thesis, Hunan University.

Yang, Z. Y. (2016). *Research on the expanding strategy of retail business in the Changsha branch of Guangdong Nanyue Bank*. Ph.D. thesis, Hunan University.

Ye, C. Q. (2017). The new generation core system of products in Guangdong Nanyue Bank: Documentary interview with Guangdong Nanyue Bank's director of science and technology – Mai Zhiwen. *Financial Times of science and Technology, 2017*(2), 10–15.

Chapter 4
Strategies and Transformations in Chinese Banking Industry: A Study of the HSBC Bank (China) Ltd. from 2010 to 2019

Bhabani Shankar Nayak and Huaihua Lai

Introduction

In spite of unfavorable international environment, HSBC Bank (China) Ltd. has expanded rapidly in China. The chapter analyses the relationship between HSBC Bank (China) Ltd's net profit and its risk management strategy. It analyses the factors that affect operational efficiency of banks in China. It focuses on the role of Chinese state policies in shaping the operational efficiency and transformation of commercial banks in the country. The chapter captures the strategies and transformations of in Chinese banking industry for last four decades.

The processes of globalisation accelerated internationalisation of trade and banking industry. The commercial banks expanded in a massive scale. Different commercial banks have taken different measures under the influence of growing international trade. Many commercial banks are actively establishing branches in other countries to expand their potential customer outreach and capture the capital market and small and large savings of people. It helps banks to avoid resource shortages while participating in international trade and commerce (Ben et al., 2018). In this case, the bank has to do more business overseas, thereby looking for more potential customers (ibid.). It also solves the problems of territorial stangnancy and demand deficiency within domestic market. The internationalisation strategies are very helpful for the banks to spread and reduce risk. One of the reasons for it is that they believe it gives them an advantage over other, less internationalized banks when competing for customers. According to Bronzini and D'Ignazio (2017), information collected by international banks in other countries is of great help to international

B. S. Nayak (✉)
Business School for the Creative Industries, University for the Creative Arts, Epsom, UK
e-mail: Bhabani.nayak@uca.ac.uk

H. Lai
University of Glasgow, Glasgow, UK

© The Author(s), under exclusive license to Springer Nature Singapore Pte Ltd. 2021
B. Shankar Nayak (ed.), *China: The Bankable State*,
https://doi.org/10.1007/978-981-16-5252-3_4

companies in terms of cost savings. International banks collect market information by setting up branches, which is very valuable to their business customers (ibid).

Some banks choose to de-internationalise due to the risks arising from the deepening of international trade. An example of de-internationalisation is Citibank, whose BII index has been declining in the past decade. According to Ben et al. (2018), their overseas branches dropped from 3200 (2012) to 2214 (2015), and the BII index fell by 11%. The reason is that the pressure generated during the 2008 financial crisis forced Citibank to shrink. Through de-internationalisation, Citibank's total overseas assets have remained stable, from US$192 billion (2010) to US$183 billion (2015). Therefore, for risk-averse commercial banks, less participation in overseas business may be a feasible strategy. However, this approach may cause banks to lose part of the market, which may result in the loss of long-term benefits.

With the increasing tolerance of the Chinese government for the foreign banking industry, China has become one of the largest markets for the banking industry. According to the CBRC (2012), the institutions of overseas banks in China rose from 188 (2004) to 412 (2012) and assets rose to 2380 billion yuan, which is almost four times as high as in 2004. For international commercial banks, China's vast market has enormous profits. For banks with a high BII index, China is an integral part of their strategy.

Therefore, how to operate in China and improve the operating efficiency may be the issues that these international commercial banks need to face. However, for these commercial banks, the macro environment, laws, business strategies and factor of production may all be factors that affect their operating efficiency. According to Luo et al. (2017), since 2006, China's laws and regulations on the banking industry and economic conditions have undergone tremendous changes. These changes have a certain role in promoting the growth of the banking industry. Additionally, according to CBRC (2012), the loan amount of the banking industry has tripled between 2007 and 2011, and the number of branches and subsidiaries have also increased significantly. This shows that the business strategies and asset investment of foreign commercial banks in China are both aggressive. In terms of improving efficiency, potential influencing factors vary in China. Therefore, it is necessary to explore how international commercial banks could improve operating efficiency in China under complex international trade conditions. Although much literature focuses on the operational efficiency of banks worldwide, there is a lack of studies on the tole of Chinese state in the internationalisation of commercial banks. This chapter focuses to address this gap within the literature.

Factors Affecting the Efficiency of Banking Industry

The banks as important financial intermediaries play a significant role in national, local and international economic systems. They can efficiently integrate funds and effectively allocate them. For the national economy, well-functioning financial institutions could promote economic development and international trade (Holod and Toma, 2018). Therefore, how to improve the efficiency of banks has become an important issue. In their study based on a sample of 240,000 companies, Shamshur and Weill (2019) conclude that the improvement of bank efficiency could effectively reduce the overall borrowing cost which means that an efficient banking system can help in the development of the real economy. In their research, if both the businesses and individuals can borrow capital at a lower cost, the country's overall investment level could be promoted (2019). Similarly, Prochniak and Wasiak (2017) also believe that the performance of financial institutions is positively correlated with GDP growth and for the overall social welfare, the efficiency of financial institutions has a substantial impact. In addition, for the stakeholders of commercial banks, the improvement of bank efficiency will also bring more profits (ibid.). Considering the importance of society and the stakeholders, the factors that affect the efficiency of the bank 'are significant to research.

Previous studies have explored the relationships between technology and bank operating efficiency. First of all, for users, the improvement and popularisation of technology may bring about an increase in operational efficiency. According to Sathye and Sathye (2017), ATM is positively related to bank operating efficiency, especially in the Asia-Pacific region. For savers, a nearby ATM limits the distance that they would otherwise have to travel to get to a physical branch to deposit their savings. As a result, the increase in technology investment will bring more convenience to customers and eventually, more benefits will be brought to the bank (ibid.). Additionally, the improvement of technology cannot only improve the efficiency of the bank's own work but also help the bank improve its security. Bilan et al. (2019) identify that Fintech also has an essential impact on the operating efficiency of banks. They point out that banks can use Fintech to efficiently access data and improve regulatory capabilities. On the one hand, fast data reading can help banks quickly find the information that customers need improving work efficiency. However, the information security and stricter risk supervision brought by Fintech can reduce the risks of banks in operation (ibid.). From the perspective of the bank, the increase in operating efficiency may be due to a reduction in costs caused by Fintech. When Fintech is successfully implemented, banks can save a lot of labour and regulatory costs and thereby gain higher profits. Nevertheless, Sathye and Sathye (2017) also state that IT decisions must be made very carefully. The reason for this is that if the overall efficiency cannot be improved, the investment in IT cannot produce the desired results (ibid.). For banks, whether technology can promote operating efficiency should be based on their specific situation to formulate appropriate IT strategies (Gai et al., 2018).

Various studies have assessed the efficacy of risk management for banking efficiency. Considering that strict regulations may lead to increased costs and reduced efficiency, strict risk management strategies may reduce the operating efficiency of banks (Andries et al., 2018). They point out that two reasons may cause a decrease in operating efficiency. Firstly, if banks implement strict risk management strategies, they are likely to reject high-risk and high-yield projects or borrowers with low credit scores; eventually, some potential customers will be rejected by the bank, which means that benefits will be reduced (ibid). Also, banks must increase related regulatory costs, such as the use of Fintech. The innovation and maintenance of these technologies require bank capital investment. However, according to Erdinc and Gurov (2016), in the later stages of the economic crisis, strict regulatory mechanisms led to a decline in total non-performing loans, thereby promoting the overall profitability and solvency of the banking industry. Andries et al. (2018) also believe that during the crisis, strict supervision will increase costs, but it will also bring better-operating efficiency. The main reason is that during the crisis, due to the increase in market risk, effective risk management can reduce banks' non-performing assets and loans. The result is that the benefit of the relative reduction of non-performing assets can make up for the increase in costs, thereby leading to a better operating efficiency (ibid.).

Several studies determined that macro factors have a meaningful impact on the efficiency of the bank. According to Yap and Sufian (2018), the reduction in tax rates and trade barriers can alleviate the decline in commercial bank interest rates. They also identify that reducing currency freedom can increase bank efficiency. Based on their research, the main reason is that the bank's after-tax profits, daily business operations and business strategies are all closely related to macro policies. When the tax rate is reduced, the tax that the bank needs to pay will be reduced. Consequently, it will bring more cash flow to the bank for investments, which can bring more benefits. They also point out that the lifting of national trade barriers will promote international trade, thereby accelerating capital flows (ibid.). Moreover, when the macro policy changes, the bank's financial level and business strategy may change thereby affecting the bank's operating efficiency (Rodriguez, 2008). As Delis and Papanikolaou note (2009), short-term interest rates and GDP have a positive correlation with the efficiency of banks. Changes in macroeconomic conditions may change the investment and consumption decisions of enterprises and individuals (ibid). According to their views, the central bank's macro-control and national economic conditions are of considerable significance to consumers and investors. They believe that a favourable macro environment for investors will promote the overall efficiency of the market.

Some researchers note that the choice of bank strategy is also a key factor affecting operating efficiency. Curi et al. (2015) identify that targeted strategy, in terms of funds, assets or income, will be more efficient than diversified strategies in the long run, especially during the financial crisis. Diversification involves reducing risks and as such, sacrificing part of the profit is its price. If banks want to make higher profits, they need to bear higher risks. The purpose of diversification is to help banks to obtain profits stably and safely. Additionally, Peng et al. (2017) draw on an extensive range of sources to assess the function of bancassurance in Taiwan. They found that the bank's active participation in bank insurance strategy can bring higher efficiency and profitability. From the perspective of the bank, bancassurance can bring commissions and additional non-monetary benefits (ibid.). The existence of bancassurance can further deepen the merger of banking and insurance companies, and thereby improves the overall efficiency of financial institutions.

Some specific methods will have to be adopted by the Bank of China in order to improve efficiency. According to Caiazza et al. (2016), usually, more efficient banks involve more MA. Their research results show that MA can help banks improve technical efficiency and reduce cost-efficiency (ibid.). For some banks, the expansion of overseas strategies is very critical. Liu states that overseas MA is significant to the Commercial Bank of China because MA can help improve internationalisation and integration. He proposes that the motivation of overseas MA is to meet the growth of demand and expand its market scale. Besides, because most of China's large banks are state-owned banks, the government will purchase their liabilities to help them improve efficiency. According to McCauley and Ma (2015), in order to make state-owned banks play an abnormal role, the Chinese government will need to purchase debts in the form of foreign exchange reserves of the central bank. In addition, asset management companies funded by the Chinese government will also need to purchase the liabilities of state-owned banks to reduce their debt ratio. They also point out that the acquisition of bank debt doubled or tripled the stock of government bonds (ibid.).

Impacts of International Trade on Banking Industry

In previous studies on bank efficiency, different variables have been found to be related to international trade. According to Niepmann and Schmidt-Eisenlohr (2017), international trade will enable many companies to purchase bank trade finance products in order to avoid import and export risks. This shows that banks will be able to provide services that they would not otherwise be able to offer without international trade. Due to the existence of international trade, the products that banks can provide will be more diverse. At the same time, it also shows that the risks caused by international trade will bring more opportunities to banks.

As banks usually act as financial intermediaries in international trade, macro-factors such as legislation, customs and economic conditions in different countries will affect their efficiency (Bhogal et al., 2019). According to their research, when a bank acts as a financial intermediary, it needs to consider the macro conditions of different countries and to fulfill its role; this is especially a case for international commercial banks who usually involve more cross-border transfers and payment business. Economic and political changes will bring them more uncertainty. According to Niepmann and Schmidt-Eisenlohr (2017), in order to solve the risk of cross-border payments, some banks have adopted many tools to reduce risks such as letters of credit which play a vital role in guarantees in cross-border transactions. They point out that the US $2.5 trillion of world exports transaction was completed utilising a letter of credit, especially in countries with higher risks. Caballero et al. (2018) point out that banks will also obtain information on the goodwill of potential purchasers through connections between different banks, thereby reducing cross-border risks due to information asymmetry.

As international trade accelerates the capital flows, banks can only gain a better competitive advantage by engaging more actively in cross-border transactions. Regarding the factor endowment theory, banks use a lot of labour and tangible resources to improve the efficiency of participating in international capital activities (Dia and VanHoose, 2017). When banks make cross-border investments or open overseas branches, they need to invest capital in obtaining information, such as market information and the goodwill of potential users, to eliminate information asymmetry (ibid.). In order to obtain more benefits in international trade, the increase in costs and expenses, such as human resources, is necessary.

Due to the complexity of cross-border transactions, the improvement of payment technology is also the result of accelerated international transactions. According to Bhogal et al. (2019), in order to cope with the needs of transactions, the form of international payment has gradually transitioned from the past bank drafts and email communication to the new types of CHIPS, EFT and other new forms of payment. They are responsible for more than 90% of international payments, especially CHIPS.

Impacts of International Trade on China

International trade has an essential impact on China's economic development. According to Zestos et al. (2018), China's GDP grew 28 times between 1978 and 2014 because of the expanding foreign trade sector, which is the most crucial factor in China's economic development. International trade has made China become the most important emerging market in the world.

The impact of international trade on China is periodic. Between 1978 and 1991, the central government of China eased restrictions on export enterprises intending to increase the country's trade freedom (Garnaut et al., 2018). The coverage of China's foreign trade control system fell from 100% of exports (1978) to 15% in 1991 (ibid.). In 1992–2000, in order to better participate in international trade, China reduced tariffs on more than 200 products and eliminated import surcharges on various products; eventually, China's non-barrier tariff restricted products dropped from 1247 to 240 (Garnaut et al., 2018). Garnaut et al. (2018) state that since China joined the WTO in 2001, it has increased the total value of imports and exports to US $4.1 trillion utilising laws, regulations, tariffs and non-trade barriers. According to their analysis, the average annual growth rate of imports and exports in China from 1978 to 2017 is much higher than the world average. Although China's economic level has developed rapidly due to its active participation in international trade, it has encountered significant challenges worldwide. Compared with other countries, China's negative international image has a more negative impact on the export price of its goods (Yan et al., 2017). Considering that China has been caught in trade disputes with the United States and other countries in recent years, China's export commodities are in a disadvantaged position in the world. China has become the country with the most anti-dumping measures (866 in 2016) (Garnaut et al., 2018). Garnaut et al. (2018) also state that in addition to the continuous deterioration of the external market environment, China's export-led growth model can no longer bring about as rapid a growth as before. Therefore, for China, how to find opportunities to promote development under the condition of deteriorating international trade conditions is the primary task for the future.

Through the analysis of the literature, it can be found that many factors affect the bank's operating efficiency, such as technology, macro environment and business strategy. These influencing factors can be universally applied to all commercial banks in the world. Nevertheless, under the influence of international trade, the prior literature summarises that more measures need to be taken by the banking industry to face the opportunities and risks brought on by international trade, such as increasing capital investment, using letters of credit and changing payment methods.

The HSBC Bank (China) Limited

The HSBC bank has a very long operating history in China. Thomas Sutherland, in 1865, established the first HSBC bank in Hong Kong and established a branch in Shanghai a month later (HSBC, 2020). Although China restricted foreign banks for a while, in the 1970s, China reopened foreign trade, and HSBC became the first foreign bank to obtain a business licence in China (ibid.). As HSBC is the first foreign bank to operate in China, it has a substantial competitive advantage in China as compared to other foreign banks. In 2007, for strategic development, HSBC Bank (China) Ltd. was established in China as a wholly-owned subsidiary of HSBC (HSBC in mainland China, 2020). HSBC Bank (China) Ltd. has more than 8000 employees in China (99% are locals) and 171 service points (located in more than fifty cities), including 34 branches and 137 sub-branches (ibid.). According to its size and coverage area, HSBC is China's most competitive foreign bank. In 2001–2006, 2008–2011, 2013–2018 and 2020, HSBC was rated as the best international bank in China by Financial Asia; in 2019, it was rated as the best onshore RMB product and service provider by Asian Currency (HSBC in mainland China, 2020). According to the 2019 annual report of HSBC Bank (China) Ltd., the assets of HSBC Bank (China) Ltd. totalled 524.8 billion yuan (increased by 10.18% compared with 2018), and the net profit reached 4455 million yuan (increased by 14.41% compared with 2018). Since the establishment of HSBC Bank (China) Ltd., it has achieved great success in China.

History of the Development of the Chinese Banking Industry

The Gradual Reform from 1979 to 1994 in the Making and Unmaking of the Single Banking System

Before 1979, China implemented a single banking system, which means that the People's Bank of China was the only bank in China. After the reform and opening up to the international markets, in order to transform into a market economy, the two-tier banking system was introduced in China (Tan, 2016). Under the two-tier banking system, China Construction Bank, Industrial and Commercial Bank of China and Agricultural Bank of China were established, and all of these banks have had particular roles in economic development. According to Jiang and Yao (2017), including the People's Bank of China, all four banks had a monopoly position in their respective regions. The purpose of the action was to make sure that the plan of China's government could be achieved without free competition among these four banks. After completing the reform of the two-tier banking system, China's market efficiency improved by decentralising China's capital distribution. According to Kwong (2011), by 1985, the share of the output value of state-owned enterprises fell from 76% (1980) to 65%; total foreign direct investment rose to US $4.291 billion (1983–1985), which was three times that of the period between 1979 and 1982. However, although these four banks were established, China still could not achieve a complete market economy due to the limitation of banks' business scope. At that point in time, the planned economy was still the main form of China's banking industry.

After 1985, joint-stock banks began to appear in the Chinese banking industry. According to Jiang and Yao (2017), unlike state-owned banks, joint-stock banks pursued profit maximisation because they needed to meet the goal of maximising the interests of shareholders. The emergence of joint-stock banks shows that market competition in China's banking industry became fiercer because joint-stock banks did not need to fully follow the government's goals. However, Jiang and Yao (2017) also point out that at that time, most of the shareholders of joint-stock banks were local governments or state-owned enterprises, although these shareholders' intervention in joint-stock banks was relatively low. After 1985, China's banking industry became more competitive and performance-oriented.

In 1985, in order to increase the degree of free competition in the market, the government of China liberalised the business restrictions on four specialised banks, which means that they could compete with other joint-stock banks and state-owned banks in the market (Jiang and Yao, 2017). Lifting the restrictions of the four large banks led to more intensive competition in the market because other joint-stock banks had to improve their services to stand out in the market. However, considering that state-owned banks had a vast market share, it was unfair on the other banks to compete with them in a market. From 1988 to 1993, the capital market share of four large banks stabilised at around 85% (Kwong, 2011). During this period, China increased its market freedom, thereby making the market more efficient. Nevertheless, the existence of oligopoly made the market competition unfair.

In addition to lifting the restrictions of four large banks, the establishment of three policy banks also helped to increase the degree of competition in the market. The three policy banks, China Development Bank, the Import-Export Bank of China and the Agricultural Development Bank of China, were established for the purpose of providing loans based on government decisions. According to He et al. (2017), the existence of policy banks turned four large banks into real commercial banks. The potential reason may be that these four banks no longer needed to carry out commercial activities in accordance with the government policies; on the contrary, they could provide commercial services according to market conditions and thus, could freely participate in market competition.

Since the 1990s, China has also opened up restrictions on commercial banks and non-bank financial institutions. According to Kwong (2011), by 1994, many regional banks and more than 60,000 rural credit cooperatives were established. He points out that the reason for this practice is that China's urban and rural areas and different regions have different borrowing needs.

During the period between 1979 to 1994, the purpose of the reform of the Chinese banking industry was mainly to increase market competition efficiency and free competition, thereby changing the market inefficiency caused by the single banking system.

The Greater Reforms from 1995 to 2002 and the Deepening of the Freedom of the Banking Industry

In 1995, the promulgation of the Law of the People's Republic of China on Commercial Banks was the beginning of the second phase of China's banking reform. According to Jiang and Yao (2017), this law made the four state-owned specialised banks more commercialised, because this law required them to be responsible for their daily operations. This reform meant that these four banks needed to assess project and customer risks rather than national policy. However, this law did not have the expected effect because these four banks were still obligated to achieve outcomes set by the government. According to Kwong (2011), although the law was promulgated, the loans of four banks were mainly based on government orders rather than profitability due to their huge market capitalisation. They also point out that due to the complexity of loan procedures, policy banks could not provide loans to fund all the government decisions. The consequence of this is that during this period, a large number of non-performing loans appeared, which caused the banking industry to become more vulnerable (ibid). According to Hsiao et al. (2015), the non-performing loans ratio of the four major banks was around 40% during this period; incidentally, in 2001, the total amount of non-performing loans reached 1.88 trillion yuan.

During this period, China also took specific measures to reduce the banks' non-performing loan ratio. According to Jiang and Yao (2017), the Chinese government invested 270 billion yuan in four commercial banks by raising the national debt. Tan (2016) points out that the four asset management companies established by the government purchased 1.4 trillion yuan of non-performing loans during this period. The government of China adopted measures to reduce the overall non-performing loan rate of state-owned commercial banks, thereby improving market stability.

Before joining the WTO in 2002, the banks' reform aims were to make the industry more commercial and reduce the non-performing loan ratio. Since the four state-owned banks still have an oligopoly in the market, the industry's adjustment target is still concentrated on these four large commercial banks.

The Period of State Led Privatisation of Banking (2002–2010)

During this period, in order to join the WTO, the privatisation of banks became the primary goal of the Chinese banking industry. First, the government injected capital into the four major state-owned banks through different channels, intending to strengthen the bank's balance sheet. According to Kwong (2011), between 2003 and 2006, the four major state-owned banks received more than $75 billion in capital injections. Eventually, in 2006, the capital adequacy ratio of state-owned banks reached international standards (8%) and the non-performing loan ratio was reduced to 7.83% (Kwong, 2011). With the help of the government, the four banks stripped a large number of non-performing loans, thereby becoming more attractive for investors.

In the next stage, the government encouraged state-owned banks to cooperate with foreign investors. According to Jiang and Yao (2017), state-owned banks cooperated with large banks such as Bank of America and Royal Bank of Scotland in order to acquire capital and banking skills. Through cooperation with large banks, China's state-owned banks gained a better reputation in the world, which laid the foundation for the next step of state-owned banks' private ownership. From 2005 to 2010, the four major banks conducted public offerings in Hong Kong and Shanghai and received a considerable market response (ibid.). By 2010, all state-owned banks became joint-stock banks, which means the market competition was more liberalised.

The privatisation of Chinese banks has its own characteristics. One of them is that after the privatisation of Chinese banks, they still have state-owned attributes. In other words, the commercial decisions of these banks are still closely related to the decisions of the government. According to Liu et al. (2018), after the privatisation reform of Chinese banks, most of the bank's loans are still allocated to state-owned enterprises. This means that the investment decisions of Chinese commercial banks are not entirely profit-oriented. According to Chen et al. (2016), China's banking industry at this stage is most helpful to state-owned enterprises; indeed, they hinder the development of private enterprises. At this stage, even if Chinese government officials are not the largest shareholders, they have significant influence on the bank's business decisions (ibid.). In this regard, China is different from other countries in the world. According to Paulet and Mavoori (2019), compared with banks in Europe or India, the Chinese government has a stronger influence on the profitability and stability of banks. They point out that the drawback of this model is that when a crisis occurs, the Chinese government's direct intervention in banks will disregard the role of the market in the evaluation of their interventions.

During this period, foreign banks began to enter China in enormous numbers because of the relaxation of restrictions on foreign banks. According to Hsiao et al. (2015), in 2001, China further relaxed the operation of foreign banks in the domestic market by relaxing restrictions on RMB deposits and loans. They also find through research that the number of wholly foreign-owned banks and joint-venture foreign banks with legal entities increased from 14 in 2006 to 28 in 2008. During this period, the WTO agreement required China to open the domestic market, thereby protecting the regular operation of foreign banks. As a result, large quantities of foreign banks began to enter China, making it an emerging market t.

By the end of 2010, the capital market share of the four major state-owned banks had decreased to 57%, while other types of banks, such as joint-stock banks, foreign banks and city banks, observed an increase (China Banking Regulatory Commission, 2010) (Hsiao et al., 2015). Through this period of reforms, China has slowly and successfully transformed into a market economy.

The Year of Risk Reduction Strategy (2010)

After the financial crisis, the reform objectives of the Chinese banking industry focused on reducing risks. According to Jiang and Yao (2017), China adopted diversified commercial banking services and reform of small and medium-sized banking institutions to provide diversified services and finally enhance stability. The financial crisis made China realise that the banking industry needed a safer business strategy. The overall efficiency of the Bank of China decreased, and the overall risk also decreased after the financial crisis (He et al., 2017).

Development of China's Banking Laws and Regulations

The laws and regulations for the banking industry in China have changed over time because the purpose of the Chinese government at each stage was different. According to the different macro-objectives of the Chinese government, the evolution of laws and regulations for the banking industry can be divided into three stages which will now be discussed in more detail.

The State Led Internationalisation

China has implemented economic reforms since 1978 and gradually changed the previous banking system. According to Jiang and Yao (2017), before 1979, the single banking system used in China was aimed at ensuring a high degree of central control. They point out that a single banking system meant that the only bank in

China at the time, the People's Bank of China, was responsible for managing foreign exchange, deposits, loans, investment and the formulation of laws and regulations. Before the implementation of reforms and the opening up to foreign markets, the single banking system ensured that the government's production and planning goals were achieved, rather than pursuing the maximisation of bank profits. Therefore, at this stage, the bank would prioritise the realisation of the government goals as their primary task without considering the risks and benefits of the project (ibid.). In order to restore the general function of banks and ensure the regular operation of the banking system, China adopted measures in the economic reform of 1979. Between 1979 and 1984, China separated the commercial functions and regulatory functions of the Bank of China. After the reform, the People's Bank of China became the central bank which supervised other financial institutions (Jiang and Yao, 2017). However, due to the poor effectiveness of the transformation, there were still some issues with this regulatory system. During this period, banks did not pay much attention to the analysis of credit and operational risks, and supervision was biased toward administrative rather than bank business (Tsai et al., 2016).

During the second stage from 1984 to 1993, the bank's regulatory system underwent essential changes in order to achieve the goal of foreign exchange control. Before the reform, China's foreign trade was mainly controlled by state-owned foreign trade companies. According to Lin and Schramm (2003), a high degree of control led to lower efficiency of China's foreign trade system due to the reduced efficiency of competition and the low degree of freedom of foreign trade. Many measures against foreign exchange were implemented in order to promote more foreign capital to flow into China. In order to establish an efficient foreign exchange market, the interbank market CFETS was established. Participants of CFETS are foreign exchange banks and approved non-bank financial institutions and foreign banks (ibid.). At this stage, in order to adapt to the foreign exchange reforms, the four major state-owned banks were established and they were responsible for monitoring and conducting specific businesses. As Tsai et al. (2016) note, according to the nature of the four state-owned banks, they are responsible for agricultural financing (Agricultural Bank of China), urban construction financing (China Construction Bank), industrial and commercial credit business and foreign exchange management (Bank of China). However, in 1998, the Asian financial crisis had a substantial impact on China's banking supervision. To maintain the stability of the RMB, China strictly limited capital outflows (Lin and Schramm, 2003). As a result of this, the Bank of China has also strengthened foreign exchange supervision by prohibiting unauthorised inter-bank currency transfers and limiting the capital account (ibid.).

China Joined the WTO and Established the CBRC

China joined the WTO in 2001 to attract more foreign investment and banking technology. In order to join the WTO, China signed an important agreement and obtained a five-year grace period, which meant that it had time to develop the domestic banking industry to ensure fair international competition (De Rambures and Duenas, 2017). Due to the grace period means, China could vigorously develop its banking industry without the competition of foreign banks. Before the end of the grace period, RMB credit services were not allowed for foreign banks if their customers were Chinese companies (ibid.). After the grace period, foreign banks would be guaranteed fair access to China's banking services market. During this period, China aimed to avoid the impact of WTO accession on its banking industry through the protection that the grace period provided.

The establishment of CBRC in March 2003 was an important milestone for the Chinese banking industry. The purpose of CBRC was to create a more complicated banking situation after joining the WTO. According to Tsai et al. (2016), CBRC oversees the People's Bank of China, other banks and financial institutions that accept deposits. They also point out that CBRC is also responsible for formulating banking regulations, market supervision and investigation of illegal activities. The establishment of CBRC helped the Chinese banking industry to face the challenges of foreign banks better and improve its own competitiveness and efficiency, especially during a period of increased market competition (the grace period for China's accession to the WTO).

China's Current Banking Supervision

The promulgation of the Regulations of the People's Republic of China on the Administration of Foreign-funded Banks indicated the beginning of a new, current phase in China's banking industry. According to Tsai et al. (2016), although these regulations allow foreign banks to set up branches, subsidiary banks can receive preferential treatment in more areas. According to He (2012), CBRC believes that branches are more difficult to control than subsidiary banks because the host country where the branches are located cannot obtain priority in the debt recovery process. It means that despite the Chinese government's concerns, it has initially accepted foreign banks to enter the Chinese market. Regardless of the form in which foreign banks enter the Chinese market, China's banking system is increasingly participating in the world market.

In this period, the regulatory system of the Chinese banking industry hopes to establish a more unified risk determination system. According to He (2012), in terms of credit risk, the internal ratings-based approach is required to be used. In terms of market risk, although no required method is given, CBRC still recommends that the method adopted between commercial banks should be standardised (ibid.).

In order to adapt to China's rapidly changing external environment, Windows Guidance is also a widely used regulatory measure. Windows Guidance has a healthy openness in terms of credit control, with its primary approach including telephone and verbal assessment (He, 2012). Window Guidance's existing scoring mechanism can affect the bank's promotion of certain products and services (ibid.). However, there are still some problems with this open regulatory approach, including the lack of mandatory and clear interpretation of the law. He (2012) points out that due to the lack of clear punishment measures by Window Guidance, its suppression of malpractice is not always effective. As the Window Guidance mainly provides oral guidance, foreign entrants and compliance personnel may misunderstand the purpose of the Guidance which will then increase the cost of time (ibid.).

Since 2006, although the supervision of the banking industry is more liberal than before, China has been taking some measures to improve the efficiency of supervision. The purpose of this is to achieve the ultimate goal of promoting national economic development in a more intense and complex environment.

The HSBC Bank (China) Ltd. has an advantage of entering the Chinese market earlier as compared to other foreign banks. At present, the scale of their operations and achievements in China are considerable. Therefore, their strategy can be a valuable example for foreign banks that want to enter China.

Since 1979, the reforms of China's banking industry have been aimed at developing the country's economy by creating a healthy market. China has created a new banking system to make the competition more liberalised, thus completing the transition from a planned economy to a market economy. After joining the WTO, the reform of China's banking industry brought China's financial system into line with the world. In the following stage, through some adjustments in banks, the overall risk of the banking industry has been reduced. In conclusion, the policies after reform and the opening up have made China's banking industry sounder. However, for banks eager to enter China, the influence of the Chinese government on their daily operations must be considered as the most important macro factor. Although the degree of privatisation of Chinese banks is gradually increasing, the government still has a high degree of control over banks.

Since the reform and the opening up, China has first divided the task of supervision to different state-owned banks according to their focus business. In the following, in order to achieve foreign exchange reform, new regulatory measures have been implemented. After joining the WTO, the supervision of foreign banks appeared in order to protect domestic banks. At the same time, the establishment of CBRC marks the emergence of a bank-independent regulatory body in China. After 2006, more regulatory measures for foreign banks have been proposed. China has also taken measures to regulate the business operations of the entire banking industry. In conclusion, China's banking laws and regulations have become more standardised. In order to achieve better operating efficiency in China, banks operating in China must improve their compliance. In addition, they must also strengthen their own risk control, especially since the supervision of China's banking industry focuses on risk management.

The HSBC Bank (China) Ltd's Strategy in China

Foreign banks need to make correct strategic arrangements to enter China in order to compete with large state-owned banks. According to Chen and Yao (2017), foreign banks must find competitive advantages to enter China. If this is impossible, cooperating with local banks can improve their operating efficiency. HSBC Bank (China) Ltd., as a 100% subsidiary of the HSBC Group, needs to formulate a more appropriate business strategy in a complex market, especially as the international situation becomes increasingly complex. According to Yin et al. (2013), China's foreign trade conditions and economic uncertainty have a certain degree of influence on banks' efficiency. In this chapter, HSBC Bank (China) Ltd's business strategy will be discussed from the perspective of risk management and daily operations and taking into account the changing international trade environment.

Credit Risk Management

Generally speaking, credit risk is the risk that banks are most concerned about. For the banking industry, proper credit management can improve banks' operational efficiency, but too loose a credit management may cause a severe crisis (like the 2007 Great Depression) (Koulafetis, 2017). According to HSBC Bank (China) Ltd. Annual Report (2013), credit risk is defined as the financial losses caused by customers or counterparties failing to fulfil their contractual obligations, mainly from loans, trade financing and other products such as guarantees and derivatives.

According to a later HSBC Bank (China) Ltd. Annual Report (2019), a series of regulations on credit risk were developed by HSBC Bank (China) Ltd. Firstly, HSBC Bank (China) Ltd. measures the credit risk based on the number of losses that may be caused when customers or counterparties fail to repay. Within the enterprise, the potential credit risk depends on three risk parameters: default probability, default risk exposure and default loss rate, which are calculated by the internal evaluation system (ibid.). After the Basel Committee introduced a standardised approach to credit risk, the sensitivity of credit risk was increased by assigning risk weights to each asset and off-balance sheet position (Koulafetis, 2017). With a reasonable credit risk quantification system, the project's approval process will be more efficient for the staff, and the cost of credit risk supervision will also be reduced. Secondly, various measures were adopted to detect credit risk, and the loans that can be provided must not exceed the limit of the person in charge. In order to address credit risk, HSBC Bank (China) Ltd. set up a clear risk monitoring framework, which can be used for risk management staff to provide guidance. Through the supervision and training of individual employees, credit risk has been contained to a certain extent, especially for large loans. Anolli et al. (2013) believe that effective internal risk monitoring can effectively reduce credit risk through business monitoring and the improvement of practitioners' level.

HSBC Bank (China) Ltd. has also adopted a series of measures to deal with credit risk arising from participation in international trade. Keatinge (2018) points out that because most money laundering activities occur through cross-border transactions, for banks, the risk of cross-border transactions continues to increase. For these transactions, HSBC Bank (China) Ltd. has set strict cross-border transaction limits and approval procedures to control cross-border risks (HSBC Bank (China) Ltd.

Annual Report, 2019). Additionally, to meet the needs of international trade, HSBC Bank (China) Ltd. has developed a credit policy that meets the requirements of local regulations, which is recorded in the group's credit management manual. Zhang et al. (2011) state that the Chinese government has introduced a green credit policy by supporting environmentally friendly companies and relaxing their loan restrictions. In response to China's call, HSBC Bank (China) Ltd. also deepened the development of green credit in 2011 and won the 'Most Socially Responsible Financial Institution' and 'Best Green Finance Award' (HSBC in mainland China, 2020). Through the positive response to local credit policies, HSBC Bank (China) Ltd. can quickly integrate into the Chinese market and gain market advantage.

Market Risk Management Strategy

HSBC Bank (China) Ltd. internally defines market risk as the risk of a reduction in earnings or portfolio market value caused by changes in market factors such as exchange rates, interest rates, credit spreads and commodity prices (HSBC Bank (China) Ltd. Annual Report, 2013). Market risk also has a particular impact on the daily operation of the banking industry. After a financial crisis, China's market risks may lead to an increase in asset prices and securitised credit, and prompt banks to take more significant risks (Geng et al., 2016).

Considering that financial services are an essential part of HSBC Bank (China) Ltd., they attach great importance to the management of market risk and divide market risk into trading use combinations and non-trading use combinations (HSBC Bank (China) Ltd. Annual Report, 2013). The primary market risk management method adopted by HSBC Bank (China) Ltd. is the use of hedging and risk mitigation strategies, including the use of diversified hedging strategies and other traditional market instruments such as interest rate swaps (ibid.). Hedging plays a significant role in reducing the foreign exchange risk of banks that manage interest rate and foreign exchange risks separately (Mun, 2016).

Due to international trade, the impact of market risks on the banking industry has become more complex. Interest rate risk and foreign exchange risk have caused many banks' equity to fall (Vuillemey, 2019). In order to monitor the market risk in China more efficiently, HSBC Bank (China) Ltd. adopted some highly effective strategies, such as setting up an independent market risk supervision department, whose main task is to monitor the market risk of each HSBC Bank (China) Ltd. product and transfer it. After the financial crisis, many commercial banks choose to establish a supervision department and continuously improve the efficiency of supervision (Tian, 2017).

HSBC Bank (China) Ltd. uses a value-at-risk model to quantify the value-at-risk and use it as an important indicator to measure risk (HSBC Bank (China) Ltd. Annual Report, 2016). By quantifying the value of the overall risk, including interest rate risk, foreign exchange risk and interest rate risk, HSBC Bank (China) Ltd. manages and controls various market risks, thereby offsetting part of the impact of international trade. The quantification of market risks has become a top priority for many commercial banks because it can improve regulatory efficiency (Tian, 2017).

Operational Risk Management Strategy

Operational risks exist in the daily operations of commercial banks. In HSBC Bank (China) Ltd., operational risk is defined as the risk that internal procedures, personnel and systems are insufficient or ineffective, or that external events prevent the company from achieving their strategy or goals (HSBC Bank (China) Ltd). Many financial institutions, especially banks, have poor management of business operations and are likely limit their economic profits (Boussemart et al., 2019). Therefore, the control of operational risks is also an important part of HSBC Bank (China) Ltd's business activities.

Internally, HSBC Bank (China) Ltd. manages operational risks through a 'three lines of defence' model. The advantage of this model is that operational risks are divided according to responsibilities. The 'three lines of defence' are the senior management team such as the board of directors, the operational risk management department and the internal audit department. They all need to identify and manage operational risks and are responsible for the formulation and implementation of policies (HSBC Bank (China) Ltd. Annual Report, 2013). Through these three lines of defence, operational risk can be reduced significantly, because each line of defence has an obligation to supervise, identify and prevent operational risks. In terms of preventing operational risks, the 'three lines of defence' model can enhance the quality of supervision through the synergy of various levels (Luburić, 2017). In addition, the internal information system, 'Helios', can also effectively reduce operational risks. The main functions of 'Helios' are to record and manage the results of risk and control assessment, operation risk loss event, operation risk tracking and rectification (HSBC Bank (China) Ltd. Annual Report, 2019). 'Helios' can effectively help reduce internal operational risks through the analysis and rectification of operational risk events that have been released. The level of advancement of the information system will affect the bank's efficiency to a certain extent because a sophisticated information system can help the management formulate more efficient strategies (Pilarczyk, 2016).

The impact of international trade on operational risks is mainly the regulatory compliance risks, which may be due to banks' inability to understand regulatory or market regulations. Lack of compliance may result in the obstruction of bank marketing and, eventually, it may lead to financial collapse (Birindelli and Ferretti, 2017). HSBC Bank (China) Ltd. offsets regulatory compliance risks by establishing efficient internal communication channels, high-level employee training and continuously updated risk monitoring (HSBC Bank (China) Ltd. Annual Report, 2015). If the risk of regulatory compliance cannot be reduced, the fines and penalties imposed on the bank may adversely affect the daily operation and reputation of the bank. Birindelli and Ferretti (2017) point out that adequate monitoring of compliance can help financial institutions make effective plans, absorb capital and increase positive image of the bank.

Human Resources Management Strategy

The emphasis on competent staff is an important means for HSBC Bank (China) Ltd. to cope with the operating risks brought on by international trade. The reason is that HSBC Bank (China) Ltd. believes that outstanding talent, especially senior managers, can help companies improve their competitiveness in response to the increasingly competitive Chinese market (HSBC in mainland China, 2020). This approach to staff is mainly reflected in the salary levels and corporate culture. In terms of remuneration, as HSBC Bank (China) Ltd. attaches great importance to the training of senior personnel, the total salary of the company's senior managers has increased, especially during the period of market expansion. Bosworth et al. (2003) propose that for banks with small assets, senior salaries are positively correlated with bank operating efficiency. In China, although HSBC Bank (China) Ltd's total assets rank first among foreign banks, it is still at a disadvantage compared with state-owned banks (China Banking Regulatory Commission, 2020). For HSBC Bank (China) Ltd., maintaining a high total executive salary may help companies improve efficiency. In this case, HSBC Bank (China) Ltd. increased the company's competitiveness by increasing salary expenditures to retain its top managers.

HSBC Bank (China) Ltd. also helps companies cope with strong market competition by improving employees' sense of self-identity and their own worth. According to HSBC in mainland China (2020), in 2016, HSBC Bank (China) Ltd. set up professional training programmes for lower-tier employees and managers and provided welfare services, including mental health counselling. In 2016, HSBC Bank (China) Ltd's staff retention rate reached 81.7% (ibid.). Anitha (2016) states that a distinctive corporate culture increases the sense of belonging and accomplishment for employees and ultimately helps the company increase the overall retention rate. The improvement of the quality of staff experience and retention rates can increase the competitiveness of the enterprise and reduce the cost of personnel training.

Revenue Management Strategy

In terms of banking business, due to the strength of state-owned commercial banks in non-interest business, traditional business is still the primary source of revenue for HSBC Bank (China) Ltd. In 2010–2019 income, the ratio of net interest income to net income remained at a high level and even increased from 60.24% (2016) to 80.65% (2013). Although, according to Puri et al. (2011), after the economic crisis, the credit risk of the traditional lending business has become the main issue that banks need to face. According to Yin et al. (2013), a study of Chinese banks, banks with sufficient capital are inefficient unless capital is sufficient to produce scale effects. This may be due to lower profit margins and higher risks of the lending business. However, the expansion of lending business can help the business enter the market quickly by actively participating in corporate lending and maintaining friendly relationships with companies (Gambini and Zazzaro, 2011). HSBC Bank (China) Ltd's strong balance sheet performance provides the basis for their business strategy. From 2010 to 2019, the average annual growth rate of HSBC Bank (China) Ltd's total assets reached 10.97%, from 205.620 billion RMB to 524,797 billion RMB. The main sources of growth are services such as loans and advances, disbursements and transactional financial assets. From the perspective of the target of loan granting, corporate loans accounted for 74%, of which import and export corporate loans accounted for the highest proportion of foreign banks (HSBC Bank (China) Ltd. Annual Report, 2017). In this case, HSBC Bank (China) Ltd. has achieved a leading position in foreign banks through its strong lending business.

Due to the high profitability of non-traditional businesses, in order to pursue higher yields, HSBC Bank (China) Ltd. has also formulated a strategy that emphasises personal financial services. According to Abedifar et al. (2018), non-interest income has no adverse effect on the bank's credit risk compared with the traditional lending business. It has a higher profit margin, especially during the economic crisis. Since 2017, HSBC Bank (China) Ltd's ROA ratio has stabilised at 0.85%, which is lower than the 1.14% of Industrial and Commercial Bank of China and China Construction Bank (China Banking Regulatory Commission, 2020). Although HSBC Bank (China) Ltd's balance sheet has performed well, it is in order to increase its presence in China. To increase competitiveness, HSBC Bank (China) Ltd. keeps strengthening the product line and efficiency of personal financial products (HSBC Bank (China) Ltd. Annual Reports, 2015). Since 2010, net fee and commission income have maintained 10.01%, reaching 1.812 billion Yuan (2019), which accounts for 15% of its total revenue. It is worth noting that the cost-to-income ratio of fee and commission income dropped from 17.05% (2010) to 15.47% which shows that HSBC Bank (China) Ltd's personal wealth management product line was upgraded. The strategic deployment of personal wealth management products may help HSBC Bank (China) Ltd. obtain higher profit margins, thereby responding to more intense market competition under international trade.

Expansion Strategy

Since HSBC Bank (China) Ltd. is the first foreign bank to enter the Chinese market, to consolidate its dominant position in foreign banks, it has implemented an active expansion policy. Within China, the total number of HSBC Bank (China) Ltd. branches increased from 23 to 34 (sub-branches increased from 83 to 137) from 2010 to 2019. Most of these banks are located in China's coastal provinces, especially Guangdong, which accounts for 10% of China's GDP (China Statistics

Bureau, 2020). According to Pan and Tan (2007), China's coastal cities are increasingly participating in international trade and gradually driving-related industries, which means that HSBC Bank (China) Ltd. can advantageously participate in lending activities in the import and export processing industry. By helping develop enterprises in coastal cities, HSBC Bank (China) Ltd. has has integrated with the market more. The increase in corporate outlets means that corporate management costs (including rent and labour costs) need to increase. From 2010, HSBC Bank (China) Ltd's administrative expenses increased from 3.420 billion Yuan to 7.561 billion Yuan (2019), which accounted for the majority of enterprise costs.

HSBC Bank (China) Ltd's business strategy in China can be divided into risk management and business strategy. In order to control risks, HSBC Bank (China) Ltd. has taken measures to control credit risk, operational risk and market risk. Firstly, HSBC Bank (China) Ltd. reduced credit risk by quantifying credit risk and internal training. Simultaneously, strict restrictions on international transactions and a positive response to Chinese regulations also helped HSBC Bank (China) Ltd. to further reduce the credit risk due to internationalisation. Secondly, market risks have also been efficiently reduced by adopting active hedging strategies, efficient market monitoring and reasonable market risk quantification. In addition, operational risks have also been effectively reduced by the effective internal control mechanism and the 'three defence lines. Combined with better compliance, the operating errors of local operators could also be effectively reduced.

HSBC Bank (China) Ltd. hopes to obtain better benefits through talent strategy, business strategy and expansion strategy, as the external environment become more complex than before. As HSBC Bank (China) Ltd. attaches great importance to the retention rate and training of talent, it pays more attention to corporate culture and the salary of senior management. In terms of business strategy and continuously consolidating the leading position of traditional businesses in foreign banks, HSBC Bank (China) Ltd. attaches importance to the development of non-traditional businesses. The purpose of this is to obtain a better ROA and eventually stand out in the fierce market competition, especially as more and more foreign banks enter the Chinese market. Because HSBC Bank (China) Ltd. was the first foreign bank to enter China, in order to consolidate its leading position in the industry, HSBC Bank (China) Ltd. adopted an aggressive expansion strategy. Since 2010, the number of HSBC Bank (China) Ltd. outlets and management fees have increased rapidly.

Factors Affecting Net Profit of the HSBC Bank in China

The factors affecting HSBC Bank (China) Ltd's net profit can be divided into three categories. The first category of data is mainly based on business strategies. Among them, interest income and fee income are used to measure the traditional lending business and non-interest business of HSBC Bank (China) Ltd., both of which have a significant influence on bank income. According to Abedifar et al. (2018), non-interest business is valued by most banks because of lower risks and higher profits; traditional lending business is the primary income of banks, which is mainly related to the bank's loan amount.

The number of service points is also an important factor and is used to evaluate HSBC Bank (China) Ltd's expansion strategy. Opening branches across the country is an essential part of the expansion strategy and their number will continue to rise as the company expands. According to the financial statements of HSBC Bank (China) Ltd., during 2010–2019, the bank's service points increased from 106 to 171.

In addition, executive compensation has also been selected as an important factor affecting ROA. This is mainly because, according to HSBC Bank (China) Ltd. Annual Report (2015), valuing sophisticated and skilful managers is an important strategy, as their professional knowledge can help companies get more profits. In order to study the influencing factors of net profits in international trade, human resource strategy, as an important strategy for HSBC Bank (China) Ltd., should be evaluated, thereby researching whether good managers could help companies get a higher net profit.

The second category focuses on the risk management of HSBC Bank (China) Ltd. in its operations. This chapter selects the capital adequacy ratio as an indicator to measure the operating risk of HSBC Bank (China) Ltd. Considering that international trade will accelerate the risk outbreak of banks (Demir et al., 2017), it is important for banks to try to balance profits and risks. According to Rafique et al. (2020), the introduction of capital adequacy ratios can help banks overcome financial risks, including credit, liquidity and operational risks, thereby improving banks' profitability.

The third type of data is macro data as it is an essential factor that affects enterprises' business decisions. To determine how macro data net profits in the context of international trade, China's total import and export volume and the proportion of companies that are keen to participate in import and export are selected as indicators. The main reason for the selection is that HSBC Bank (China) Ltd. is the foreign bank that participates in import and export trade lending most frequently (HSBC Bank (China) Ltd. Annual Report, 2018). On the one hand, China's total import and export volume can reflect the macroeconomic environment facing Chinese export companies. On the other hand, China's foreign trade environment has deteriorated in recent years, caused by the deterioration of Sino-US relations and the increase in export tariffs. Consequently, the proportion of companies having an optimistic attitude towards import and export can be selected as an indicator to evaluate the macro-political environment because it can reflect the judgment of export companies on the international trade situation.

Considering that HSBC Bank (China) Ltd. was established in 2007, the financial crisis's impact may cause higher volatility in the sample. This article focuses on analysing the influencing factors of HSBC Bank (China) Ltd's net profits from 2010 to 2019. The research data is the relevant annual data from between 2010 and 2019, coming from the financial statements and the China Statistics Bureau. For empirical analysis, data applied in the regression is tested for stationarity, in order to make this analysis more practical.

Empirical Analysis

In the analysis, the net profit of HSBC Bank (China) Ltd. is selected as the explained variable. The following table shows the symbols and units of each explanatory variable (Table 4.1).

First, the unit root test is used to determine whether the variable has non-stationary problems. Since some data, such as the total import and export volume, are relatively large, their logarithm is used for analysis. The unit root test results of the dependent variable and all explanatory variables are shown in the following table (Table 4.2).

It can be seen from the above table that only the variables, $\ln x_3$, x_4 and $\ln y$, are stable, because their DF test value is less than 5% significant level. The DF test values of other variables, $\ln x_1$, $\ln x_2$, x_5, $\ln x_6$ and x_7 are all greater than their 5% level t-statistic. This result shows that these variables have the unit root; in other words, these time series are not stationary. Therefore, the stationarity test of the first-order difference is required for these variables. Consequently, the first-order difference DF test values of these variables are all less than their 5% significant level, which

Table 4.1 Independent variable name, symbol and unit

Variables	symbol	unit
Executive compensation	x_1	RMB
Fee income	x_2	RMB
Interest income	x_3	RMB
Number of service point	x_4	/
Capital adequacy ratio	x_5	%
Total export and import	x_6	RMB
Confidence in export situation (enterprises)	x_7	%

Table 4.2 Variable unit root test results

Variable	Test mode	DF test statistic	5% level t-statistic	Probabilities	Result
$\ln x_1$	(C,0,0)	−2.485254	−3.259808	0.1486	Non-stationary
$D(\ln x_1)$	(C,0,1)	−3.451878	−3.403313	0.0471	Stationary
$\ln x_2$	(C,0,0)	−1.376556	−3.259808	0.5449	Non-stationary
$D(\ln x_2)$	(C,0,1)	−3.328684	−3.320969	0.0495	Stationary
$\ln x_3$	(C,0,0)	−5.808597	−3.259808	0.0018	Stationary
x_4	(C,0,0)	−11.15674	−3.320969	0.0000	Stationary
x_5	(C,0,0)	−1.962575	−3.259808	0.2947	Non-stationary
$D(x_5)$	(C,0,1)	−3.465602	−3.403313	0.0464	Stationary
$\ln x_6$	(C,0,0)	−2.202495	−3.320969	0.2182	Non-stationary
$D(\ln x_6)$	(C,0,1)	−3.735558	−3.403313	0.0336	Stationary
x_7	(C,0,0)	−2.485254	−3.259808	0.1486	Non-stationary
$D(x_7)$	(C,0,1)	−3.451878	−3.403313	0.0471	Stationary
$\ln y$	(C,0,0)	−9.298656	−3.259808	0.0000	Stationary

indicates that the first-order difference of these variables is stationary at the 5% significant level. Therefore, the time series data are all first-order single integers and have stationarity.

According to the analysis, the influencing factors of net profits are stable time series after the first-order difference. Therefore, these time series can be used for a multiple linear regression analysis. The regression analysis is established in the following form:

$$\ln y = c + \beta_1 \ln x_1 + \beta_2 \ln x_2 + \beta_3 \ln x_3 + \beta_4 x_4 + \beta_5 x_5 + \beta_6 \ln x_6 + \beta_7 x_7 + \varepsilon$$

The data was entered into Eviews for analysis, and the results are shown in the following table:

As the above regression analysis shows, $R^2 = 0.998842$ and Adjusted $R^2 = 0.990738$, which indicates that the model is appropriate for the sample. Additionally, the interpretability of the regression model for the sample is 99.0738%. Therefore, the explanatory variables in the model can accurately explain the explained variables and net profit of HSBC Bank (China) Ltd. In addition, the Durbin-Watson statistic equals to 3.088994, which is significantly greater than R^2, which means that there is no spurious regression in this model. Consequently, this model is of research significance.

Due to the lack of quarterly data of HSBC Bank (China) Ltd., the small sample size prevents the model from being tested within the 95% confidence interval. Therefore, the analysis of the model is based on the 10% significance level. From the results of the appeal analysis, it can be seen that $\ln x_1$ (executive compensation), $\ln x_2$ (fee income), $\ln x_3$ (interest income), x_5 (capital adequacy ratio), $\ln x_6$ (total export and import) and x_7 (the proportion of companies with a positive attitude) all pass the test because their probability is less than 10%. By contrast, x_4 (number of service points), with a higher probability (0.4261,) failed the significance test. However, this result does not affect the overall accuracy of the model because the overall probability of the model is equal to 0.069251 which is less than 10%. On the whole, $\ln x_1$, $\ln x_2$, $\ln x_3$, x_5, $\ln x_6$ and x_7 have a significant linear effect on $\ln y$, while x_4 has no significant effect on $\ln y$.

From Table 4.3, it can be concluded that the regression equation is:

$$\ln y = -0.337524 + 3.78636 \ln x_1 + 1.813708 \ln x_2 + 1.323126 \ln x_3$$
$$- 0.004234 x_4 + 25.92493 x_5 + 3.143943 \ln x_6 + 4.513962 x_7 + \varepsilon$$

The results of the regression equation show that, except for x_4 which is less significant, the influence coefficients of the other explanatory variables on $\ln y$ are all positive, which means that they have a positive correlation with $\ln y$. When these variables increase, the explained variable $\ln y$ will also increase.

Table 4.3 Multiple linear regression results

Variable	Coefficient	Std. Error	t-Statistic	Prob.
C	−0.337524	0.034154	−9.882562	0.0642
$\ln x_1$	3.786361	0.290781	13.02137	0.0488
$\ln x_2$	1.813708	0.229503	7.902748	0.0801
$\ln x_3$	1.323126	0.085838	15.41413	0.0412
x_4	0.004234	0.003349	−1.264142	0.4261
x_5	25.92493	3.190114	8.126646	0.0779
$\ln x_6$	3.143943	0.483932	6.496657	0.0972
x_7	4.513962	0.594303	7.595381	0.0833
R-squared	0.998842	Mean dependent var		0.159302
Adjusted R-squared	0.990738	S.D. dependent var		0.498931
S.E. of regression	0.048017	Akaike info criterion		−3.653954
Sum squared resid	0.002306	Schwarz criterion		−3.478643
Log likelihood	24.44279	Hannan-Quinn criter.		−4.032274
F-statistic	123.2462	Durbin-Watson stat		3.088994
Prob(F-statistic)	0.069251			

Empirical Results

According to the analysis, except for the x_4 (number of service points) which has a poor influence, other variables have a significant linear effect on y. The equation is as follows:

$$\ln y = -0.337524 + 3.78636 \ln x_1 + 1.813708 \ln x_2 + 1.323126 \ln x_3 \\ - 0.004234 x_4 + 25.92493 x_5 + 3.143943 \ln x_6 + 4.513962 x_7 + \varepsilon$$

First of all, senior managers' salary is positively correlated with HSBC Bank (China) Ltd's net profit, which is consistent with their strategic goals. According to the model, when top managers' total salary increases by 1%, the company's net profit will increase by 3.78636%. This shows that the incentives of senior managers will promote the profitability of the enterprises.

Second, interest income and HSBC Bank (China) Ltd's net profit are also positively correlated. The reason is that the traditional lending business of banks is their main source of income. Although the profit margin of interest income is low, HSBC Bank (China) Ltd. has sufficient capital to guarantee the loan volume, thereby increasing the total income. According to the model, when interest income increases by 1%, the company's net profit will increase by 1.813708%. The reason for the increase may be that sufficient capital allows companies to carry out a large number of lending operations, thereby increasing total revenue. In this case, although the profit margin of interest income is low, it can also create a lot of income.

The growth of non-interest income can also increase the net profit of the company. Non-interest income has the characteristics of high yield and low cost. The net profit of a company will also increase when the total amount of non-interest income increases. Although the proportion of non-interest income is less than that of interest income, it also has a very significant impact on the company's net profit due to its high-profit rate. According to the model, when a company's non-interest income increases by 1%, its net profit will increase by 1.323126%.

The relationship between expansion strategy and the company's net profit is not significant. The reason may be that although the expansion strategy could bring more revenue, the price of doing so is the increase in cost. In a short period, the impact of expansion strategies on a company's net profit may be difficult to judge. Expansion strategies may have a more extended return period, so its impact on net profit may not be significant in a small sample size.

From the perspective of macro variables, the total amount of imports and exports and the optimism of import and export enterprises are directly proportional to the total net profit. When the total import and export volume increases by 1%, the net profit will increase by 3.143943%; when the enterprises that are optimistic about the form of import and export increase by 1%, the net profit will increase by 4.5139625%. When the macro environment is more positive, export companies will be more involved in the lending business, thereby promoting the rise of bank profits. A better import and export environment are more favourable to HSBC Bank (China) Ltd. because they are the foreign banks that are most actively involved in the production and operation of import and export enterprises.

According to the regression model, except for the number of service points, explanatory variables are positively correlated with net profit. Evaluating the explanatory variables of a company's business strategy is an effective practice to consider for experienced managers because it has a positive impact on net profit. In addition, HSBC Bank (China) Ltd. should also pay attention to traditional lending and non-interest income, especially traditional business with a higher correlation coefficient. However, companies should carefully evaluate the impact of expansion strategies on net profit because the significance of the number of service points and net profit is not apparent. For HSBC Bank (China) Ltd., the asset adequacy ratio should be taken seriously because the explanatory variables have the highest impact coefficient. The macro market environment should also be considered. When the market environment is more positive, HSBC Bank (China) Ltd's net profit will also increase.

In this analysis, there are also some limitations. Firstly, the sample data for this regression analysis is not sufficient. The main reason is that HSBC Bank (China) Ltd. is not a listed company, and it is difficult to find financial data in a quarterly form from their financial statements. Another reason is that HSBC Bank (China) Ltd. was formally established in 2007. Considering that the economic crisis will increase the chance of the sample, the data can only be selected from the annual data of 2010–2019 which results in a smaller sample size. In addition, due to the small sample size, the confidence interval of this regression model is 90%. The result of doing so may lead to some limitations in the use of the model.

Since the international political situation facing China is difficult to quantify, the macro-political environment's indicators may have certain quality problems.

Nevertheless, this problem is not severe. The reason is that when China faces detrimental economic conditions, such as higher export tariffs, the proportion of import and export companies that maintain a positive attitude towards the future business will decrease. In other words, it can judge the macro-political environment from the perspective of enterprises.

Some factors that can affect a company's net profit are not considered in this study, such as the company's technology investment and shareholder behaviour because these variables are difficult to find or quantify in financial statements. Nevertheless, these factors may have a significant impact on the company's net profit.

According to the regression model, except for the number of service points, other explanatory variables are positively correlated with net profit. Evaluating the explanatory variables of a company's business strategy is an effective business strategy to attach importance to experienced managers because it has a positive impact on net profit. In addition, HSBC Bank (China) Ltd. should also pay attention to traditional lending and non-interest income, especially traditional business, with a higher correlation coefficient. However, companies should carefully evaluate the impact of expansion strategies on net profit, because the significance of the number of service points and net profit is not apparent. For HSBC Bank (China) Ltd., the asset adequacy ratio should be taken seriously because the explanatory variables have the highest impact coefficient. The macro market environment should also be considered. When the market environment is more positive, HSBC Bank (China) Ltd's net profit will also increase.

In this analysis, there are also some limitations. First, the sample data for this regression analysis is not sufficient. The main reason is that HSBC Bank (China) Ltd. is not a listed company, and it is difficult to find financial data in a quarterly form from the financial statements. Another reason is that HSBC Bank (China) Ltd. was formally established in 2007. Considering that the existence of the economic crisis will increase the chance of the sample, the data can only be selected from the annual data of 2010–2019, Which leads to the decrease of the sample size. In addition, due to the small sample size, the confidence interval of this regression model is 90%. The result of doing so may lead to some limitations in the use of the model.

Since the international political situation facing China is difficult to quantify, the macro-political environment's indicators may have certain quality problems. Nevertheless, this problem is not severe. The reason is that when China faces a relatively bad international situation, such as higher export tariffs, the proportion of import and export companies that maintain a positive attitude towards the future will decrease. In other words, it can judge the macro-political environment from the perspective of enterprises.

Some factors that can affect a company's net profit are ignored, such as the company's technology investment and shareholder behavior. Because these variables are difficult to find or quantify in financial statements, these explanatory variables cannot be included in the model. These factors may have a significant impact on the company's net profit.

Conclusion

The purpose of this chapter was to explore how banks can improve their operating efficiency under international trade. Through the analysis of HSBC Bank (China) Ltd., this article aimed to draw a general recommendation that would be relevant to the banking industry in terms of operating in the operating on the international market. There are many ways to improve operating efficiency for the banking industry, including strategic adjustments and risk aversion. The business strategies shown in the financial statements of HSBC Bank (China) Ltd., combined with the macro data of China's foreign trade, were used to discover the extent to which the company's strategy and macro environment affect the company's net profit. If HSBC Bank (China) Ltd's strategy is effective, it will have a positive effect on the net profit. At the same time, if the macro environment is favourable to import and export, it is also advantageous for HSBC Bank (China) Ltd., because they are extensively involved in the lending to import and export enterprises. However, although the macro-environment analysis results often correlated with the forecasts, some strategies of HSBC Bank (China) Ltd. did not have the expected effect.

2010–2019 financial data was chosen for this paper as the index for evaluating HSBC Bank (China) Ltd's strategy, and some annual macro data was used to assess the macro-environment. The results of multiple linear regression showed that most of the strategies adopted by HSBC Bank (China) Ltd. have a positive effect on net profit, except for the rapid expansion of service points. This shows that in a situation where the macro environment becomes gradually unfavourable, a quick exaggeration strategy may be unwise. The increase in the number of service points will increase the risks faced by the company, which in turn may cause the increased costs of the company. Therefore, when a foreign banking company enters the market, especially in a country that is deeply involved in international disputes like China, they need to consider whether the increased profits can compensate for the increase in costs caused by the rise in the number of service points.

Through the analysis, it was found that other strategies of HSBC Bank (China) Ltd., including risk management and control, human resources strategies and business strategies, are all successful when faced with global risks. After the financial crisis, regulatory agencies around the world attached greater importance to risks. In China, CBRC also put forward many requirements for banks' risks. HSBC Bank (China) Ltd. successfully dealt with this aspect through strong capital injection. Compared with CBRC's requirements, HSBC Bank (China) Ltd's capital coverage ratio is much higher than the standard. In this case, the company can guarantee the company's risks without affecting its daily operations as much as possible. The case gives other banks an example of how strong capital can help banks overcome global risks and obtain better benefits.

When entering a market, management talents can help companies operate better. When HSBC Bank (China) Ltd. entered the Chinese market, it put forward a strategy of valuing employees and senior personnel. Through analysis, it was found that executive compensation is positively correlated with corporate net profit. Therefore, it can be speculated that for banks, recruiting experienced and capable managers can help better adapt to the environment, especially when they enter an unfamiliar market.

Banks also need to pay attention to traditional profitable projects as traditional interest income is an important, primary profit method for banks. HSBC Bank (China) Ltd. provides a guarantee for interest income through a strong capital injection. In other words, HSBC Bank (China) Ltd's interest income can be guaranteed when the loan amount is sufficient. In addition, to increase corporate profits, HSBC Bank (China) Ltd. attaches great importance to non-interest income. Since the cost of non-interest income is lower, it can make a higher profit for the enterprise when the market size is formed. HSBC Bank (China) Ltd's income strategy shows that in a complex external environment, the banking industry can increase lending with sufficient capital. At the same time, companies also need to pay attention to the creation of non-interest income, even if the market competition is fierce.

The macro trading environment also has a significant impact on banks. Considering that import and export trade has become an economic stimulus for many countries, especially China, a favourable import and export conditions can help banks operate better. The case of HSBC Bank (China) Ltd. shows that when the country is in a positive import and export environment, its performance will increase. When companies evaluate the impact of international trade on their operations, analysing the terms of trade of the host country is very important.

This chapter has used regression model to analyse the impact of different net profit strategies when companies face international trade risks. However, due to lack of data, the confidence level of regression analysis has certain defects. It may lead to some limitations in the applicability of the analysis results. Also, case analysis may cause the analysis results to be inapplicable under inapplicable universally conditions. Therefore, more extensive research needs to be carried out to obtain universally meaningful conclusions.

Appendices

Appendix 1: Unit Root Test-Executive Compensation

Null Hypothesis: X1 has a unit root				
Exogenous: Constant				
Lag length: 0 (automatic – based on SIC, maxlag = 0)				
			t-statistic	Prob.*
Augmented dickey-fuller test statistic			−2.485254	0.1486
Test critical values:	1% level		−4.420595	
	5% level		−3.259808	
	10% level		−2.771129	

		t-statistic	Prob.*
Null Hypothesis: D(X1) has a unit root			
Exogenous: Constant			
Lag length: 0 (automatic – based on SIC, maxlag = 0)			
Augmented dickey-fuller test statistic		−4.051836	0.0194
Test critical values:	1% level	−4.582648	
	5% level	−3.320969	
	10% level	−2.801384	

Appendix 2: Unit Root Test- Fee Income

		t-statistic	Prob.*
Null Hypothesis: X2 has a unit root			
Exogenous: Constant			
Lag length: 0 (automatic – based on SIC, maxlag = 0)			
Augmented dickey-fuller test statistic		−1.376556	0.5449
Test critical values:	1% level	−4.420595	
	5% level	−3.259808	
	10% level	−2.771129	

		t-statistic	Prob.*
Null Hypothesis: D(X2) has a unit root			
Exogenous: Constant			
Lag length: 0 (automatic – based on SIC, maxlag = 0)			
Augmented dickey-fuller test statistic		−3.328684	0.0495
Test critical values:	1% level	−4.582648	
	5% level	−3.320969	
	10% level	−2.801384	

Appendix 3: Unit Root Test- Interest Income

		t-statistic	Prob.*
Null Hypothesis: X3 has a unit root			
Exogenous: Constant			
Lag length: 0 (automatic – based on SIC, maxlag = 0)			
Augmented dickey-fuller test statistic		−5.808597	0.0018
Test critical values:	1% level	−4.420595	
	5% level	−3.259808	
	10% level	−2.771129	

Null Hypothesis: D(X3) has a unit root				
Exogenous: Constant				
Lag length: 0 (automatic – based on SIC, maxlag = 0)				
			t-statistic	Prob.*
Augmented dickey-fuller test statistic			−6.168086	0.0017
Test critical values:	1% level		−4.582648	
	5% level		−3.320969	
	10% level		−2.801384	

Appendix 4: Unit Root Test- Number of Service Point

Null Hypothesis: X4 has a unit root				
Exogenous: Constant				
Lag length: 1 (automatic – based on SIC, maxlag = 0)				
			t-statistic	Prob.*
Augmented dickey-fuller test statistic			−11.15674	0.0000
Test critical values:	1% level		−4.582648	
	5% level		−3.320969	
	10% level		−2.801384	

Null Hypothesis: D(X4) has a unit root				
Exogenous: Constant				
Lag length: 1 (automatic – based on SIC, maxlag = 0)				
			t-statistic	Prob.*
Augmented dickey-fuller test statistic			−3.775741	0.0321
Test critical values:	1% level		−4.803492	
	5% level		−3.403313	
	10% level		−2.841819	

Appendix 5: Unit Root Test- Capital Adequacy Ratio

Null Hypothesis: X5 has a unit root				
Exogenous: Constant				
Lag length: 0 (automatic – based on SIC, maxlag = 0)				
			t-statistic	Prob.*
Augmented dickey-fuller test statistic			−1.962575	0.2947
Test critical values:	1% level		−4.420595	
	5% level		−3.259808	
	10% level		−2.771129	

Null Hypothesis: D(X5) has a unit root				
Exogenous: Constant				
Lag length: 1 (automatic – based on SIC, maxlag = 0)				
			t-statistic	Prob.*
Augmented dickey-fuller test statistic			−3.465602	0.0464
Test critical values:	1% level		−4.803492	
	5% level		−3.403313	
	10% level		−2.841819	

Appendix 6: Unit Root Test- Total Export and importExogenous: Constant

Lag Length: 1 (Automatic – based on SIC, maxlag = 0)				
			t-statistic	Prob.*
Augmented dickey-fuller test statistic			−2.202495	0.2182
Test critical values:	1% level		−4.582648	
	5% level		−3.320969	
	10% level		−2.801384	

Null Hypothesis: D(X6) has a unit root				
Exogenous: Constant				
Lag length: 1 (automatic – based on SIC, maxlag = 0)				
			t-statistic	Prob.*
Augmented dickey-fuller test statistic			−3.735558	0.0336
Test critical values:	1% level		−4.803492	
	5% level		−3.403313	
	10% level		−2.841819	

Appendix 7: Unit Root Test- Confidence in Export Situation (Enterprises)

Null Hypothesis: X7 has a unit root				
Exogenous: Constant				
Lag length: 0 (automatic – based on SIC, maxlag = 0)				
			t-statistic	Prob.*
Augmented dickey-fuller test statistic			−2.348439	0.1486
Test critical values:	1% level		−4.420595	
	5% level		−3.259808	
	10% level		−2.771129	

Null Hypothesis: D(X7) has a unit root				
Exogenous: Constant				
Lag length: 1 (automatic – based on SIC, maxlag = 0)				
			t-statistic	Prob.*
Augmented dickey-fuller test statistic			−3.451878	0.0471
Test critical values:	1% level		−4.803492	
	5% level		−3.403313	
	10% level		−2.841819	

Appendix 8: Unit Root Test- Net Profits

Null Hypothesis: Y has a unit root				
Exogenous: Constant				
Lag length: 0 (automatic – based on SIC, maxlag = 0)				
			t-statistic	Prob.*
Augmented dickey-fuller test statistic			−9.298656	0.0000
Test critical values:	1% level		−4.420595	
	5% level		−3.259808	
	10% level		−2.771129	

Null Hypothesis: D(Y) has a unit root				
Exogenous: Constant				
Lag length: 0 (automatic – based on SIC, maxlag = 0)				
			t-statistic	Prob.*
Augmented dickey-fuller test statistic			−6.022015	0.0020
Test critical values:	1% level		−4.582648	
	5% level		−3.320969	
	10% level		−2.801384	

References

Abedifar, P., Molyneux, P., & Tarazi, A. (2018). Non-interest income and bank lending. *Journal of Banking and Finance, 87*, 411–426.

About.hsbc.com.cn. (2020). *HSBC In Mainland China*. [online] Available at: <https://www.about.hsbc.com.cn/>. Accessed 7 Aug 2020.

Andries, A. M., Capraru, B., & Nistor, S. (2018). Corporate governance and efficiency in banking: Evidence from emerging economies. *Applied Economics, 50*(34–35), 3812–3832.

Anitha, J. (2016). Role of Organisational culture and employee commitment in employee retention. *ASBM Journal of Management, 9*(1).

Anolli, M., Beccalli, E., & Giordani, T. (2013). *Retail credit risk management*. Palgrave Macmillan.

Ben, S., Yu, J., Gu, Y., Lv, J., Zhang, L., Gong, H., Gu, H., Shuai, Q., & SpringerLink (Online service). (2018). *In pursuit of presence or prominence?: The Prospect of Chinese banks' global expansion and their benchmarks.* Springer.

Bhogal, T., Trivedi, A., & SpringerLink (Online service). (2019). *International trade finance: A pragmatic approach* (2nd ed.). Springer.

Bilan, A., Degryse, H., O'Flynn, K., Ongena, S., & SpringerLink (Online service). (2019). *Banking and financial markets: How banks and financial technology are reshaping financial markets* (1st ed.). Springer.

Bosworth, W., Mehdian, S., & Vogel, T. (2003). Executive compensation and efficiency: A study of large and medium sized bank holding companies. *American Business Review, 21*(1), 91.

Boussemart, J., Leleu, H., Shen, Z., Vardanyan, M., & Zhu, N. (2019). Decomposing banking performance into economic and credit risk efficiencies. *European Journal of Operational Research, 277*(2), 719–726.

Bronzini, R., & D'Ignazio, A. (2017). Bank internationalization and firm exports: Evidence from matched firm–Bank data. *Review of International Economics, 25*(3), 476–499.

Caballero, J., Candelaria, C., & Hale, G. (2018). Bank linkages and international trade. *Journal of International Economics, 115*, 30–47.

Caiazza, S., Pozzolo, A. F., & Trovato, G. (2016). Bank efficiency measures, M&a decision and heterogeneity. *Journal of Productivity Analysis, 46*(1), 25–41.

Chen, X., & Yao, L. (2017). Foreign banks' entry and local banks' strategies in China. *Asia-Pacific Journal of Financial Studies, 46*(4), 635–660.

Chen, Z., Li, Y., & Zhang, J. (2016). The bank–firm relationship: Helping or grabbing? *International Review of Economics and Finance, 42*, 385–403.

China Banking Regulatory Commission. (2020). [online] Available at: <http://www.cbrc.gov.cn/>. Accessed 20 July 2020.

China Banking Regulatory Commission (CBRC). (2012). CBRC Annual Report 2012, Beijing, available at: <http://www.cbrc.gov.cn/showannual.do>. Accessed 5 August 2020.

Curi, C., Lozano-Vivas, A., & Zelenyuk, V. (2015). Foreign bank diversification and efficiency prior to and during the financial crisis: Does one business model fit all? *Journal of Banking and Finance, 61*, S22–S35.

De Rambures, D., Duenas, F. E., & SpringerLink (Online service). (2017). *China's financial system: Growth and inefficiency.* Springer.

Delis, M. D., & Papanikolaou, N. I. (2009). Determinants of bank efficiency: Evidence from a semi-parametric methodology. *Managerial Finance, 35*(3), 260–275.

Demir, B., Michalski, T. K., & Ors, E. (2017). Risk-based capital requirements for banks and international trade. *The Review of Financial Studies, 30*(11), 3970–4002.

Dia, E., & VanHoose, D. (2017). Capital intensities and international trade in banking services. *Journal of International Financial Markets, Institutions & Money, 46*, 54–69.

Erdinc, D., & Gurov, A. (2016). The effect of regulatory and risk management advancement on non-performing loans in European banking, 2000–2011. *International Advances in Economic Research, 22*(3), 249–262.

Gai, K., Qiu, M., & Sun, X. (2018). A survey on FinTech. *Journal of Network and Computer Applications, 103*, 262–273.

Gambini, A., & Zazzaro, A. (2011). Long-lasting bank relationships and growth of firms. *Small Business Economics, 40*(4), 977–1007.

Garnaut, R., Song, L., & Fang, C. (Eds.). (2018). *China's 40 years of reform and development: 1978–2018.* ANU Press.

Geng, Z., Grivoyannis, E., Zhang, S., & He, Y. (2016). The effects of the interest rates on bank risk in China: A panel data regression approach. *International Journal of Engineering Business Management, 8*, 184797901666261.

He, W. (2012). Banking regulation in China: What, why, and how? *Journal of Financial Regulation and Compliance, 20*(4), 367–384.

He, L., Chen, L., & Liu, F. H. (2017). Banking reforms, performance and risk in China. *Applied Economics, 49*(40), 3995–4012.

Holod, D., & Torna, G. (2018). Do community banks contribute to international trade? Evidence from U.S. data. *Journal of International Financial Markets, Institutions & Money, 57*, 185–204.

HSBC. (2020). *HSBC Group Corporate Website | HSBC Holdings Plc.* [online] Available at: <https://www.hsbc.com/>. Accessed 4 August 2020.

Hsiao, C., Shen, Y., & Bian, W. (2015). Evaluating the effectiveness of China's financial reform—The efficiency of China's domestic banks. *China Economic Review, 35*, 70–82.

Jiang, C., Yao, S., & SpringerLink (Online service). (2017). *Chinese banking reform: From the pre-WTO period to the financial crisis and beyond.* Springer.

Keatinge, T. (2018). We cannot fight cross-border money laundering with local tools, FT.com, [Online].

Koulafetis, P., & SpringerLink (Online service). (2017). *Modern credit risk management: Theory and practice.* Palgrave Macmillan UK.

Kwong, C. C. L. (2011). China's banking reform: The remaining agenda. *Global Economic Review: Finance and Economic Development in China, 40*(2), 161–178.

Lin, G., & Schramm, R. M. (2003). China's foreign exchange policies since 1979: A review of developments and an assessment. *China Economic Review, 14*(3), 246–280.

Liu, Q., Pan, X., & Tian, G. G. (2018). To what extent did the economic stimulus package influence bank lending and corporate investment decisions? *Evidence from China, Journal of Banking and Finance, 86*, 177–193.

Luburić, R. (2017). Strengthening the three lines of Defence in terms of more efficient operational risk Management in Central Banks. *Journal of Central Banking Theory and Practice, 6*(1), 29–53.

Luo, D., Dong, Y., Armitage, S., & Hou, W. (2017). The impact of foreign bank penetration on the domestic banking sector: New evidence from China. *The European Journal of Finance: Third Conference on the Chinese Capital Markets University of Edinburgh Business School, 1st-2nd July 2013, 23*(7–9), 752–780.

McCauley, R., & Ma, G. (2015). Transforming central Bank liabilities into government debt: The case of China. *China and the World Economy: English Version, 23*(4), 1–18.

Mun, K. (2016). Hedging bank market risk with futures and forwards. *Quarterly Review of Economics and Finance, 61*, 112–125.

Niepmann, F., & Schmidt-Eisenlohr, T. (2017). International trade, risk and the role of banks. *Journal of International Economics, 107*, 111–126.

Pan, S., & Tan, Y. W. (2007). An empirical analysis of the relationship between international trade and economic growth in Guangdong Province. *International Economics and Trade Research, 23*(12), 24.

Paulet, E., & Mavoori, H. (2019). Globalization, regulation and profitability of banks: A comparative analysis of Europe, United States, India and China. *The European journal of comparative economics : EJCE, 16*(2), 127–170.

Peng, J., Jeng, V., Wang, J. L., & Chen, Y. (2017). The impact of bancassurance on efficiency and profitability of banks: Evidence from the banking industry in Taiwan. *Journal of Banking and Finance, 80*, 1–13.

Pilarczyk, K. (2016). Importance of management information system in banking sector, Annales Universitatis Mariae curie-Skłodowska. Sectio H. *Oeconomia, 50*(2), 69.

Prochniak, M., & Wasiak, K. (2017). The impact of the financial system on economic growth in the context of the global crisis: Empirical evidence for the EU and OECD countries. *Empirica, 44*(2), 295–337.

Puri, M., Rocholl, J., & Steffen, S. (2011). Global retail lending in the aftermath of the US financial crisis: Distinguishing between supply and demand effects. *Journal of Financial Economics, 100*(3), 556–578.

Rafique, A., Quddoos, M. U., & Akhtar, M. H. (2020). Impact of financial risk on financial performance of banks in Pakistan; the mediating role of capital adequacy ratio. *Journal of Accounting and Finance in Emerging Economies, 6*(2).

Rodriguez, G. (2008). Stability of central bank preferences, macroeconomic shocks, and efficiency of the monetary policy: Empirical evidence for Canada. *Applied Economics Letters, 15*(6), 437–441.

Sathye, S., & Sathye, M. (2017). Do ATMs increase technical efficiency of banks in a developing country? Evidence from Indian banks. *Australian Accounting Review, 27*(1), 101–111.

Shamshur, A., & Weill, L. (2019). Does bank efficiency influence the cost of credit? *Journal of Banking and Finance, 105*, 62–73.

Stats.gov.cn. 2020. *China Statistics Bureau.* [online] Available at: <http://www.stats.gov.cn/>. Accessed 20 July 2020.

Tan, Y. (2016). The impacts of risk and competition on bank profitability in China. *Journal of International Financial Markets, Institutions & Money, 40*, 85–110.

Tian, W., & SpringerLink (Online service). (2017). *Commercial banking risk management: Regulation in the wake of the financial crisis.* Palgrave Macmillan US.

Tsai, S., Chen, K., Zhao, H., Wei, Y., Wang, C., Zheng, Y., Chang, L., & Wang, J. (2016). Using a mixed model to explore evaluation criteria for Bank supervision: A banking supervision law perspective. *PLoS One, 11*(12), e0167710.

Vuillemey, G. (2019). Bank Interest Rate Risk Management. *Management Science, 65*(12), 5933–5956.

Yan, Z., Bao, D., & Luo, C. (2017). Economic value of country image: Evidence from international trade and implications for China. *China and the World Economy: English Version, 25*(3), 87–111.

Yap, W. K., & Sufian, F. (2018). Bank's profit efficiency under China economic structure rebalancing: Empirical evidence using index of economic freedom. *The Chinese Economy, 51*(1), 20–44.

Yin, H., Yang, J., & Mehran, J. (2013). An empirical study of bank efficiency in China after WTO accession. *Global Finance Journal, 24*(2), 153–170.

Zestos, G. K., Guo, W., & Patnode, R. (2018). Determinants of real Chinese GDP 1978–2014. *Atlantic Economic Journal, 46*(2), 161–177.

Zhang, B., Yang, Y., & Bi, J. (2011). Tracking the implementation of green credit policy in China: Top-down perspective and bottom-up reform. *Journal of Environmental Management, 92*(4), 1321–1327.

Chapter 5
Mapping the Relationship Between Financial Developments and Economic Growth in China

Bhabani Shankar Nayak and Zhong Yingnan

Introduction

There are many burgeoning literatures dominate the debates on relationship between financial developments and economic growth in China. It has always been a contagious one. The Chinese state is making coordinated effort for the development of the financial sector for economic growth to address issues of local development. Since the reforms of 1978, the Chinese economy has witnessed rapid growth. This chapter explores the relationship between financial development and economic growth in China. It argues that there is a bidirectional causality between financial development and economic growth in China.

The impact of financial development on economic growth has always been controversial among various theoretical and empirical studies. Although there are different voices in academic communities, the existing studies generally confirm the role of financial development on economic growth. There are also some empirical researches supporting such a view. King and Levine (1993), Jalilian and Kirkpatrick (2002), pointed out that financial development had a promoting effect on economic growth. By contrast, Shan et al. (2001), Rioja and Neven (2004) argued that things are different in different countries, for example, financial development deterred economic growth in some Latin American countries. All these studies suggest that financial development has various effects on economic growth in different countries at different times and stages of development (Rioja & Valev, 2004).

In the about 40 years of reform and opening up, China has been experiencing rapid economic growth and a vast expansion of the financial sector. Having been

B. S. Nayak (✉)
Business School for the Creative Industries, University for the Creative Arts, Epsom, UK
e-mail: Bhabani.nayak@uca.ac.uk

Z. Yingnan
Adam Business School, University of Glasgow, Glasgow, UK

© The Author(s), under exclusive license to Springer Nature Singapore Pte Ltd. 2021
B. Shankar Nayak (ed.), *China: The Bankable State*,
https://doi.org/10.1007/978-981-16-5252-3_5

classified as emerging financial sector, China has been defined as "high performing economies" by the World Bank (Shan et al., 2001). Since the economic reform starting in 1978, the annual growth rate of the Chinese economy has maintained to be about 10%, and the total economic output has ranked the second highest in the world. At the same time, the Chinese government has also carried out large-scale of financial reforms, which has led to the development of the financial industry. It seems that financial development goes hand in hand with the higher-speed economic growth (Jordan & Qi, 2006). With the consistent fast-growing economy and the increasing development of the financial system, China has been drawing more and more attention as a compelling case for researchers to find the relationship between financial development and economic growth.

Since the reform and opening up of China in 1978, there are more and more metropolitan cities with high speed of economic development and social progress. The emergence and development of the metropolis not only represent the level of a country's economic growth but also become the driving force to improve the quality of domestic economic growth (Scott, 2008). At the same time, the financial industry has been developing at a higher speed, gradually contributing to the development of those metropolises and economic prosperity. Specifically, the effective operation of financial institutions provides more financing approaches for firms, which reduces the cost of firms' development and the risk of the operation (Hao, 2006). It also provides a large number of jobs and opportunities, which contributes to economic growth in many aspects. Besides, financial institutions can accumulate capital which can be invested in emerging high-tech industries, like the computer and internet, which can surge economic growth (ibid).

Critical Reflections on Financial Development and Economic Growth

In the literature, the causality issue between financial development and economic growth has been examined by both theoretical and empirical evidence. However, there are different conclusions of these studies on "the finance-led growth hypothesis" (Jordan & Qi, 2006). Back in 1993, King and Levine pointed out that financial development could lead to economic growth, and the development of financial intermediation including the stock market and the banking system could positively associate with economic growth. A well-developed financial system plays a vitally important role in mobilizing savings and facilitating investments (Levine & Zervos, 1998). Afterward, Arestis et al. (2001) indicated the critical role of banks and stock markets on economic growth, and they also stressed that banks were much more important to economic growth. Jalilian and Kirkpatrick (2002) and Kang and Sawada (2000) also supported the idea that financial development led economic growth through increasing the benefits of capital investment, which can also reduce the poverty level in some developing countries. Furthermore, through the study of both developed and developing countries in different stages of development, Nourzad (2002) finds that financial deepening can increase the efficiency of productivity, thus promoting economic growth.

However, some other economists argued that economic growth could also provide more demands for financial services, which in turn can lead to a more developed financial sector (Singh and Weisse, 1998). Further, Shan and Morris examined the causal relationship between financial development and economic growth in some developing countries and some OECD countries, supporting the fact that there existed the bi-directional causality between finance and growth, but there are no "one-size-fits-all" conclusions across countries. There is also some empirical and theoretical evidence showing that there is no causal relationship between finance and growth (Al-Tamimi et al., 2001). They do not find evidence whether financial development is affected or can influence economic growth in their selected countries. Deidda and Fattouh (2002) also presented that there is no linear relationship between finance and growth.

In those works of literature, there is a controversial debate regarding the direction of causality. On the one hand, some economists support the finance-lead-growth hypothesis. On the other hand, there is evidence of reverse causality in some countries and bidirectional causality in others. That is to say, the relationship between financial development and economic growth might be country-specific (Shan et al., 2001). And Rioja and Valev (2004) used an extensive panel data set of 74 countries which are at different level of economic growth covering 1961–1995 to test the relationship between financial development and economic growth. It turns out that the effect of financial development on economic growth is various in different countries, which depends on the level of financial development. In countries with the relatively low level of financial development, the effect on economic growth is uncertain. Financial development may spur economic growth or deter growth; while in countries with a higher level of financial development, there is a significant positive effect on economic growth; moreover, in countries with a significantly high level of financial development, financial development also increases growth, but not that obvious as relatively high level of financial development countries (Rioja & Valev, 2004). They also find that financial development affects the sources of economic growth differently in developing countries and industrial countries. In developing countries which are behind "technological frontier", financial development has a strong positive influence on economic growth mainly through capital accumulation. Conversely. In industrial countries that at the technological frontier, financial development can increase the funding for innovative activities, which can lead to more considerable productivity growth (ibid).

Among those kinds of finance-growth literature, most empirical researches based on cross-country data suggests a positive relationship between financial intermediations and economic growth (Hao, 2006). The development of financial sector has the function to mobilize savings and allocate capital more efficiently, which can have a positive effect on savings decisions and promote better investments, and therefore spur economic growth in the long-run. According to Levine (2005), there are five major channels through which financial systems can influence economic growth. First, financial development can produce information about more productive investments and allocate capital more efficiently. Second, the emergence of some financial arrangements can improve corporate governance. Third, a more developed financial market can diversify risk to encourage individuals to invest in projects with higher risks and higher production efficiency. Forth, financial development can increase the rate of savings. Last, financial development can make the exchange of goods and services more accessible. Financial intermediations, regarded as the medium in the saving-investment process, play an important role in resource allocation (Zhang et al., 2012). They can acquire information at a lower cost and allocate capital from less productive investments to relatively more productive ones, which improve resource allocation (Patrick, 1966). They can also make capital allocation more efficient by changing its ownership and composition (ibid).

The emergence and expansion of financial intermediations represents financial development. Sound financial intermediations are efficient in obtaining more resources and the allocating capital (Hao, 2006). And Odedokun (1996) explored that financial intermediations can prosper the economy in most developing countries. Besides, Becker and Knudsen (2002) stressed that the development of the banking system plays a vital role in economic growth. Furthermore, Levine and Zervos (1998) added that stock market development was also positively correlated with economic growth.

Finance and Economic Growth in China

With the rapid development of the financial sector and the fast-growing economy, China draws much interest of economists all over the world. However, the findings are quite different according to the finance-growth literature. In the view of Allen et al. (2005), the financial sector is still under-developed with the state-controlled banking system and weak stock and bonds markets, which might hinder economic growth due to the distorting nature of the government. Even though China has experienced fast economic growth for nearly 40 years, they believe there exists the negative relationship between financial development and economic growth. According to Jordan and Qi (2006), the substantial government ownership of banks in China is believed to be one of the reasons for the slow economic growth. Hasan et al. (2009) and Boyreau-Debray (2003) also supported the negative impact of the financial sector on economic growth by using provincial data over the period from the early 1990s to the early 2000s. They attribute the adverse effect on economic growth to the banking sector's support of loss-making state-owned enterprises.

In contrast, Hao (2006) found that China's financial development did contribute to economic growth during the period 1985–1999, he also indicated that the financial sector in China contributed to economic growth by the "mobilization of savings and the substitution of loans for budget appropriation". Furthermore, Degryse and Cheng

(2010) confirmed these findings, showing that the development of the banking sector in China has a significantly positive impact on economic growth. Guariglia and Poncet (2008) showed that some activities taken by the Chinese government as state intervention in finance hindered economic growth, while other activities taken to develop financial markets by the government spurred economic growth positively. Besides, data from the firm level can also indicate that the formal financial system was positively associated with firm's growth, while informal financing did not have such an effect on growth (Ayyagari et al., 2010).

However, Zhang et al. (2012) use the city-level data from 286 Chinese cities with more local information for the period 2001–2006 to suggest that financial development has a positive relationship with economic growth. They mainly focus on the period after China's access to the World Trade Organization (WTO) in 2001, which is the big difference from previous studies that only covered the years before 2001 (Zhang et al., 2012). Their findings show that the financial reform after 2001 goes in the right direction, which leads to the economic prosperity in China (ibid). And Yuan (2014) uses the data from Jiangsu province to test whether financial development can lead economic growth in a Granger causality sense. He finds that Financial Interrelation Ratio is the primary factor to lead economic growth, while Financial Efficiency and the development of capital markets have little effect on economic growth in Jiangsu province (Yuan, 2014).

Financial economists from China and abroad study the relationship between financial development and economic growth in the overall China or different regions of China and have striking findings. Hao (2006), Jordan and Qi (2006) and Zhang et al. (2012) use the dataset from all regions of China to find financial development influence economic growth in China positively. Ma and Jalil (2008) launch a comparative study between China and Pakistan to find the positive and significant relationship in Pakistan but negative relationship between loans to the private sector and economic growth in China. Chen and Jiang (2018) conduct research on specific provinces and cities in western China from 2010 to 2015 to find the positive relationship between financial development and economic growth. It shows that the relationship is different in different regions at various stages of development, which is the result of different economic and financial performance of those regions. However, there are few studies on the relationship between financial development and economic growth in the metropolis and megacities of China during recent years.

In China, financial development contributes a lot to economic growth. Since the economic reform in 1978, a series of economic and financial reforms took place in China, which lead to a more deregulated financial system and a more prosperous financial market, hence spurs significant economic growth in China (Jordan & Qi, 2006).

Before the reform, China's financial system was a mono-bank system, which restricted resource allocation extremely. The People's Bank of China functioned as both the central and commercial bank in the financial sector, and it only distributed working capital (Hao, 2006). Over the period from the economic reform in 1978–1984, both the gross national income and GDP increase slowly through the liberation of prices which increases agricultural products' prices and thus raises rural household's income (Hao, 2006). Meanwhile, the rapid emergence of non-state enterprises intensifies the competition with state-owned enterprises, which increase the profit of those enterprises and increase the earnings of their employees (ibid). The increases in households' income also contribute to the increase in savings deposits during that period.

From 1984 to 1994, the Big Four state-owned commercial banks and other financial institutions were established as the new commercial banks, and foreign banks were allowed to participate in the banking sector. Further, some non-banking financial institutions emerged in the financial market. All these development in the financial institutions in this period extended loans to state-owned enterprises and intensified the competition in the financial sector (Zhang et al., 2012). Therefore, investment and credit in the financial sector increase rapidly, and resource allocation became more efficient, which promote the steady growth of GDP.

From 1994, a series of financial reforms aiming at the more liberalized banking system has taken place. A large number of new banks appeared, and commercial banks gained more substantial autonomy of financial operation. Furthermore, restrictions on foreign banks were relaxed. All these contribute to the increase in the total financial assets in China. Meanwhile, Chinese monetary policy focused on indirect monetary control and indirect monetary instruments played an important role in credit planning (Zhang et al., 2012). However, this bank-nominated financial sector is inefficient in capital allocation. For example, a significant share of household savings, allocated mainly by the four state-owned banks, were into inefficient state sectors (Hao, 2006). These state banks also produced a large quantity of NPLs which hinder efficient performance (Iftekhar et al., 2006).

However, after 2001 when China entered the WTO, financial liberalization process plays an important role, including the relaxation of restrictions on ownership takeovers, on foreign banks entries and interests of loans and deposits (Zhang et al., 2012). Financial liberalization can help improve the efficiency of resource allocation and boost technology innovation. Moreover, the strengthening of financial regulation and supervision can also monitor state-owned banks, improve corporate governance and alleviate NPLs problems. Furthermore, foreign banks' presence can fierce the competition, which encourages the Chinese banking sector to perform more efficiently (Zhang et al., 2012). From 2001 to 2016, Chinese GDP witnessed a significant increase and the figure in 2016 is almost 6.7 times of that in 2001 (Chinese Statistic Yearbook, 2017). The rapid economic growth is the achievement of a series of 5-Year Plan for the development of domestic economy and society.

The development of Chinese financial markets goes smoothly. In the early 1990s, the stock market began to take shape. Two stock exchanges were established, which are the Shanghai Stock Exchange and the Shenzhen Stock Exchange. As for bond markets, government bond takes a larger share than corporate bonds in China. However, the stock market capitalization and the total value of corporate bonds only account for 15.1% and 1.1% of GDP respectively. Although Chinese stock and bond markets enjoyed rapid expansion, their effect on the real economy is insignificant (Hasan et al., 2009). And Hao (2006) pointed out that there are two major channels for financial sectors to promote economic growth, which are "the mobilization of household savings and the substitution of loans for budget appropriation". He also uses GMM-system estimator to testify that savings and loan/budget have the positive and significant relationship with growth regression (Hao, 2006).

Before the reform, state-owned enterprises were the primary source of government revenue, at an average of 50.1% during 1952–1977, while household savings has been accounting an increasing share in national income after the reform (Hao, 2006). In 1993, household total financial savings only accounted for 43.02% of GDP, while the figure almost doubled in 2013, at 82.1% of GDP and household savings added up to 46703.1 billion yuan. It appears that financial development promotes the households' savings potential and increase savings. In the meanwhile, the expansion of household savings contributes a lot to financial deepening (Hao, 2006). In 2016, household savings deposits accounted for 56.7% of quasi-money and 38.9% of M2 (China Statistic Yearbook, 2017). The increase of quasi-money can be used as an indicator of financial development (Zhang et al., 2012). Also, the ratio of M2 to GDP used to measure financial depth has increased dramatically from 24.6% in 1978 to 208.3% in 2016(China Financial Statistics: 2016). Therefore, financial deepening is impressive in China from 1978 to 2016.

Furthermore, in China, due to the fact that non-state enterprises have limited access to bank loans, while household savings can be converted through some informal channels into the investments of non-state enterprises which spur economic growth more efficiently than state sectors (Hao, 2006). Therefore, financial development can channel those savings into more productive and promising investment, which improves the efficiency of capital allocation and promotes economic growth.

With the successful process of a series financial reforms, domestic loans have expanded increasingly. The empirical research shows that domestic loans, including RMB loans, credit loans, and entrusted loans replaces state budget, becoming the larger source to finance the economy, with 10.9% of actual funds financed investment in 2016. According to Hao (2006), most self-raised funds are from loans. Therefore, we can conclude that domestic loans are the primary source of financing the economy, which can lead to economic growth, because loans need the payment of interests, which can constrain firms' budget and therefore encourage them to allocate capital to more promising investments (Hao, 2006). Empirically, Liu and Li find that domestic loans, as a means of external financial sources, are more efficient in economic growth compared to state appropriation.

Financial Developments in China

Financial development can be reflected by the increase of total financial assets, the expansion of the number of financial institutions, as well as the growth of financial efficiency which is reflected by the degree of financial contribution to the needs of economic growth (Singh, 2008). According to Goldsmith (1969), the Financial

Interrelation Ratio (FIR) can be used to measure the degree of financial intensity to an economic system in that country. It refers to the ratio of the total amount of financial activities to the total amount of economic activities in a certain period, which can be expressed by the ratio of the financial assets to the wealth of the whole economy (Singh, 2008). Generally, it can be simplified as the ratio of total financial assets to the gross domestic product.

$$\text{FIR} = (\text{M2} + \text{L} + \text{D})/\text{GDP}$$

In this expression, M2 refers to broad money, L refers to the balance of loans in domestic and foreign currencies in financial institutions, D refers to the balance of savings deposit in domestic and foreign currencies in financial institutions, and GDP refers to the gross domestic product. Singh (2008) believes that financial interrelation ratio reflects the magnitude of the actual funds to the investment and can link investment and growth directly, which can be seen as a characteristic of financial development. It is universally acknowledged that finance can affect the economy through the accumulation and the usage of capital, while the main approach is financial intermediaries and financial markets.

Efficiency of Financial Developments in China

Capital formation and capital accumulation are core issues of economic growth. Without capital accumulation, there will be no economic growth. Savings is the ultimate source of capital. Whether savings can be effectively converted into investment plays an essential role in the healthy and stable development of the economy (Hao, 2006). When a country has enough amount of savings resources, and the savings resources can be converted into investment through effective channels, the country's economy can maintain healthy and stable development. On the contrary, if a country's savings resources are unreasonably distributed, or there are obstacles in the channel of converting savings into investments, economic growth will also be affected adversely (Chang et al., 2010). And McKinnon (1973) also confirmed this in the theory of financial repression: the development of most developing countries is lagging behind because of insufficient savings resources and the lack of smooth flow of savings to investment.

The efficiency of financial development refers to the efficiency of financial intermediations to absorb capital and reallocate those resources into productive investment, which can be expressed by the Loan–Deposit Ratio (LDR) (Chang et al., 2010).

$$\text{LDR} = \text{L}/\text{D}$$

Since indirect financing is the major way to finance the economy in China in the long run, therefore bank's lending behavior has become the dominant factor for the smooth conversion of savings into investment. Which is to say, bank lending is the main approach to transfer savings into investment (ibid). Thus, the decreasing ratio of loans to savings means that there are more and more savings not able to be transferred into investment, and the channel for allocating savings into investment is blocked. The smaller the LDR, the smaller the amount of savings converted into investment and the more inefficient of financial development.

Development of Financial Markets in China

According to Patrick (1966), one of the significant contributions of financial development to economic growth is to encourage savers to transfer their unproductive tangible assets into savings in the form of financial assets, such as the capital stock which is of higher liquidity and can achieve more productive uses. The private market mechanism can be sufficient to allocate scarce capital in their most productive uses (Patrick, 1966). It can achieve its functions more broadly compared with traditional financial institutions which avoid taking risks. In China, the investments for infrastructure construction, agriculture mechanism, and technological innovation are highly needed, which requires a large number of long-term funds to finance these kinds of productive investment. A well-functioning financial market can encourage people more willingly to buy long-term securities like stocks and bonds because shareholders can sell their stakes easily if they need their savings, and this can provide abundant funding to those investments (ibid).

Financial markets provide important services for economic growth, and stock markets can provide financial services which are different from banking services (Levine & Zervos, 1998). Further, Levine and Zervos (1998) find a strong and positive connection between stock markets development and economic growth. With the continuous optimization of the financial development environment, all kinds of financial institutions including banks, securities, insurances emerge quickly, and the scale of financial markets is getting larger (Guo & Zhao, 2011).

Financial markets play an important role in resource allocation, providing substantial capital supply. During 2011–2015, the 12th Five -Year Plan guided the financial market as one of the major players in the process of China's economic and social development. As the core of the capital market, the development of securities markets in Beijing from 2010 to 2016 is significant. The Chinese government data shows that the total trading volume of securities markets increased almost three times from 8757.54 billion yuan in 2010 to 23231.86 billion yuan in 2016, which indicates that the securities market in Beijing becomes more active. Stock trading and bond trading account for a large proportion of the total trading volume of securities markets in Beijing. By the end of 2016, the volume of stock trading and bond trading increases to 13589.09 billion yuan and 24068.96 billion yuan respectively.

The active insurance market also has a positive influence on economic growth, which can transfer and manage different risks more efficiently and accumulate and mobilize domestic savings into more productive uses (Arena, 2008). And Webb et al. (2002) further explained that life insurance activity can contribute to economic growth by increasing productivity. Beides, property insurance can promote economic growth by protecting individuals from taking risks in different economic activities, and provide "risk-financing choice" for firms to reduce the probability of suffering losses, which can affect investment decisions (ibid).

At the meanwhile, Arena (2008) also finds that both life and non-life insurance has an effective impact on economic growth, and there is evidence to support the large effect of non-life insurance on economic growth in developing countries. Normally, life insurance companies can provide funds to facilitate long-term investments, while non-life insurance companies usually facilitate short-term investments (Arena, 2008). Also, according to Han et al. (2010), the development of overall insurance business including life and non-life insurance plays a more important role in the process of economic growth in developing countries than in developed countries (Han et al., 2010).

In 2011, credit insurance bore the venture capital of more than 30,000 RMB in the international trade, which enabled Chinese foreign trade to develop steadily in a safe and reliable environment (Commision, 2011). Besides, the insurance industry has also created liability insurance, and the amount of liability risk is about 30 trillion, which provides the necessary conditions for social reform and enterprise innovation (ibid). Furthermore, the insurance industry is also actively involved in financial reforms. In the bonds market, insurance institutions are the second largest investors, and large amounts of funds are put into use (ibid).

More importantly, the aggravating trend of an aging population in China's economic development brings tremendous pressure on China's social security, but the development of the insurance business can provide support for the elderly care. In 2011, there are 289.91 million policyholders of endowment insurance and 473.43 million policyholders of medical insurance (ibid). It seems that the development of the insurance industry has further solved the problem of old-age care and medical care in China. Therefore, the development of insurance business has guaranteed people's livelihood, driven China's consumption level to a certain extent, stimulated people's consumption demand and led to economic development. At the same time, it has also promoted China's social security system, increased people's welfare level continuously, and made social development more harmonious.

Economic Structure and Growth of Total Investments in Fixed Assets in China

The 12th Five-Year Plan (2011) insists to optimize the primary industry, strengthen the second industry, expand the tertiary industry, promote the industrial integration and develop the modern industrial system of the capital. At the end of 2016, the 13th Five-Year Plan points out that the transformation of "full-industrial-chain" and upgrading a saturated sector are the top priority of economic development. It aims to construct an "innovation-led, technology-intensive" and high-grade economic structure. Recent years, financial services contribute a lot in support of emerging sectors of strategic importance and high-end manufacturing sectors.

Fixed-asset investment is the workload of building and purchasing fixed-asset activities in monetary performance, and infrastructure investment is the key factor to facilitate the rapid development of economic activities (Qin & Song, 2009). The 12th Five-Year Plan (2011) infers that investment is the primary force to improve economic growth. Therefore, it is important to make the coordinated development of increasing investment, promoting consumption, rising employment and improving people's livelihood. It is also important to actively adjust investment structure to expand investment in producer services industries, strategic emerging industries, high-end manufacturing, cultural industries, and tourism to increase infrastructure investment in transportation, energy and environment, and to optimize investment structure in the real estate (Beijing Government, 2011).

Financial Developments, Economic Growth and its Positive Impacts on people's Livelihood in China

During the 12th Five-Year Plan period, people's living standard has been improved thoroughly, with a more stable employment environment, more comprehensive public service system, smaller income gap, modern education system, improved health care and old-age service system, and a more harmonious society (Beijing Government, 2016). Consumption plays an increasingly important role in economic development. In the 12th Five-Year Plan (2011), the government promotes rapid economic development through sustained expansion of consumption. Therefore, it is necessary to follow the guidance of the national income distribution policy to improve the income level of residents, alleviate the inequality between the rich and poor, stabilize household consumption expectations, and enhance their consuming capacity (ibid).

According to Table 3.6, per capita disposable income of urban household keeps increasing from 29,073 yuan in 2010 to 52,530 yuan in 2016, but after deducting the price factor, the actual growth rate is 6.9%, which is 0.1% lower than that in 2015. During the 12th Five-Year Plan period, the annual actual growth rate of per capita disposable income of the urban household is 7.2%, increasing by 1% in 2010, which indicates that people's living standard is improving at a higher speed. Meanwhile, per capita disposable income of urban household is an important indicator of people's consumption capacity, the higher actual growth rate also means the higher speed of economic growth in that period. Regarding per capita consumption expenditure of urban household, the figure is 38,256 yuan in 2016, increasing by 92% compared with that in 2010, which also indicates the higher speed of economic growth in Beijing from 2010 to 2016.

Besides, the employment situation is quite stable during the 12th Five-Year Plan period, with an average of 433,400 persons being newly employed in the urban area. This is the effort of the 12th Five-Year Plan which implements affirmative employment policies by creating more employment opportunities, targeting employment supports, perfecting public employment services networks and strengthening the regulation of labor markets (Beijing Government, 2011).

Conclusion

The financial industry is the driving force for China's economic development and social progress. Currently, the Chinese financial industry has become the industry with the largest proportion of the tertiary industry, especially after the 2008 financial crisis, the development of financial industry entered into a new booming stage and has achieved excellent results. In the meanwhile, it is of great significance for the government to formulate economic and fiscal policies, aiming to provide guidance for the healthy and rapid development of metropolis and megacities represented by further spur Chinese economic growth. Moreover, there is no significant relationship between economic growth and the improvement of financial efficiency, and to some degree, the efficiency of financial development can affect economic growth adversely. It is also important to increase the capacity of the banking system to allocate resources efficiently, and to broaden financing channels to the economy with prosperous and diversified financial markets, which can increase the direct investment to the economy.

References

Allen, F., Qian, J., & Qian, M. (2005). Law, finance, and economic growth in China. *Journal of Financial Economics, 77*(1), 57–116.

Al-Tamimi, H., Al-Awad, M., & Charif, H. (2001). Finance and growth: Evidence from some Arab countries. *Journal of Transnational Management Development, 7*, 3–18.

Arena, M. (2008). Does insurance market activity promote economic growth? A cross-country study for industrialized and developing countries. *Journal of Risk & Insurance, 75*(4), 921–946.

Arestis, P., Demetriade, P., & Luintel, K. (2001). Financial development and economic growth: The role of stock markets. *Journal of Money, Credit and Banking, 33*(1), 16–41.

Ayyagari, M., Demirgüç-Kunt, A., & Maksimovic, V. (2010). Formal versus informal finance: Evidence from China. *Review of Financial Studies, 23*(8), 3048–3097.

Becker, M., & Knudsen, T. (2002). Schumpeter 1911: Farsighted visions on economic development. *American Journal of Economics and Sociology, 61*(2), 387–403.

Beijing Government. (2011). *The 12th five-year plan for the development of domestic economy and society in Beijing* (pp. 1–133). The Beijing Government.

Beijing Government. (2016). *The 13th five-year plan for the development of domestic economy and society in Beijing* (pp. 1–148). The Beijing Government.

Boyreau-Debray, G. (2003). *Financial intermediation and growth: Chinese style*. Working paper series 3027. The World Bank, Policy Research.

Chang, P., Jia, C., & Wang, Z. (2010). Bank Fund reallocation and economic growth: Evidence from China. *Journal of Banking & Finance, 34*(11), 2753–2766.

Chen, H., & Jiang, N. (2018). *The relationship between financial development and economic growth in Western China.* In Jiangsu: 2018 3rd international conference on social society and economics development, pp. 509–513.

China Insurance Regulatory Commission. (2011). *China insurance regulatory commission-statistics.* [Online] Available at: http://bxjg.circ.gov.cn/web/site0/tab5179/. Accessed 15 Dec 2011.

Degryse, H., & Cheng, X. (2010). The impact of banks and non-bank financial institutions on local economic growth in China. *Journal of Financial Services Research, 37*(2–3), 179–199.

Deidda, L., & Fattouh, B. (2002). Non-linearity between finance and growth. *Economics Letters, 74* (3), 339–345.

Goldsmith, R. (1969). *Financial structure and development* (pp. 232–245). Yale University Press.

Guariglia, A., & Poncet, S. (2008). Could financial distortions be no impediment to economic growth after all? Evidence from China. *Journal of Comparative Economics, 36*(4), 633–657.

Guo, X., & Zhao, H. (2011). *Co- Integration analysis of development of security market and economic growth: A case study of Beijing.* Research of Finance and Education, pp. 43–47.

Han, L., Li, D., Moshirian, F., & Tian, Y. (2010). Insurance development and economic growth. *The Geneva Papers on Risk and Insurance – Issues and Practice, 35*(2), 183–199.

Hao, C. (2006). Development of financial intermediation and economic growth: The Chinese experience. *China Economic Review, 17*(4), 347–362.

Hasan, I., Wachtel, P., & Zhou, M. (2009). Institutional development, financial deepening and economic growth: Evidence from China. *Journal of Banking & Finance, 33*(1), 157–170.

Iftekhar, H., Paul, W., & Mingming, Z. (2006). Institutional development, financial deepening and economic growth: Evidence from China. *Journal of Banking & Finance, 33*(1), 157–170.

Jalilian, H., & Kirkpatrick, C. (2002). Financial development and poverty reduction in developing countries. *International Journal of Finance & Economics, 7*(2), 97–108.

Jordan, S., & Qi, J. (2006). Does financial development 'Lead' economic growth? The case of China. *Annals of Economics and Finance, 1*, 197–216.

Kang, S., & Sawada, Y. (2000). Financial repression and external openness in an endogenous growth model. *Journal of International Trade & Economic Development, 9*(4), 427–443.

King, R., & Levine, R. (1993). Finance, entrepreneurship and growth. *Journal of Monetary Economics, 32*(3), 513–542.

Levine, R. (2005). Finance and growth: Theory and evidence. In Handbook of economic growth (1 (A), 866–923).

Levine, R., & Zervos, S. (1998). Stock markets, banks, and economic growth. *The American Economic Review, 88*(3), 537–558.

Ma, Y., & Jalil, A. (2008). Financial development, economic growth and adaptive efficiency: A comparison between China and Pakistan. *China & World Economy, 16*(6), 97–111.

McKinnon, R. (1973). Inflation as a global problem. *Journal of International Economics, 3*(4), 397–398.

Nourzad, F. (2002). Financial development and productive efficiency: A panel study of developed and developing countries. *Journal of Economics and Finance, 26*(2), 138–148.

Odedokun, M. (1996). Financial policy and efficiency of resource utilization in developing countries. *Growth and Change, 27*(3), 269–297.

Patrick, H. (1966). Financial development and economic growth in underdeveloped countries. *Economic Development and Cultural Change, 14*(2), 174–189.

Qin, D., & Song, H. (2009). Sources of investment inefficiency: The case of fixed-assets investment in China. *Journal of Development Economics, 90*(1), 94–105.

Rioja, F., & Neven, V. (2004). Does one size fit all?: A reexamination of the finance and growth relationship. *Journal of Development Economics, 74*(2), 429–447.

Rioja, F., & Valev, N. (2004). Finance and the sources of growth at various stages of economic development. *Economic Inquiry, 42*(1), 127–140.

Scott, A. (2008). Resurgent Metropolis: Economy, society and urbanization in an interconnected world. *International Journal of Urban and Regional Research, 32*(3), 548–564.

Shan, J., Morris, A., & Sun, F. (2001). Financial development and economic growth: An egg-and-chicken problem? *Review of International Economics, 9*(3), 443–454.

Singh, A., & Weisse, B. (1998). Emerging stock markets, portfolio capital flows and long-term economy growth: Micro and macroeconomic perspectives. *World Development, 26*(4), 607–622.

Singh, T. (2008). Financial development and economic growth nexus: A time-series evidence from India. *Applied Economics, 40*(12), 1615–1627.

Webb, I., Grace, M. F., & Skipper, H. D. (2002). *The effect of banking and insurance on the growth of capital and output.* Working paper 02, Center for Risk Management and Insurance.

Yuan, J. (2014). *An empirical research on Jiangsu's financial development affects economic growth.* Postgraduate. Hunan University.

Zhang, J., Wang, L., & Wang, S. (2012). Financial development and economic growth: Recent evidence from China. *Journal of Comparative Economics, 40*(3), 393–412.

Chapter 6
Financial Development and National Economic Growth in China: A Beijing Praxis

Bhabani Shankar Nayak and Hao Chen

Introduction

This chapter outlines theoretical and empirical works on the relationship between financial development and economic growth within the context of China. It critically evaluates different theories to understand different linkages between financial development and national economic growth in China. The article investigates the causal relationship between regional financial development and economic growth in China. The article attempts to find the development characteristics of regional finance and interaction mechanism between financial development and economic growth from microeconomic perspective with a special reference to Beijing.

The relationship between financial development and economic growth has attracted a lot of attention among economists for a long time. It has been well documented in the literature that financial development has a strong positive relationship with economic growth (Goldsmith, 1969; Levine, 2005; Andini, 2011). Some studies also claim that economic growth may be the major driving force behind the financial development. A large number of researchers have attempted to decipher causality patterns, which can help to adjust the financial structure, improve the efficiency of resources allocation and further promote regional economic growth.

China is an ideal avenue for investigating possible causality switches due to the sequential implementation of economic reform among Chinese provinces, and the determinants of such extraordinary growth are far from certain. Since the start of its market-oriented reforms in 1978, China has experienced a persistent and impressive

B. S. Nayak (✉)
Business School for the Creative Industries, University for the Creative Arts, Epsom, UK
e-mail: Bhabani.nayak@uca.ac.uk

H. Chen
Adam Smith Business School, University of Glasgow, Glasgow, UK

growth rate globally. After nearly four decades of economic reform, China has become the second largest economy in the world, and its GDP accounted for 15% of global total GDP (Gross Domestic Product) in 2016 (Jiang & Yao, 2017). In a similar sense, the financial system of China is also in the process of reform, while it remains under state control and underdeveloped relative to most western economies (Xu et al., 2018). In the past few decades, China's urbanization process has been accelerating, and many major cities have emerged. For example, Beijing, the capital of China, is the centre of commercial and financial activity.

The Chinese Praxis

The level of economic growth of these major cities is not only a reflection of the economic growth of a country, but also has a guiding role in improving the quality of national economic growth.

For example, McKinnon (1973) and Shaw (1973) challenge the case for financial repression and advocate financial liberalization and development as growth enhancing economic policies. This is because that financial liberalization causes interest rates to rise towards market-clearing levels and makes bank deposits more attractive, which will raise the demand for money and lead to a higher level of investment and economic growth. In addition, Roubini and Sala-i-Martin (1995) present a model that the government policies of financial repression tend to reduce the efficiency of the financial sector, increase the costs of intermediation, and reduce aggregate investment and the growth rate of the economy. Levine (2005) lists five possible channels through which financial development may influence economic growth. These channels include: (i) producing ex ante information about possible investments and capital allocation; (ii) monitoring firms and exerting corporate governance after providing finance; (iii) facilitating the trading, diversification and management of risks; (iv) mobilizing and polling savings; (v) easing the exchange of goods and services. In addition, Cihak et al. (2013) define the concept of financial function and construct an improved measure to quantify the functioning of financial institutions and financial markets via four dimensions below: (i) financial depth – the size of financial institutions and markets; (ii) financial access – the ability of individuals or enterprises to obtain financial services; (iii) financial efficiency – the efficiency of financial institutions in providing financial services and products; (iv) financial stability – the stability of financial institutions and markets. Their study (Cihak et al., 2013) compare 205 economies using time series data from 1960 to 2010, and their results show that financial sectors differ widely in accordance to their performance.

There are many empirical literatures on the relationship between financial development and economic growth. Early cross-country studies suggest a positive relationship between these two factors. Goldsmith (1969), using cross-country data from 1860 to 1963, claims a positive correlation between the size of financial intermediary sector and the level of economic activity. However, there is no evidence on whether financial development causes economic growth. In addition, several problems exist in Goldsmith's work, for example, only 35 countries are investigated and other factors influencing economic growth are not systematically controlled. King and Levine (1993) build on Goldsmith's work and then analyze whether the level of financial development predicts long-term economic growth. They examine it from three aspects: *Depth, Bank, Privy,* and the results of econometric tools show that the relationship between the initial level of financial development and economic growth is economically significant (King & Levine, 1993).

To answer the question of whether financial development is a leading indicator or a fundamental factor of economic growth, instrumental variables are employed in several cross-country studies. Levine et al. (2000a, b) use the measures of legal origin as instrumental variables for financial intermediation indicators to control for simultaneity bias, which improves King and Levine (1993) work's. They find a very strong connection between the exogenous component of banking development between per capita income growth, capital accumulation and productivity improvement. La Porta et al. (2002) use an alternative indicator of financial development to investigate the degree of public ownership of banks around the world. The authors show that higher degrees of public ownership of banks are associated with lower levels of bank development and high levels of public ownership of banks are associated with slower economic growth.

Studies of financial development and economic growth have also employed panel data techniques, pure time-series methods and case studies to ameliorate a number of statistical problems with pure cross-country investigations. Using a panel Generalized Method of Moments (GMM) estimator can improve pure cross-country work in three aspects. The first benefit is the ability to exploit the time series and cross-sectional variation in the data. The second benefit from moving to a panel is that it takes account the unobserved country-specific effect. The third benefit is that it permits the use of instrumental variables for all regresses and thereby providing more precise estimates of the finance-growth relationship. Liang (2005) uses the GMM techniques to test the model in a panel data set covering 29 Chinese provinces over the period of 1990–2001. Empirical results show that financial development and government deregulation in the financial sector significantly promote China's economic growth. Zhang et al. (2012) focus on the years after China's admission to the World Trade Organization (WTO) and then investigate the relationship between financial development and economic growth at the city level in China. They suggest that most traditional indicators of financial development are positively associated with economic growth, which means that the financial reforms after China's admission to the WTO are in the right direction. This is because that China began to take many steps to promote financial liberalization after 2001, including more interest rate liberalization, less restriction on ownership takeovers, and greater freedom to foreign banks and so on. Thus, freedom and competition jointly promote further deepening reforms and economic progress.

In addition, a substantial time-series literature use Granger-type causality tests and *Vector Autoregressive (VAR)* procedures to examine the nature of the finance-growth relationship. Chen et al. (2013), using cross-provincial data over the period

1978–2010, find that finance has strong positive influence on growth in high-income provinces, but a strong negative impact on growth in low-income provinces. The main reason for the negative impact is that the economic structure of low-income provinces with small portion of private sector, and a large number of shares of bank loans were used by government to support inefficient state-owned enterprises. As a consequence, non-performing loans have a tendency to accumulate and distort the allocation of capital in the economy. The *Granger causality tests* are used to estimate the finance-growth nexus of different bank types, using data from 1997 to 2008 of China's banking sector. Their results show that State-owned commercial banks do not Granger-cause GDP growth while joint stock commercial banks promote economic growth (Andersson et al., 2016). Additionally, Zhao (2017), using city-level data from 2007 to 2014, claims the results from different regressions all show that financial development does not have any significant positive effects on economic growth, while some indicators of financial development show negative effects. The author suggests that if the financial sector aims to play a more efficient role in promoting real economic growth, China has to further reform its financial system.

Apart from cross-country studies, there are also many researchers who focus on specific countries like United State and Japan. Since different countries have their own particular characteristics, an increasing number of researchers have to find empirical evidence that financial development affects the economic growth of one country (Xu, 2011). Compared with cross-country studies, in studies of an individual country, researchers can design specific measures of financial development according to the particular characteristics of country, which can examine an individual country in much greater depth. For example, Rousseau and Sylla (1999) find evidence consistent with the view that the financial development stimulates economic growth in United States. Besides, Rousseau (1999) uses the VAR procedures and concludes that financial sector is crucial in promoting Japan's explosive growth prior to the Frist World War.

To improve the understanding of the relationship between financial development and economic growth, researchers have employed more micro-level data, such as Industry-level and firm-level data across a broad cross-section of countries. These studies seek to resolve causality issues and to document in great detail of the mechanisms. Rajan and Zingales (1998) argue that better-developed financial intermediaries and markets help overcome market frictions, and lower costs of external finance facilitate firm growth and new firm formation. That is to say, the firms that are highly dependent on external financing grow more rapidly in countries with more developed financial institutions. Using a different strategy, Wurgler (2000) also employs industry-level data across 65 countries for the period 1963–1995 to explore the international differences in the efficiency of capital allocation. The author shows that countries with higher levels of financial development increase more investment in growing industries and decrease more investment in declining industries than financial underdevelopment economies. In other words, developed financial markets are associated with a better allocation of capital. Demirgüç-Kunt and Maksimovic (2001) examine whether financial development influences the degree to which firms are constrained from investing in profitable growth opportunities. The firm-level data consist of accounting data for the largest publicly traded manufacturing firms in 26 countries. They find both banking system development and stock market liquidity are positively associated with the excess growth of firms, and better developed financial systems eased external financing constraints, particularly on small firms.

Most existing studies have concentrated on the variations of the finance-growth relationship across countries (Goldsmith, 1969; Levine, 2005; La Porta et al., 2002), and these countries have different legal systems or various stages of economic development. However, few studies have paid attention to certain regions within a country. It focuses on within-country differences, rather than cross-country variations, in the finance-growth relationship. This is because that specific financial indicators might not be equally suitable for all countries. By focusing on city-level samples, factors that determine the relationship between financial development and economic growth can be effectively examined, which may help to establish a viable and efficient financial system and maintain fast regional economic growth.

Theoretical Foundations of Financial Development and National Economic Growth

Many researchers have different views on how to measure financial development. There still exists a gap between the roles finance plays in economic growth and the indicators in the empirical analysis. Since the data used to do research is usually limited, it may not measure the level of financial development in a region completely and accurately. Goldsmith creates a new indicator, *Financial Interrelations Ratio* (FIR), to measure the financial structure and financial development level of a country. In addition, China's financial system is regarded as a prototype described by the financial repression theory. For example, interest rates are still controlled by government, and credit allocation is heavily influenced by political factors rather than commercial motives. However, China has achieved remarkable success in economic growth in spite of its repressed financial system. This result is contrary to financial repression theory, but it may be due to China's special national conditions. Suggest that financial repression have some negative impacts on economic growth. Thus, a process of financial liberalization may be necessary to promote economic growth in most developing countries.

Theories of Finance and Economic Growth

Financial markets play an important role in producing strong economic growth by diverting financial funds from unproductive uses to productive ones. The origins of this role of financial markets may be traced back to the work of Schumpeter.

In his study, Schumpeter proposed that the banking system is a crucial factor for economic growth due to its role in the allocation of savings, the encouragement of innovation, and the funding of productive investments. From the late 1960s to the early 1970s, some western economists began to work on the relationship between financial development and economic growth. For example, Goldsmith (1969), McKinnon (1973) and Shaw (1973) put forward considerable evidence that financial development has a positive effect on economic growth. According to different research perspectives, financial development theory can be divided into three phases: (i) financial structure theory; (ii) financial repression theory; (iii) financial function theory.

Financial Structure Theory

Financial structure refers to the mixture of financial instruments, markets, and intermediaries operating in an economy. Goldsmith (1969) has examined financial development from the perspective of the relative structures of financial institutions and instruments. This research mainly aimed to analyse the evolution direction of financial system. Different financial structures lead to different resources allocations, which results in the difference of resources utilization efficiency (Liu & Li, 2010). Goldsmith (1969) also proposed that financial development refers to changes in financial structures, and research on financial development must be based on the changes of financial structure in the short and long term. From this point of view, a new indicator, Financial Interrelations Ratio (FIR), was created to measure the financial structure and financial development level of a country. Afterwards, he pioneered the application of cross-country data for empirical research. An empirical study was conducted, using cross-country data from 1860 to 1963, and the results show that the period of rapid economic growth is normally accompanied by the rapid development of finance.

As we know, the banking sector is the predominant channel of financing investment in China. Zhao (2017) claimed that a state-ruled banking sector, such as that of China, hinders economic growth because of the distorting nature of the government. They also suggested that China has to further reform its financial system and financial structure and make the financial sector more efficient. In addition, using a panel data of 29 provinces in China, the empirical results show that financial structure has a significant impact on economic growth, and the effect of financial structure on regional economic growth varies at different stages of financial development (Liu & Zhang, 2018). These studies are consistent with Goldsmith's (1969) point of view, and suggest forming a balanced financial structure, which will help better resource allocation.

Financial Repression Theory

Financial repression refers to a set of government regulations, laws and other non-market restrictions, which prevent the financial intermediaries of an economy from functioning at their full capacity (Xu & Gui, 2013a, b). Pervasive restrictions include high reserve requirements, interest rate ceilings, directed credit policies, restriction on market entry into the financial sector, exchange rate restrictions, capital controls, and government ownership or control of banks etc. The financial repression theory has its origins in the work of McKinnon (1973) and Shaw (1973). They further studied the financial structure from the perspective of financial repression and financial deepening. According to their argument, a repressed financial sector discourages both savings and investment because the rates of return are lower than those could be obtained in a competitive market. Thus, a process of financial liberalization is necessary to promote economic growth in developing countries. For example, When the interest rate is set at a level below the market-clearing equilibrium rate, the demand for credit will greatly exceed the available supply, which may lead to inefficient economic outcomes. McKinnon and Shaw believed that the relationship between financial development and economic growth is not a one-way causal relationship. They claimed that financial development is the power of economic growth, and economic growth is also the foundation of financial development.

Based on China's growth experience, the connection between financial repression and economic growth is more complicated. Financial repression, particularly the interest rate controls, has contributed to China's extraordinary economic growth performance by promoting investment and production, because those restrictions lower the cost of capital for the corporate sector (Xu & Gui, 2013a, b). This phenomenon is exactly what can be witnessed in China today. A repressed financial system acts as a double-edged sword: on the one hand, the system may help China accomplish extraordinary economic growth by subsiding investment and production. On the other hand, it endangers China's economic health by damaging economic efficiency. Therefore, a more market-oriented financial system is required to rebalance China's distorted economy and make China's economic growth more sustainable (Xu & Gui, 2013a, b). Financial liberalization is undoubtedly desirable given its positive effects on savings, investment, and economic development in China, which is the same as McKinnon (1973) and Shaw's (1973) point of view.

Endogenous Financial Development Theory

Endogenous financial development theory refers to the theory of the relationship between financial development and internal factors in the region. In 1990s, some financial theorists developed the theories of McKinnon and Shaw. On the one hand, they agreed with the idea of the interaction between financial development and economic growth. On the other hand, they discovered some deeper points of view. For example, what are the endogenous roots of financial development? The financial systems of different countries are various, some have greatly helped their economic to grow, while others have not. Some real economic factors were introduced, including information asymmetry, supervision costs and many uncertain factors. Although the models are more complex than before, they have made their policy proposals more in line with the actual situation in different countries. For example, Liang (2005) analyzed the relationship between finance and growth in the context of an endogenous growth model with government regulation and intervention. Based on the empirical results, they suggested that financial development and government deregulation in the financial sector significantly promote China's economic growth.

Trends of Financial Development and Economic Growth in China

When studying the finance-growth nexus in China, it is important to highlight certain specific characteristics of the Chinese financial system. Since the beginning of economic reforms in 1978, China has experienced the fastest economic growth the world has ever seen. It is undeniable that the average annual GDP growth rate from 1978 to 2006 was 9.6% (Liang & Teng, 2006; Holz, 2008). China's financial sector has also flourished as it successfully implemented a series of reforms. Before the economic reforms at the end of 1978, there was only one financial institution in China, the People's Bank of China (PBOC), which played the dual roles of both a central bank and a national commercial bank (Huang & Wang, 2017). There was an urgent need for a financial system, as growing economic activities would require effective financial intermediation. Thus, four state-owned commercial banks, the Bank of China, the China Construction Bank, the Agricultural Bank of China and the Industrial and Commercial Bank of China were split off from PBOC and PBOC retained its central banking role. To promote competition in the banking sector, the Chinese government began to establish some new banks, known as joint-equity commercial banks in 1986, and there was a total of 12 joint-equity commercial banks by the end of 2007 (Zhang et al., 2012).

Despite multiple market-oriented reforms, China's financial sector remains dominated by a few large banks, which are regulated by the government and differ from the financial system of Western economies (Söderlund & Tingvall, 2016). This implies that the government's mission to build an efficient financial system has only been partially accomplished. It created a very comprehensive financial system, but did not let the market mechanism work freely. For example, PBC regularly decides on base deposit and lending rates, although commercial banks' freedom in setting their own rates has increased over time (Huang & Wang, 2017).

Additionally, China established two stock exchanges, the Shanghai Stock Exchange and Shenzhen Stock Exchange in 1990 and 1991 respectively. The total market capitalization of the two exchanges was 10.9 billion Yuan in 1991, and it skyrocketed to 32,714 billion Yuan in 2007 (Chang et al., 2010). In spite of the fast growth, the ratios of stock market capitalization over GDP and total value traded over GDP in China are still lower compared to most of the countries with publicly-traded companies. In China, the banking system plays dominating force in financial intermediation, which is much more important than the stock market.

Although financial system is relatively weak and heavily intervened, China has experienced remarkable economic growth over the past three decades and has surpassed Japan to become the World's second largest economy (Xu & Gui, 2013a, b; Xu et al., 2018). While many economists and politicians have paid much attention on its remarkable economic performance, few have looked into China's various regional growth in details. During the reform period, the Chinese per capita GDP increased by almost eightfold, and China has transformed from one of the poorest countries into a major economic power (Xu, 2011). In fact, the overall high growth rate at the national level has never been evenly experienced at the provincial level. The actual economic growth and the level of income vary significantly among provinces due to their unique economic and financial conditions. For example, the highest provincial per capital GDP was 51,583 Yuan in Shanghai, almost ten times the GDP of Guizhou province, which is 5222 Yuan in 2005 (Chen et al., 2013). In this section, we provide a brief overview of the economic growth and financial conditions at the regional level. Then we pay attention to the economic growth and financial development in Beijing.

Nature of Economic Growth in Beijing

This part provides an insight into the recent dynamics of China's capital city. Beijing is not only the political and cultural center of China, but also the economic hub of north and west of the country. In the early 1980s, China's transition process from a planned to a market economy started to deeply affect the urban economy of Beijing, so that the city is on its way to become one of the world's leading cities.

Economic Growth in Beijing

The economic growth trend in terms of GDP shows that there is accelerated economic growth in Beijing from 2001 to 2016.

Figure 6.1 shows the trend of the nominal GDP and the growth rate of nominal GDP in Beijing from 2001 to 2016. As can be seen from the figure, Beijing's GDP has been rising since 2001, from 376.99 billion yuan in 2001 to 2566.91 billion yuan in 2016. This is consistent with the general trend of China's rapid economic development after the market-oriented reforms in 1978. In addition, the growth rate of GDP peaked in 2004 and 2007, at 14.3% and 14.4% respectively, and the

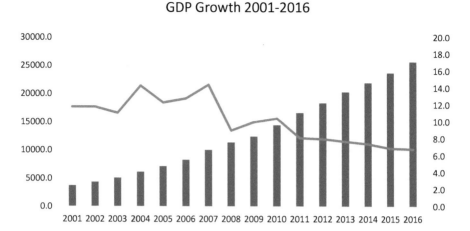

Fig. 6.1 Beijing nominal GDP and nominal GDP growth rate (2001–2016)
Source: Beijing Statistical Yearbook 2017

average annual growth rate is around 10.2%. However, the growth rate fell sharply in 2008, which may be affected by the global economic crisis. The global economic downturn also slowed the economic growth of Beijing. In the most recent years, particularly since 2012, when China entered a period of "new normal", economic growth has slowed down to a single-digit level (Jiang & Yao, 2017). Beijing also follows the national trend and pays more attention to the quality of economic growth rather than speed. This is the reason why Beijing's economic growth rate has been declining since 2010. Although the growth rate has decreased since 2010, Beijing's GDP has kept rising steadily and the economic aggregates has been increasing.

Economic Growth Structure in Beijing

The analysis of growth structure in Beijing shows that the primary sector is in the bottom of the growth ladder whereas secondary sectors are declining. The tertiary sector composed of financial sector is growing continuously as documented in the following graph.

Figure 6.2 shows the trend of the proportion of GDP in Beijing's three strata of industry, which reflects the structure of economic growth. It is obvious that, from 2001 to 2016, the proportion of primary industry and secondary industry in Beijing is a downward trend, while the tertiary industry has been rising and its contribution to GDP has reached 80.2% in 2016. The tertiary industry is in a dominant position, which is related to Beijing's industrial policy of building an international financial center and focusing on the development of tertiary industries such as service sector.

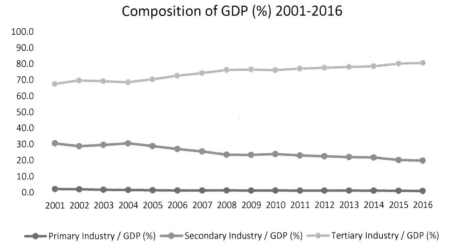

Fig. 6.2 Composition of GDP (2001–2016)
Source: Beijing Statistical Yearbook 2017

Meanwhile, as an international metropolis, the proportion of primary industry has remained at a very low level because the Beijing city has no extra land to develop agriculture. In recent years, the industrial structure is also gradually optimized. For example, a large number of high-pollution and heavy energy-consumption enterprises have been shut down or relocated and more high-tech industries are being introduced (Xu et al., 2018). These are the reasons why the proportion of the primary and secondary industries is declining. This change is also consistent with new normal economy, where the market further promotes the development of the tertiary industry and high-tech industries, and reduces the proportion of low value-added industries.

Total Investment in Fixed Assets in Beijing

The following graph shows that the investments in fixed assets are growing but the growth rate of investment has declined.

Fixed asset investment is a measure of capital spending. It refers to any investment within the measurement period in physical assets, such as real estate infrastructure, machinery etc. Additionally, it can also be a good indicator for measuring how much investment is occurring in a country or region. In general, when a local infrastructure and production technology are invested, it will promote local economic development. According to Fig. 6.3, apart from an obvious decline in 2008 due to the impact of the economic crisis, the total investment in fixed assets in Beijing has continued to expand, and the average annual growth rate is more than 13%.

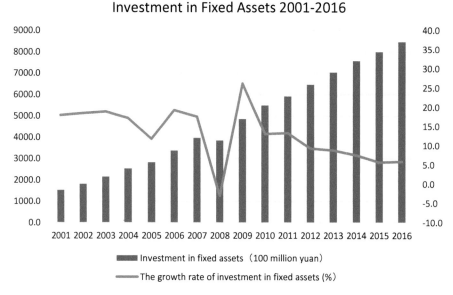

Fig. 6.3 Investment in fixed assets (2001–2016)
Source: Beijing Statistical Yearbook 2017

Living Standard in Beijing

The living standard in Beijing in terms of per capital disposable income is growing. The urban households have higher disposable income than the rural households in Beijing as outlined in the following graph.

Per capita disposable income is an important indicator to reflect people's living standards and the level of regional economy, because this indicator represents the spending power of urban and rural households. The faster the disposable income grows, the faster the living standards improve, which means regional high-speed economic growth. As shown in the Fig. 6.4, the per capita disposable income of Beijing residents has steadily increased, and the gap between urban and rural households has gradually narrowed. In 2016, it reached 52,721 yuan and 24,285 yuan respectively. This is similar to the per capita disposable income of residents in Shanghai, which is 57,692 yuan in 2016 (Shanghai Statistical Yearbook, 2017). Generally speaking, the growth of regional economy has promoted the improvement of people's living standards.

In general, the degree of Beijing economic development is reflected in the above four aspects: economic aggregates, economic growth structure, total investment in fixed assets and people's living standards. It can be seen that under the new normal economy, Beijing's economic growth has been continuously improved, and the structure of economic growth has become more reasonable.

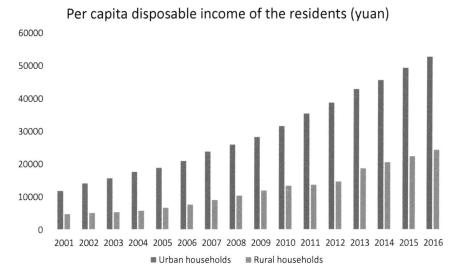

Fig. 6.4 Per capita disposable income of the residents (2001–2016)
Source: Beijing Statistical Yearbook 2017

Nature of Financial Development in Beijing

Financial development is characterized by the expansion of financial assets and the number of financial institutions. It refers not only to quantity of financial expansion, but also to the efficiency of financial improvement. The 30 years of reform and opening up has promoted the rapid financial development. A relatively well-rounded financial system with three pillars of banking, securities and insurance has gradually formed, and the status of Beijing's political and economic center has been further consolidated. The following part will describe the development of financial system in Beijing from those three pillars.

Growth of Banking in Beijing

The previous reform of mono-bank system has been transformed into a more sophisticated and diversified financial system. However, it can be seen that banks still play a vital role in Beijing's financial system. Until the end of 2016, there are 4303 banking institutions in Beijing, with a total of 191,529 employees (National Bureau of Statistics of China, 2018). Additionally, the amount of deposits has increased from 1222.34 billion yuan in 2001 to 13,064.80 billion yuan, which increased more than ten times. A study suggests that private savings rate rises with the level and growth rate of real per capita income (Loayza et al., 2000). Therefore, the growth of deposits in Beijing's banking system has also benefited from economic

Year	Total deposits (100 million yuan)	Total Loans(100 million yuan)	Sum of deposits and loans	GDP (100 million yuan)	Sum / GDP =FIR
2001	12223.4	7202.9	19426.3	3769.9	5.15
2002	15392.7	9230.8	24623.5	4396.0	5.60
2003	18321.9	11314.7	29636.6	5104.1	5.81
2004	21625.9	12600.2	34226.1	6164.9	5.55
2005	26731.3	13792.2	40523.5	7141.4	5.67
2006	31179.2	15486.9	46666.1	8312.6	5.61
2007	35014.1	17360.2	52374.3	10071.9	5.20
2008	41500.0	19431.1	60931.1	11392.0	5.35
2009	53428.8	24805.1	78233.9	12419.0	6.30
2010	63025.2	28748.1	91773.3	14441.6	6.35
2011	70985.1	32434.6	103419.7	16627.9	6.22
2012	79620.6	35441.7	115062.3	18350.1	6.27
2013	85897.2	39557.5	125454.7	20330.1	6.17
2014	93326.0	44438.8	137764.8	21944.1	6.28
2015	121878.9	49530.8	171409.7	23685.7	7.24
2016	130648.0	55553.2	186201.2	25669.1	7.25

Fig. 6.5 Total deposits and total loans in financial institutions (2001–2016)
Source: Beijing Statistical Yearbook 2016

development. In addition, Financial Interrelationship Ratio (FIR), which is the ratio of the sum of deposits and loans to nominal GDP, also increases year by year and reached 7.25% in 2016, except for a significant decline in the world economic crisis. This indicator is used to measure the degree of financial deepening in Beijing, and the higher the FIR is, the more important the financial system is in the economy. As shown in Fig. 6.5, Beijing's financial deepening is progressing rapidly.

Trading in the Securities Market in Beijing

From Fig. 6.6 above, it can be seen that, the turnover of various securities in the securities market was 42196.29 billion yuan in 2016, a decrease of 29.3% over the previous year, but the total turnover is still enormous. Due to the late establishment of China's stock market, the development of stock market is relatively slow. The state carried out a series of policy improvements such as the shareholding system reform. Although the stock market raised only 533.96 billion yuan in 2001, its scale has increased more than twentyfold, reaching 13589.09 billion yuan in 2016. The

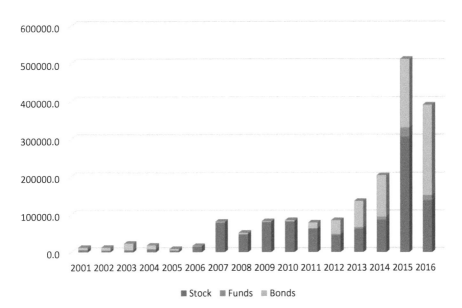

Fig. 6.6 Turnover in the securities market (2001–2016)
Source: Beijing Statistical Yearbook 2017

increasing of people's disposable income has generated more investment demand, and the diversification of investment choices has attracted more investors. There are the driving forces for the booming securities market. In addition, the bonds market issued a total 24068.96 billion yuan of bonds in 2016, an increase of 31.9% over the previous year. The bonds market has been growing rapidly in recent years, and market investor structure was further diversified. However, compared with Shanghai, the overall size of Beijing's securities market is relatively small. Because of Shanghai's history and locational advantages, the turnover of all SSE (Shanghai Stock Exchange) securities in 2016 reached 283872.4 billion yuan. Among them, the total bond turnover amounted to 224717.5 billion yuan, accounting for 79% of the total turnover (Shanghai Statistical Yearbook, 2017).

Insurance Business Situation in Beijing

With a population of more than 1.3 billion and a dynamically growing economy, China is expected to become one of the world's most important insurance markets (Chen & Lai, 2011). Beijing, as one of the largest cities, also has a large population, but the insurance market is still relatively underdeveloped compared to that of developed countries. According the Fig. 6.7, the original insurance premium income

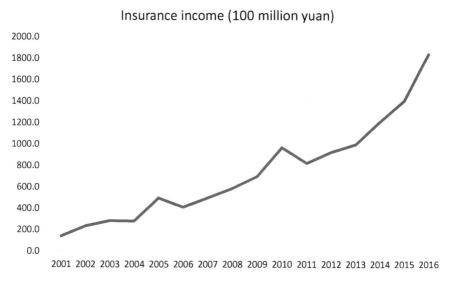

Fig. 6.7 Insurance income (2001–2016)
Source: Beijing Statistical Yearbook 2017

was 183.9 billion yuan in 2016, an increase of 31% over the previous year. There were 648 insurance institutions in Beijing, and the number of employees has also increased steadily. The insurance industry has been increasingly valued by investors, and it may become a new growth point for Beijing's financial development.

Conclusion

In general, it can be concluded that the development of the three pillars of financial system, Beijing's financial industry has flourished in recent years. However, it is uncertain whether there is a casual link or fundamental relationship between stable economic growth and financial development. The fictitious global finance makes it difficult to develop a strong link between financial growth and economic development within Chinese context. However, Beijing praxis of financial industry has potential to contribute to economic development due to regulatory mechanisms developed by People's Republic of China.

References

Andersson, F., Burzynska, K., & Opper, S. (2016). Lending for growth? A granger causality analysis of China's finance–growth nexus. *Empirical Economics, 51*(3), 897–920.

Andini, C. (2011). Financial development and long-run growth: Is the cross-sectional evidence robust? *Applied Economics, 43*(28), 4269–4275.

Chang, P., Jia, C., & Wang, Z. (2010). Bank fund reallocation and economic growth: Evidence from China. *Journal of Banking & Finance, 34*(11), 2753–2766.

Chen, L., & Lai, G. (2011). The Chinese insurance market and the WTO. *The Chinese Economy, 44* (6), 6–14.

Chen, K., Wu, L., & Wen, J. (2013). The relationship between finance and growth in China. *Global Finance Journal, 24*(1), 1–12.

Cihak, M., Demirguc-Kunt, A., Feyen, E., & Levine, R. (2013). Financial development in 205 economies, 1960 to 2010. *Journal of Financial Perspectives, 1*(2), 17–36.

Demirgüç-Kunt, A., & Maksimovic, V. (2001). *Firms as financial intermediaries: Evidence from trade credit data.* World Bank mimeo.

Goldsmith, R. W. (1969). *Financial structure and development.* Yale University Press.

Holz, C. (2008). China's economic growth 1978–2025: What we know today about China's economic growth tomorrow. *World Development, 36*(10), 1665–1691.

Huang, Y., & Wang, X. (2017). Building an efficient financial system in China: A need for stronger market discipline. *Asian Economic Policy Review, 12*(2), 188–205.

Jiang, C., & Yao, S. (2017). *Chinese banking reform: From the pre-WTO period to the financial crisis and beyond* (The Nottingham China Policy Institute Series). Springer.

King, R. G., & Levine, R. (1993). Finance and growth: Schumpeter might be right. *Quarterly Journal of Economics, 108*, 717–738.

La Porta, R., Lopez-de-Silanes, F., & Shleifer, A. (2002). Government ownership of commercial banks. *Journal of Finance, 57*, 265–301.

Levine, R. (2005). Chapter 12: Finance and growth: Theory and evidence. In *Handbook of economic growth*, vol. 1, 1. Elsevier, pp. 865–934.

Levine, R., Loayza, N., & Beck, T. (2000a). Financial intermediation and growth: Causality and causes. *Journal of Monetary Economics, 46*, 31–77.

Levine, R., Loayza, N., & Beck, T. (2000b). Financial intermediation and growth: Causality and causes. *Journal of Monetary Economics, 46*(1), 31–77.

Liang, Z. (2005). Financial development, market deregulation and growth: Evidence from China. *Journal of Chinese Economic and Business Studies, 3*(3), 247–262.

Liang, Q., & Teng, J. (2006). Financial development and economic growth: Evidence from China. *China Economic Review, 17*(4), 395–411.

Liu, Y., & Li, W. (2010). Regional financial development and regional economic growth: An empirical analysis of Suzhou City, China. *Chinese Geographical Science, 20*(3), 269–274.

Liu, G., & Zhang, C. (2018). Does financial structure matter for economic growth in China. *China Economic Review.* https://doi.org/10.1016/j.chieco.2018.06.006

Loayza, N., Schmidt-Hebbel, K., & Servén, L. (2000). What drives private saving across the world? *Review of Economics and Statistics, 82*(2), 165–181.

McKinnon, R. I. (1973). *Money and capital in economic development.* Brookings Institution.

National Bureau of Statistics of China. (2018). [Online] Available at: http://www.stats.gov.cn/. Accessed 6 July 2018.

Rajan, R. G., & Zingales, L. (1998). Financial dependence and growth. *American Economic Review, 88*, 559–586.

Roubini, N., & Sala-i-Martin, X. (1995). A growth model of inflation, tax evasion, and financial repression. *Journal of Monetary Economics, 35*(2), 275–301.

Rousseau, P. L. (1999). Finance, investment, and growth in Meiji-era Japan. *Japan and the World Economy, 11*, 185–198.

Rousseau, P. L., & Sylla, R. (1999). *Emerging financial markets and early U.S. growth.* National Bureau of Economic Research working paper no. 7448.

Shanghai Statistical Yearbook. (2017). [Online] Available at: http://www.stats-sh.gov.cn/html/sjfb/201701/1000339.html. Accessed 20 July 2018.

Shaw, E. S. (1973). *Financial deepening in economic development.* Oxford University Press.

Söderlund, B., & Tingvall, P. (2016). Capital freedom, financial development and provincial economic growth in China. *The World Economy, 40*(4), 764–787.

Wurgler, J. (2000). Financial markets and the allocation of capital. *Journal of Financial Economics, 58*, 187–214.

Xu, C. (2011). The fundamental institutions of China's reforms and development. *Journal of Economic Literature, 49*(4), 1076–1151.

Xu, G., & Gui, B. (2013a). The connection between financial repression and economic growth: The case of China. *The Journal of Comparative Asian Development, 12*(3), 385–410.

Xu, G., & Gui, B. (2013b). The connection between financial repression and economic growth: The case of China. *The Journal of Comparative Asian Development, 12*(3), 385–410.

Xu, Z., Tang, Y., & Cao, Y. (2018). Promoting China's financial market reform and innovation with opening-up policies. *China Economic Journal, 11*(1), 71–80.

Zhang, J., Wang, L., & Wang, S. (2012). Financial development and economic growth: Recent evidence from China. *Journal of Comparative Economics, 40*(3), 393–412.

Zhao, S. (2017). *Does financial development necessarily Lead to economic growth? Evidence from China's cities, 2007–2014*. In MATEC web of conferences, 100, p. 05032.

Chapter 7
Role of State and Innovative Agricultural Technology in Poverty Alleviation in China: A Study of Hebei Province

Bhabani Shankar Nayak and Xinying Wang

Introduction

Since the reform and opening up, China has developed and implemented a poverty alleviation strategy on a large scale, which has lifted 700 million rural poor people out of poverty and has achieved great achievements that attract worldwide attention (Ministry of Agriculture and Rural Affairs of the People's Republic of China, 2017). The Eighteenth Congress of the Party and the 18th Central Committee of the Second, Third, Fourth, and Fifth Plenary Sessions clearly pointed out that it is necessary to make accurate poverty alleviation and accurate poverty eradication the basic strategy of the country's poverty alleviation strategy. It is necessary to help more than 70 million people from poor rural areas by 2020 to get rid of poverty (China Central People's Government, 2017). Hebei region, as the primary target area for the national development strategy, should actively respond to the call of the "13th Five-Year Plan" to realize innovative agricultural technology and drive the goal of accurate poverty alleviation (Jin, 2011: 58–65). To get rid of this hard bone and fight this tough battle, we must find the root of "poverty" and seize the source of "difficulties." Because of the village's policy, households cast spells, prescribe the right medicine, and apply precision.

At present, precision poverty alleviation faces two major challenges: first, most of the current poor population is in the "corner" of the central and western regions (Zhang, 2015). It is more difficult to alleviate poverty and overcome poverty than ever before. Second challenge is addressed by the fact that the poorer population has sought to solve the problem of food and clothing (Liu, 2009: 55–58). The poor

B. S. Nayak (✉)
Business School for the Creative Industries, University for the Creative Arts, Epsom, UK
e-mail: Bhabani.nayak@uca.ac.uk

X. Wang
Coventry Business School, Coventry University, Coventry, UK

populations must consolidate the fruits of food and clothing, speed up poverty alleviation, improve the ecological environment, enhance the ability to develop, and narrow the development gap (Li et al., 2011: 44–45). In order to achieve the goal of alleviating poverty for the "Thirteenth Five-Year Plan", China needs to improve the production conditions in impoverished areas, increase the productive capacity and fully mobilize the resources to empower poor by alleviating poverty (Fan, 2010: 48–49). The growth and application of agricultural science and technology will surely become an effective weapon for poverty alleviation (Yang, 2011: 22–24).

As the coordinated development of China's strategic development in the Beijing-Tianjin-Hebei region, Hebei, a poverty-stricken area in China, has caused difficulties in the development of Beijing, Tianjin, and Hebei. Agricultural science and technology will surely become effective weapons for achieving accurate final poverty reduction. It has summarized the role of state and agricultural science and technology innovation in poverty alleviation and development.

The popularity of agricultural technological innovation in China began in the 1990s. Different scholars have different understandings in the field of agricultural technological innovation, and their research areas are different. Xiong (2013) divided agricultural technological innovation into two categories, namely agricultural technology innovation in the broad sense and narrow sense. From a broad perspective, agricultural technology innovation is rich in content, including agricultural technology development and scientific research and its application research and promotion. These include innovating agricultural knowledge, resource development and technological means, agricultural innovation, innovative products, innovative materials, etc... Understanding in the narrow sense looks at innovating agricultural technology, but agricultural research and innovation research refers to this research. Bin believes that China's innovative agricultural technology faces many problems: lack of investment in agricultural research, lack of incentives for agricultural technology supply, and adoption of new agricultural technologies by farmers, seeking stability. China's agricultural science and technology innovations must raise farmers' awareness of science and technology to become rich, cultivate the farmers' ability to apply scientific agricultural innovation techniques, increase investment in agricultural research, and improve agricultural scientific research systems. Lu believes that the essence of wealth growth is the growth of knowledge, but such growth needs to be created. Technology can be effectively realized. It has become the most powerful driving force for social and economic development. Knowledge can create wealth, technology can innovate agriculture, and labor. The dual integration of technology and innovation is the basic path of China's agricultural development. Technological innovation is knowledge and the core of agriculture.

In addition to the current reasons for the supply of agricultural technology in China, the spread of agricultural technology is also an important factor. For the research of agricultural technology promotion, many domestic scholars are committed to studying the basic issues in the promotion and dissemination of agricultural technology. Kang believed that China's agricultural technology promotion system and mechanism are not suitable for the market economy, lack of demand, insufficient funds for agricultural promotion, low quality of promotion staff, and incomplete policies. Shi thinks that the effective operation mechanism of technological diffusion of Chinese agricultural innovative enterprises has not yet formed a practice. Its role in the promotion of agricultural technology is not significant. Therefore, one of the important means to develop the promotion of agricultural technology is the future of China. It is necessary to establish an agricultural enterprise. As the main body, the modern agricultural technology innovates the diffusion system. Dong believes that the organizational structure of China's agricultural technology promotion department is relatively single, limited to promotion, and does not involve providing training for farmers. Therefore, China's agricultural technology promotion department is not perfect, and the level of peasant education is relatively low. These factors have affected the promotion of China's agricultural technology.

In the agricultural technological innovation system, most foreign scholars mainly discuss institutional design issues related to agricultural technological innovation. Both, Ban and Hawkins believe that the goal of agricultural technology promotion is to pass all possible technical information to farmers, so that farmers can clearly understand their goals and the possibility of their realization and cultivate farmers to create more appropriate capabilities. Making decisions and achieving satisfactory agricultural development are additional goals that it might help achieve.

The establishment of the agricultural science and technology extension system in the United States took place relatively early. It began in the 1860s and experienced three important development stages. It forms a "three-in-one" agricultural science and technology extension system integrating scientific research, promotion and education, and involves universities, governments, enterprises and county extension stations (Li, 2009: 18–20). The US agricultural research system consists of a three-level structure of national, state, and private levels. Private, providing new knowledge and new technologies needed to solve a wide range of technical agricultural problems and nationally urgently needed projects, ensuring adequate production of quality food and agricultural products, and promoting food and agricultural economy. The structure continues to develop and helps solve some long-term, national major strategic issues.

Another advantage of the US agricultural science and technology extension system is the adequacy of research funding. The US Department of Agriculture's system research funding is based on state funding, and the National Science Foundation and other agencies also provide 2.6% support for cutting-edge technology research, as well as corporate funding of 0.4%. American agricultural companies invest heavily in agricultural research, focusing on agricultural products, post-harvest and food processing, veterinary technology, machinery and plant breeding techniques. In addition, the federal government assumes 50%, and the state and county governments each bear 25% of the agricultural extension services, and the funds are sufficient (Seevers et al., 2007).

China has established an administrative agricultural science and technology extension system, and in its core of operation is the government agricultural science and technology promotion agency. The agricultural science and technology extension service network with Chinese characteristics makes the agricultural extension institutions at all levels not only led by the agricultural administrative departments at the same level but also led by the business leaders of the higher-level promotion agencies, forming a dual leadership model, which leads to poor communication and contact between different departments (Zen et al., 2010: 428–431). Obstacles are prone to mutual excuse in the promotion work. The interests of the department and the overall agricultural science and technology promotion benefits are difficult to coordinate, and the overall benefits of promotion are low.

At the same time, because the agricultural science and technology extension institutions at all levels are affiliated to the government, the government formulates relevant policies on agricultural science and technology promotion, and organizes the implementation of promotion work in the form of administrative science and technology promotion, which leads to the disconnection of agricultural science and technology supply and demand, and many agricultural scientific and technological achievements are difficult to transform. For the actual productivity, the lack of farmers' interest expression mechanism is also the drawback caused by this administrative-centered agricultural science and technology promotion system.

In the administrative-led agricultural science and technology extension system, the main source of promotion funds is the government financial sector funding, and the fund-raising channels for promotion funds are relatively simple. The agricultural science and technology promotion funds in developed countries generally account for 0.6% ~ 1% of the total agricultural production value, and in the developing countries they account for about 0.5%, but China's agricultural science and technology promotion funds are only 0.2% (Kong & Lou, 2012: 12–23), although the promotion funds for township agricultural technology promotion stations are raised. The government allocates funds in full, but the finances are only responsible for their basic wages. The funds for their public welfare functions are not settled. The contradiction between insufficient investment in agricultural extension funds and increasingly heavy promotion tasks has become more prominent, leading to agriculture. Most of the science and technology promotion work is "in the village, empty in the village, and cannot be implemented in the hands of farmers" (Yu, 2012: 17–21). At the same time, insufficient investment in agricultural science and technology promotion funds has made the infrastructure and office conditions of agricultural science and technology extension institutions relatively backward, and the promotion work has been difficult.

As a basic industry of the national economy, agriculture also needs technological innovation to support its development. The "family co-production contract responsibility system", which was widely implemented in China in the early 1980s, greatly improved the enthusiasm of Chinese farmers for production, and made China's grain output continue to grow for 30 years (Duan, 2016: 6–11). However, 30 years later, this system dividend has been basically exhausted. China's agriculture is facing a series of new development problems including high agricultural product costs, serious rural environmental pollution, and the quality and safety of agricultural products are so worried (Long, 2016: 1–4). The further development of Chinese agriculture.

Under such a situation, agricultural science and technology innovation is undoubtedly an important means to solve China's three rural issues (Fan, 2014: 17–18). Promoting agricultural science and technology innovation plays a vital role in building modern agriculture, increasing farmers' income, and strengthening the core competitiveness of the country's agricultural industry.

Firstly, the level of technological innovation determines the level of agricultural development in a country (Fan, 2014: 17–18). The competition in the new era is the competition of science, technology and talents. The application of new technologies can fundamentally change the agricultural form of a country, all of which need to be supported by a strong level of technological innovation. Secondly, agricultural science and technology innovation is an effective way to increase farmers' income (Yang, 2015: 22–24). With the continuous development of society, the way of increasing farmers' income is also changing. The traditional resource-investment-increasing method is no longer adapted to the new stage. The increase of farmers' income is more dependent on the input of agricultural technology (Liu, 2012). The level of production technology directly determines the actual situation of farmer's income. Increasing investment in science and technology, taking a road of techno-logical conservation, reducing the cost of agricultural production, and improving economic efficiency are the direction for farmers to increase production and income in the future. Thirdly, the level of agricultural science and technology innovation is a manifestation of the core competitiveness of a country's agricultural industry (Yang, 2017: 254–256). Agriculture will change from the traditional resource dependency type to the intelligent dependency type. Natural resources are no longer the most important factor affecting agricultural development (Zhi & Guo, 2014: 68–69). The level of science and technology and the quality of workers ultimately determine the level of agricultural development in a country.

At this stage, Hebei has unbalanced numbers of impoverished people. They are characterized by very good performance: lack of agricultural instructors in poor areas, lack of agricultural science and technology, and unreasonable agricultural technological innovation compared with developed regions (The People Govern-ment of Hebei Province, 2018).

In response to the problems of agricultural science and technology in the impoverished areas of Hebei, corresponding countermeasures have been put for-ward: vigorously developing agricultural science and technology and promoting the construction of a well-to-do society (Hu, 2012); the development of innovative agricultural education as a key method (Hui, 2012); increasing investment in agri-cultural science and technology in impoverished areas as a guarantee for improve-ment (Hu, 2012).

At present, all-around poverty alleviation work has been carried out across the country, which has created tremendous achievements for more than 700 million poor rural people in poverty alleviation (Hu, 2012). However, there are more than 2 million poor people in Hebei Province (The People Government of Hebei Prov-ince, 2018). The number of poor people is high. More seriously, these poor people are located in remote areas and contiguous areas. There is a shortage of agricultural resources and a shortage of available resources. The poor are deeply impoverished.

Moreover, the poor population in Hebei Province has a low-income level. The per capita net income of the millions of poor people in the rural areas is very different from the per capita income of the country. Even some extremely poor households do not have other stable sources of cash income, outside of government relief subsidies. Poor population of Hebei faces livelihood issues and problems. In 2015, more than 2 million poor people were located in Hebei. The total area of 8.3 square kilometers, is residence for more than 2.7 million poor people, their per capita annual income of less than 625 yuan (The People Government of Hebei Province, 2018).

Role of Agricultural Science and Technology in Poverty Alleviation in China

At present, most of the agricultural production in poor areas of Hebei is still in the traditional stages of agriculture (Chen, 2016a, b: 6–8). Weak industrial foundation, the destiny of the people, the labor force of human and livestock, and the training of experience are still evident, and production efficiency is generally low. The fundamentals of agricultural science and technology innovation lie in stimulating the potential of self-development, improving the safety production capacity, and improving the production efficiency of agriculture and animal husbandry (Huang, 2013: 5–8).

The achievement of self-development and self-reliant is the key objective of agricultural science and technology innovation. Only by continuously tapping the potential of self-development can impoverished areas fundamentally escape poverty (Yang, 2011: 26–27). Although the poverty-stricken areas in Hebei Province are located in remote mountainous areas, where traffic is inconvenient and information is hindered, the agricultural and animal husbandry resources in the region have obvious advantages. Hebei's geographical location is close to a big city like Beijing (Chen, 2016a, b). The potential for self-development is enormous, but due to the lack of technical support, it is difficult to form a stable industry. Special cultivation techniques are combined with local resource conditions in Hebei i.e. application of modern planting techniques, and measures to increase the yield and quality of specialty agricultural products such as vegetables, edible fungi, Chinese herbs, black goats and rabbits (Shi et al., 2013: 79–80).

The characteristic cultivation techniques will effectively support the development of agricultural special industries in poor areas in Hebei and promote the income growth of farmers and herdsmen. In 2013 and 2014, Hebei Province held an agricultural innovation technology exhibition. According to statistics, the number of visitors exceeded 2 million. The direct revenue of the exhibition was 70 million yuan, which led the sales revenue of surrounding towns and villages to 400 million yuan, further illustrating the huge potential of Hebei's agricultural products market (Hebei Provincial Department of Agriculture, 2014).

Pest Control and Animal Epidemic Prevention Technology in China

Safe agricultural production is an important condition for agricultural science and technology innovation. Due to the weak ability of Hebei poverty-stricken areas to bear risks, it is vulnerable to agricultural production. In 2014, Hebei Province discovered 1.75 million hectares of American white moths. In the same period, the area of arable land was reduced by 420,000 hectares. Qiu – director of the Hebei Provincial Forest Diseases and Pest Control Station – pointed out that in recent years, the province's insect prediction accuracy rate reached 99.32%, and the quarantine rate of seedling production areas reached 95%; the introduction of pine wood nematode disease was effectively controlled, and no epidemic was found in the province. The white moth epidemic was effectively contained. The average leaf retention rate was around 99% on both sides of major scenic spots and around the major traffic points around the main activity points, and the average leaf retention rate was over 90% in each village and other areas. Pest control techniques refer to techniques that reduce or prevent pathogenic microorganisms and pests from harming crops or human bodies through physical, chemical, biological, and other means (Hammond, 2015). Animal epidemic prevention technology refers to prevention, control and elimination of animal epidemics and animal product quarantine (Bi, 2009: 15–16). Pest control technology and animal epidemic prevention technology will effectively promote the smooth development of agricultural and animal husbandry production activities in Hebei poverty-stricken areas and improve the ability of poor areas to resist agricultural production risks. According to the Hebei Forestry (2017), Hebei province has established more than 40,000 inspectors, more than 4000 suspension insect traps and more than 1500 moth traps and monitored areas in the United States. In the main pine forest areas, scenic areas and forest parks, 69 key pine disease prevention and control areas were established, 118 monitoring sites were established, and pine disease was investigated every September. These measures have provided strong support for the prevention and control of pests and diseases and have increased the safety production capacity in poor areas.

Agricultural Mechanization and Technology in China

Raising agricultural and animal husbandry production efficiency is the key to achieving agricultural science and technology innovation. The backward way of picking things up with physical strength, pulling donkeys, and manual labor has greatly hampered the improvement of production efficiency in agriculture and animal husbandry (Yan, 2017: 32). Agricultural mechanization technology can replace human and animal labor. Use agricultural machinery for land consolidation, sowing, plant protection, irrigation, harvesting and processing, can effectively reduce the labor intensity of farmers and herdsmen, and increase agricultural production capacity and professionalism. In precision poverty, the poverty-stricken areas of Hebei agricultural machinery and equipment may be suitable according to local geographical landscape, arable land type, area size, breeding varieties to choose from. In practical applications, agricultural mechanized production methods have significantly increased labor productivity in poor areas. For example, the application of corn grain mechanical direct harvest technology can reduce the cost of corn grain harvest by about 200 yuan per ton (Jin & Zhao, 2010: 36–38); the application of mechanized production technology for rapeseed can reduce the need for workers in the traditional planting of rapeseed from 10 to 0.8 workers (Wang, 2015).

Agricultural Science and Technology Are a Sight for Precision Poverty Alleviation

The core of accurate poverty alleviation is precise identification, precise management and precision assistance. In recent years, the rapid development of agricultural information technology, such as big data technology, information analysis, and intelligent decision-making, have provided new ideas and new methods for precision poverty alleviation, effectively improving the pertinence, timeliness, and foresight of precision.

The basic work of accurate poverty alleviation is to accurately find the poor population in Hebei and their poverty levels. Since the implementation of the regional coordination and poverty alleviation and development strategy in Hebei Province, a relatively complete poverty identification system and population identification standard have been established (Liu, 2015). However, there are subjective judgments, false reports and black box operations. Manual inspection of poverty information requires a large workload, high costs, and is characterized by poor accuracy. Since 2014, the implementation of the rural poor household card system in Hebei Province has initially included the basic records of poverty-stricken counties, development status, infrastructure, public services and poverty alleviation effectiveness (Chen, 2016a, b). At the same time, it also records the characteristics of population structure, education culture, and labor employment. The proportion of planting structure, sources of economic income, health status, and medical endowment insurance data have laid a solid foundation for the application of agricultural big data technology (Sun, 2017: 72–73). Agricultural big data technology is a large amount of data that is widely used. It is diverse in variety, complex in structure, and of great potential and difficult to process using traditional methods and techniques. It can be quickly used for data discovery, data mining and data visualization methods, as well as accurately locking and visually presenting modern information technology of this kind of function (Lin et al., 2017: 907–913).

In data-driven poverty alleviation, the use of agricultural big data and technology eliminates human interference through multi-dimensional, multi-level, and multi-position comprehensive processing, enabling a large amount of poverty data to "speak" and realize the distribution of poverty-stricken areas, deeply population poverty and other refined information. Accurate judgments and accurate guidance have confirmed "real poverty", effectively promoted poverty alleviation, and objectively, fairly and transparently searched for "diseases" and identified "rooted diseases" (Lv et al., 2017: 59–67).

An important guarantee for accurate poverty alleviation is to scientifically manage the poor and conduct dynamic monitoring. Poverty alleviation is a dynamic development process. With the implementation of an accurate poverty alleviation strategy, the number of poor people will continue to decrease, but due to poor policy implementation, poverty may also occur from time to time. In recent years, Hebei's poverty alleviation funds have been on the rise (Zhang & Xu, 2014). To ensure that the poverty relief fund has comprehensive and affordable benefits for the actual location and those who need help, it is necessary to conduct systematic, scientific, and effective information analysis, and to accurately, timely, and comprehensively grasp the progress, speed, and trend of poverty alleviation. Efforts are made to ensure the authenticity of information and reduce the reliability and practicality of poverty. Agricultural information analysis technology is the use of real-time monitoring, dynamic tracking and scientific analysis and other methods a large number of known agricultural information processing and abstract summary, through intertwining various relationships from the complex representation to grasp its essence (Xu, 2009).

In the accurate poverty alleviation process, through the tracking of data flow, the agricultural information analysis technology has realized the implementation of the poverty alleviation policy, the implementation progress of the project, the effect of vocational training and the real-time monitoring of the living conditions of the poor (Han et al., 2018). It laid the foundation for the approval, evacuation and adjustment of poor areas and poor people in Hebei. To prevent misappropriation and embezzlement of poverty-reducing funds, new ways and means are provided.

The key measure for accurate poverty alleviation is to effectively assess the causes of poverty and make different decisions based on different circumstances. Due to the great differences in the natural endowment, historical conditions and population quality of poverty-stricken areas in Hebei Province need to be considered. The policies and measures for poverty alleviation and development must adapt to local conditions, adapt to the needs of the times, adapt individuals to maximize the role of fixed-point assistance, and ensure maximum support needs (Han et al., 2013:100–103). Support staff should go where people need it most. As of 2017, a total of 143 agencies, state-owned enterprises, and state key scientific research institutes in Hebei Province sent 1300 cadres to poverty-stricken areas to carry out targeted poverty alleviation work, achieving remarkable results. However, it has also been found that the basic conditions of different impoverished counties and the poverty alleviation needs are significantly different, which sets a high standard for formulating contemporary social differential poverty alleviation policies and measures. Agricultural intelligent decision-making technology is based on the decomposition of agricultural problems and agricultural data analysis, establishing an overall framework model for solving agricultural problems, calculating the objectives, functions, data and solution requirements for solving various parts of agricultural issues, and obtaining solutions or providing decision-making information feedback to decision makers (Chen, 2011). In precision poverty alleviation, based on the analysis of a large number of poverty information, agricultural intelligent decision-making techniques are clustered using poverty alleviation development policy simulation and effect assessment models, giving full play to the unique advantages of computer expert systems, machine learning and the implementation of poverty alleviation policies. Further improving the "one village, one policy, one family, one law" supporting measures, provide scientific basis for dynamic comparative analysis, assessment, prediction, optimization and improvement to provide scientific basis (Li et al., 2016: 61–66).

Integrated Approach to Poverty Alleviation in China

Promoting the integration of primary, secondary and tertiary industries, monitoring agricultural product market information, and implementing "Internet plus Agriculture" are important forces for promoting accurate poverty alleviation work (Wang, 2016). Agricultural science and technology, through agricultural product processing, agricultural monitoring and early warning, along with rural e-commerce have changed the production methods in Hebei backward areas, mobilized the production enthusiasm of poor farmers and herdsmen, and activated the advantages of poverty-stricken areas (Deng et al., 2011:106).

Industrial poverty alleviation is the core content of poverty alleviation and development. In the United States, only 0.9% of the population is engaged in agriculture, but the number of people employed in the secondary and tertiary industries around farmers and agriculture is as high as 16.7% (Tang, 2000: 59). The relationship between Chinese farmers and agricultural product processing companies is relatively relaxed. In Hebei's poverty-stricken areas, the degree of closeness between agriculture and secondary and tertiary industries is relatively low, and a large number of agricultural products cannot effectively enter the processing and circulation links (Han et al., 2013: 100–103).

Promoting the development of integrated agriculture, rural areas, and agriculture in rural areas can broaden the channels for farmers to increase income and accelerate the transformation of agricultural development patterns in Hebei's poverty-stricken areas. This is an inevitable choice for the industry to help the poor. The key to establishing an industrial system combining modern agriculture with the secondary industry and the tertiary industry lies in the mechanism and the technical point of support (Yuan, 2009). Agricultural product processing technology is a series of technologies for industrial production activities that use artificial agricultural products and wild animal and plant resources as raw materials. It infiltrated the primary, secondary and tertiary industries in rural areas, followed by the pre-production of agricultural products, medium-term production and post-production (Yuan, 2009).

A comprehensive solution to the problems of agriculture, rural areas and farmers is of great strategic importance. In precision poverty alleviation, the application of agricultural product processing technology, especially the application of deep processing technology for specialty agricultural products (Lei & Zhang, 2017: 74–76), has led to the intensification, improvement in quality, and branding of the deep processing of agricultural products in poor areas, but also increased the added value of products, and increased the income of farmers and herdsmen.

The market is a "hematopoietic factory" for accurate poverty alleviation. Poor areas in Hebei have poor basic conditions, and farmers and herders have poor access to agricultural production, circulation, and trade information (Gong and Wang 2012:41-45). They often face the impact of price fluctuations in the agricultural product market. In the 2 weeks before December 2014, the average price of main raw milk-producing areas was 3.81 yuan/kg, which was 9% lower than the average price at the beginning of the year. This is the lowest level since October 2013, which has caused huge losses to some families in poor areas in Hebei Province (Ministry of Agriculture and Rural Affairs of the People's Republic of China, 2017). Without large-scale production, circulation, and trade information guidance, poor farmers and herdsmen face enormous market risks. Agricultural monitoring and early warning technology are a technological system integrating agricultural information collection, information processing and information service technology. It collects, analyzes, forecasts and warns using information on agricultural production, market circulation, and import and export trade throughout the industrial chain (Sun, 2018: 62).

To provide decision-making reference for decision-making departments and production and operation managers, and effectively manage agricultural production and market circulation, it is an effective means of realizing the effective docking of production and sales, orderly guidance of agricultural production, and stabilizing agriculture. In precision poverty alleviation, agricultural monitoring and early warning technologies can provide timely, accurate and reliable market information for production and management decisions of farmers and herdsmen in poverty-stricken areas, which can be used to rationally arrange planting and breeding programs, and increase risk-tolerant agricultural production, circulation and lower the trade risks in poor areas (Chen, 2017:43). The capacity has greatly enhanced the ability of impoverished farmers and herdsmen to participate in market activities and has formed a good situation of "hematopoiesis" to help the poor.

Agricultural and Rural E-Commerce in China

Changing production and management methods is one of the important ways to accurately reduce poverty. With the rapid development of "Internet Plus", the "e-commerce poverty alleviation project", one of China's ten poverty reduction projects, has played an increasingly important role in the development of agriculture and rural economy in poor areas of Hebei Province (Li, 2016a, b: 27–28). E-commerce not only has a profound and far-reaching impact on the production, processing, and sales organization of agricultural products in many aspects such as industrial chain, supply chain, and value chain, but also enhances the brand characteristics of specialty agricultural products. According to the 2014 China E-commerce Market Data Monitoring Report, the transaction volume of China's e-commerce market reached 13.4 trillion yuan, an increase of 31.4% year-on-year. China's existing public service platform for agricultural products and business information has contributed a total of more than 23 million tons of agricultural and sideline products, with a turnover of more than 88.0 billion yuan.

Hebei has a weak economic foundation in Beijing, Tianjin and Hebei. Compared with Beijing and Tianjin, Hebei lacks the economic development models that it can rely on. The old resource economy cannot support the sustainable development of Hebei (Lv, 2008). The major trend of economic development determines that Hebei must vigorously develop the e-commerce economy. E-commerce has a comprehensive quality and is the best development mode for adapting to the economic development in the new period. Especially under the general trend of Beijing-Tianjin-Hebei integration development, around the Beijing-Tianjin economic structure characteristics and development types, using Hebei e-commerce as a carrier, will help Hebei use its position and successfully undertake Beijing and Tianjin (Zhao, 2017).

The production capacity has achieved the goal of reasonable optimization of economic development in the three places. Rural e-commerce is a cross-border integration of agricultural science and technology, such as making full use of Internet e-commerce platforms and new agricultural production technologies (green agricultural technologies, featured agricultural technologies, etc.), agricultural product processing technologies, agricultural product storage and transportation technologies, in coordination with intensive rural chain stores. Form a compact and orderly commercial complex. E-commerce in rural areas has changed the traditional way of production and management of farmers and herdsmen and opened up "double channels" for sales of "on-line and off-line" agricultural products (Zhang et al., 2011), breaking market space restrictions, lowering the threshold for entry of agricultural products, and bringing farmers and pastoralists behind the scenes to the stage. At the same time, rural e-commerce has changed the way of life for poor farmers and herders in Hebei, promoted two-way circulation of "industrial products to the countryside, and farm products into the city" and expanded the rural market (Tu et al., 2011), which in turn led to entrepreneurial innovation and boosted the emergence in recent years. The development of such as "Internet Plus" exerts its power to accurate poverty alleviation.

Since the reform and opening up, the party and the country have always attached great importance to poverty alleviation and development work, especially the development concept of functional areas in the Jing-Jin-Ji region, and carried out a series of targeted research, planning and organization of large-scale poverty alleviation and development projects, and achieved remarkable results. Since 2011, the Party Central Committee and the State Council have successively promulgated the

"China Rural Poverty Alleviation and Development Outline (2011-2020)", "Opinions on the Innovation Mechanism, Solidly Promote Rural Poverty Alleviation and Development Work" and "Decisions on Poverty Alleviation and Poverty Alleviation" (Ministry of Agriculture and Rural Affairs of the People's Republic of China, 2017). The tasks and requirements of the poverty alleviation work in the new era have been clarified, and the key deployment of poverty alleviation work has improved. Technical poverty alleviation and special industries, infrastructure, education, culture, health, social security and ecological environment should be listed as the seven key areas for poverty alleviation and development. Solving the poverty problem in Hebei Province is the key to the coordinated development of the Jing-Jin-Ji region. For the internationalization of the Beijing-Tianjin-Hebei region, the promotion of precision poverty alleviation will inevitably require innovation in agricultural science and technology. Promoting poverty alleviation through agricultural science and technology is an important measure for the implementation of poverty alleviation policies in the new era. This is also an inherent requirement for accelerating agricultural development and transformation in poor areas in Hebei. In particular, agricultural research institutions in the new period are an important political task (Dai et al., 2003: 48–50).

Whether or not the implementation of the various policies for the implementation of the Beijing-Tianjin-Hebei poverty alleviation and development work will ultimately depend on the improvement of the production and living of the broad masses of people in poor areas in Hebei (Zhao, 2017). The farming and animal husbandry in poor areas of Hebei Province, as the basic industry, is the main source of income for poor farmers and the most important factor in improving the quality of life of farmers and herdsmen. Due to natural conditions, historical culture, and economic and social reasons, Hebei's poverty-stricken areas still suffer from backward infrastructure, backward agricultural skills, low cultural quality, and lagging industrial development (Yuan, 2009). From the past experience, in order to better solve these problems, traditional relief methods and welfare poverty alleviation methods can no longer adapt to the new situation. It is necessary to vigorously promote the "two-wheel drive" of technological innovation and institutional innovation, and further strengthen the poverty alleviation work of agricultural science and technology (Wang, 2012). Promoting poverty alleviation through agricultural science and technology, speeds up the transformation of poverty alleviation from "blood transfusion" to "hematopoiesis", and effectively improves the self-quality of the population in poor areas of Hebei Province, changes production conditions, and increases production and sustainable development capabilities. It is an important way to accelerate the development of agriculture and animal husbandry in impoverished areas in Hebei Province and to promote poverty alleviation for farmers and herdsmen (Jin & Zhang, 2014: 215–219).

Sustainable Development of Agriculture in Poor Areas of Hebei Province

The poverty-stricken areas and poor people in Hebei Province are mostly located in the western regions (Zhao, 2013a, b). They are generally faced with fragile ecological environment and limited resource carrying capacity, especially soil salability, soil erosion, land sand and petrochemical and non-point source pollution (Hebei Provincial Department of Land and Resources, n.d.). With excessive planting, excessive logging and other phenomena occurring from time to time, the production and living environment and the sustainable development of agriculture in the region are all facing severe challenges (Li, Kadambot and Neil). Practical experience shows that the development of poverty-stricken areas must be adapted to local conditions, and in accordance with their own basic conditions, adhere to the path of sustainable development of humans and nature, and promote the harmonious development of agricultural traditions. Promoting poverty alleviation through agricultural science and technology, further implementing the concept of "innovation, harmony, green, openness, and sharing" and further transforming the development of agriculture and animal husbandry in the poverty-stricken areas of Hebei is likely to promote the positive interaction between the region's agriculture and the ecological environment, and sustainable development in poverty-stricken areas (Li, 2017). The important embodiment of coordinated development is also an important way to speed up agricultural reforms in poor areas, reorganize and supplement short boards, and promote income.

Problems of Poverty Alleviation Through Agricultural Science and Technology in Hebei Province

The national development strategy centered on the coordinated development of the Beijing-Tianjin-Hebei region is to ease Beijing's non-capital functions, promote regional coordinated development, and form a new growth pole (Zhao, 2017). At present, the huge gap between Beijing, Tianjin and Hebei makes it difficult for the region to coordinate development. In Hebei Province in particular, there are 39 impoverished counties across the country, and there are a large number of poverty belts in the surrounding areas of Beijing and Tianjin (Zhao, 2017). In order to overcome the difficulties and overcome this difficult battle, we must find the root cause of the "poor people" and seize the root causes of "difficulties." As the village implements policies, it uses family spells, prescribes remedial measures and precise treatment (Wu, 2002).

Poverty in Hebei Province

In 2017, Hebei Province adjusted the key poverty alleviation and development counties according to the relevant requirements of the Chinese government, and identified 62 key poverty alleviation and development counties and 327 key villages. Among them, there are 39 key poverty alleviation and development counties in the country and 17 key poverty alleviation and development counties across the province, mainly in Yanshan, Taihang Mountain and Heilonggang. According to the special difficulties policy supported by the state, a total of 22 counties have been incorporated into the Yanshan-Taihang Mountains, with a total area of 93,000 square kilometers and a population of 10.975 million. Among them, there are five counties in Chengde City, nine counties in Zhangjiakou City, and eight counties in Baoding City. There are 36 counties in the Heilonggang area, with a total area of 24,000 square kilometers and a population of 14.173 million people (The People's Government of Hebei Province, 2018).

The current situation in poverty-stricken areas in Hebei Province is mainly reflected in the high incidence of poverty, deep levels, and high rates of return on poverty. According to the country's new annual poverty alleviation standard of RMB 2300 (China Central People's Government, 2017), Hebei Province has a total of 7.95 million rural impoverished people, of whom 5.61 million are in poverty, accounting for 10.1% of the rural population (Ministry of Finance, Division of Poverty Alleviation, Agricultural Division, 2017). Among them, according to the report (Hebei Province Adjusts Key Counties for National and Provincial Poverty Alleviation and Development Work, 2017), there are 2.718 million people in poverty-stricken areas in the Yanshan- Taihang Mountain area, accounting for 38.7% of the rural population in the area. The per capita net income of farmers is 3442 yuan, which is equivalent to 57.8% of the province's average. The total number of impoverished people in Heilongjiang is 3.5517 million, accounting for 25.8% of the rural population in the area. The per capita net income of farmers is 4698 yuan, which is equivalent to 78.9% of the provincial average. At the same time, due to unpredictable disasters, about a quarter of the poor will return to poverty every year.

Agricultural Science, Technology and Poverty Alleviation in Hebei

Historically, northern Hebei and southern Hebei have always been military bases, and they are supply areas for agricultural products. In terms of natural conditions, Hebei Province, Beijing, and Tianjin both belong to the warm-temperate continental climate arid agricultural regions of the North China Plain (China Geological Survey, n.d.). Therefore, the integration process of the Beijing-Tianjin-Hebei integration is based on the same agricultural natural conditions (Zhao, 2017). The foundation and guarantee of Beijing-Tianjin-Hebei integration depends on the safety of agriculture in Hebei Province and the healthy development of agricultural science and technology. Therefore, if we want to manage the poverty belt in Hebei Province, the development of agricultural science and technology is the best way.

Due to the lack of agricultural technology in poverty-stricken areas in Hebei Province, and its agricultural structure is an independent development of self-contained system and self-financing, the surrounding developed cities of Beijing and Tianjin rarely give technical support (Chen, 2016: 6–8); although Beijing and Tianjin have strong agricultural products demand, it has limited use in the impoverished areas of Hebei Province. Huge regional differences and imbalances between urban and rural areas constitute the greatest threat to Beijing-Tianjin-Hebei integration. The proportion of agriculture in poverty-stricken areas in Hebei Province has been declining compared with other cities in the Beijing-Tianjin-Hebei metropolitan area (Zhao, 2017). Plus, Hebei poverty area has not been taken seriously by Beijing and Tianjin, which has led to shortages in agricultural science and technology.

Problems of Agricultural Science and Technology Poverty Alleviation in Hebei Province

Poverty alleviation is both cruel and hopeful for poor areas in Hebei. The poor areas in Hebei must strive to overcome the hard battle of poverty alleviation and earnestly implement the spirit of the key instructions of the General Secretary General Xi Jinping on poverty alleviation and development (Report of the 19th National Congress of the Communist Party of China, 2017). This combined with the increasingly abundant agricultural science and technology resources and the goal of a comprehensive well-off society, with the aim of synchronizing the poverty-stricken areas of Hebei Province with other regions can help achieve a well-off society. An important breakthrough in poverty alleviation in Hebei Province, which should take place as soon as possible, is the development of agricultural science and technology. Today, there are many problems in the development of agricultural science and technology in poverty-stricken areas in Hebei Province (Liao et al., 2013: 98–100).

The most impoverished areas in Hebei Province are mainly located in deep mountainous areas with an altitude of more than 1000 m. There are more than 5000 mountains in the region with a height of more than 2000 m (Hebei Provincial Department of Land and Resources, 2018). The geographical conditions are poor and the area suitable for cultivated land is small. Most of them are in high mountains. Due to the steep cliffs, they have poor water retention and fertility, therefore, they are not suitable for agricultural production (Li, 2014: 133–137).

Poor areas in Hebei Province often cause major economic losses due to natural disasters such as droughts, floods, windstorms, frost damage, frost damage, hail and pests. The frequency of droughts is highest, and droughts of varying degrees occurred from 2008 to 2017 each year. On average, more than 40% of the population each year is affected by drought (Zhuang et al., 2013: 37–40). The conditions and capabilities of rural water supply, water storage, and flood control projects are limited and are not sufficient to withstand multiple natural disasters.

The impoverished mountainous areas in Hebei have made great contributions in the construction of ecological barriers around the capital. In order to guarantee the water supply in Beijing and Tianjin, the agricultural production water in the region is restricted. Affected by the "siphon effect", the outflow of talents and other factors of production in Hebei Province is serious (Zhang, 2014). Some poor counties are relatively backward and missed the period of strategic opportunities for the state to increase the investment in basic agricultural science and technology and the development of advanced agricultural science and technology. This has led to a serious lag in agricultural science and technology in some regions, and a large difference from the counties and counties in Beijing and Tianjin. Per capita GDP in poorer counties accounts only for 1/3 of the GDP in the suburbs of Beijing (Zhang, 2014).

Most of the poverty-stricken areas in Hebei Province are located in the mountainous areas, where the agricultural technology base is weak. After decades of development, the level of agricultural science and technology is still far below that of other cities (Liu & Guo, 2013: 43–48). Severe shortage of agricultural science and technology is a prominent manifestation of weak agricultural science and technology. Traffic inconvenience and information obstruction are all inevitable and important limiting factors for the shortage of agricultural science and technology, agricultural resource development and agricultural science as well as technology project construction (Gu, 2008).

The lack of agricultural knowledge and the shortage of talents in agricultural science and technology are another important reason for limiting the development of agricultural science and technology in poverty-stricken areas in Hebei Province (Bo, 2011). Due to the limitation of natural conditions, poverty-stricken areas in Hebei Province are not only unable to attract agricultural science and technology talents to work here but are also losing a large number of local talents. At present, in agricultural science and technology, there are an average of 0.8 scientific and technical personnel per 10,000 mu of cultivated land in poverty-stricken areas in Hebei Province. Few researchers at the municipal level have a master's degree or above (Niu et al., 2017: 110–115). The development of regional agricultural science and technology can rely on the labor force and natural resources, but with the development of agricultural science and technology, the role of talent is increasingly important in the development of regional agricultural science and technology. Especially in this era of knowledge-based development, knowledge is the most important factor. Knowledge poverty is not only a low level of education, but also a lack of ability to acquire, absorb and exchange knowledge. These reasons made some people in poverty-stricken areas in Hebei Province obsolete and conservative in their thinking (Hu & Li, 2012). They were completely out of the market's agricultural science and technology innovation system, which further deteriorated the development of their agricultural science and technology and offset their advantages in labor, land, and resource prices. Making it more and more backward and becoming a vicious circle.

Due to the small size of towns in poor areas in Hebei (Hebei Provincial Department of Land and Resources, 2018), the aggregation effect is difficult to achieve. Cities and towns are the bridges and ties between urban and rural areas. The development of agricultural science and technology occupies a very important position in promoting the construction of local agriculture and has great potential in poverty alleviation. The poverty-stricken rural areas in Hebei are sparsely populated and the villages are far apart and scattered. It is difficult to achieve economies of scale. Moreover, its infrastructure is backward, the rural community environment is poor, education and welfare development are slow, and transportation and communication are lagging behind. It is therefore difficult to obtain the latest agricultural science and technology (Chen & Zhao, 2007: 298–302).

State Led Strategy for Accurate Poverty Alleviation in Hebei Province

In view of the future development of Hebei Province, accelerating the implementation of the precise poverty alleviation strategy and the goal of poverty alleviation, is inseparable from the innovative research and development and application of agricultural science and technology (Guo & Ye, 2017), which in turn is inseparable from the continuous improvement of agricultural science and technology conditions and the unremitting efforts of the majority of scientific researchers. It is even more inseparable from the continuous improvement of the self-development ability of poverty-stricken areas and poor people. In the coming period, more attention should be paid to the role and status of agricultural science and technology in poverty-stricken areas in Hebei in the precise poverty alleviation, and the three key works and tasks will be solidly promoted (Liu et al., 2017:47–48).

Eliminating poverty and improving people's livelihood is not only an important goal of building a well-off society in an all-round way, but also a concrete manifestation of agricultural science and technology services. In view of the development of poverty-stricken areas in Hebei Province, the backward agricultural technology faced in the process of precision poverty alleviation, strengthen the innovation, promotion and application of agricultural science and technology, and give full play to the supporting role of science and technology in precision poverty alleviation (Guo & Ye, 2017).

The problems faced by different poverty-stricken areas in Hebei Province should adopt different agricultural practical technologies. To address the problem of soil erosion in some poverty-stricken areas it would be beneficial to promote the techniques of no-tillage, straw stubble and land reclaiming, and control soil wind erosion and water erosion (Sun, 2011: 16–17). Promoting soil testing and fertilizer technology could help improve soil fertility in response to some problems in poor land in poor areas (Han, 2016: 138). To address water scarcity problem in some poverty areas, promotion of sprinkler irrigation, drip, drip irrigation under mulch, fertilizer and other water-saving agricultural technology integration as well as promoting the "five small water conservancy" project, improve water use efficiency and improve water supply in farmland could be implemented (Yang & Gao, 2011: 98). For use of unique agricultural resources advantages in some poverty areas, promotion of Chinese herbal medicine, specialty fruits and vegetables, edible fungus, flowers, nursery stock, woody oil, cattle and sheep breeding and other specialty products processing technology, playing special cards, ecological cards, green cards, organic brand, can be used and could help the farmers to get rich quickly (Li et al., 2015:1–6).

For the development of poor areas of Hebei, it is vital to follow the trend of development of agricultural science and technology, precision targeting poverty reduction needs, and it is necessary not to focus on the present, but also look to the future. The government should focus on the current needs of agricultural development but the bottlenecks in technology, or the current frontiers and leading development areas, do a good job of technical reserves, and provide guarantees for the sustainable development of agriculture in poverty-stricken areas (Zhao, 2010: 5–8). Strengthening technical support and research, and sending technicians from the Technical Center of the Chinese Academy of Agricultural Sciences could be beneficial as well. Genetic engineering, cell engineering, enzyme engineering, fermentation engineering and other modern biotechnology innovation research and development, can actively develop and utilize germplasm resources in poverty-stricken areas (Tang, 2000: 5–8); strengthen agricultural information technology innovation R&D, promote accurate identification, precise service and precisely management the poverty alleviation work, as well as improve poverty alleviation efficiency (Li, 2016: 44–47). Moreover, they can strengthen research and development of facility agriculture and processing technology, and comprehensively promote agricultural production efficiency improvement and industrial upgrading in poverty-stricken areas of Hebei (Feng, 2011: 22–23).

Accurate poverty alleviation requires diverse and comprehensive agricultural technologies to meet the different development requirements of resources, manpower and technology (Duan et al., 2016: 42–47). In strengthening the agricultural science and technology R & D and innovation are crucial in order to strengthen the comprehensive integration of agricultural science and technology. In the application of technology, the integration of technologies such as soil improvement, water-saving irrigation, breeding and seedling cultivation, planting and breeding, and deep processing will be strengthened to increase production, improve quality, and obtain added value, and promote the increase of farmers' income in poverty-stricken areas in Hebei (Feng, 2011: 22–23).

While the state continues to increase special funds for poverty alleviation and related agricultural investment, it should be consciously directed at the characteristics of high agricultural efficiency, long development period, many influencing factors and large material input for agricultural science and technology innovation research and development in Hebei (Zhao, 2013). Accurate poverty alleviation related technologies or agricultural science and technology research, as well as development and promotion projects in poverty-stricken areas will promote the development of relevant important platforms and projects.

"Horizontal integration, vertical through" principle, and active integration of pro-poor agricultural science and technology (Wang & Wang, 2014) can be used to build the coordinated development of information-sharing platform in Hebei. In the horizontal direction, the first-line regions and key areas integrate the data information of the Ministry of Agriculture, the Ministry of Science and Technology, the State Council Poverty Alleviation Office, the Forestry Bureau, the Statistics Bureau and other relevant departments (People.cn, 2014). It will achieve data sharing and information exchange, and the lower-level local governments integrate the data of the corresponding departments according to the same model. Information, forming a local information sharing platform; in the vertical direction, unified statistical indicators system, statistical standards, statistical caliber and statistical scope of provinces, cities, counties, townships, and villages in the areas of precision poverty alleviation, agricultural science and technology, etc. (Zhang, 2016: 24–25). The provincial data sharing platform ensures the consistency, compatibility and accuracy of data information, and realizes the vertical communication of information.

According to the characteristics of the dynamic development of poverty alleviation work, based on the various information collected and collected in the precision poverty alleviation, the agricultural information analysis technology is used to construct the agricultural science and technology poverty alleviation simulation evaluation system to realize real-time monitoring, dynamic tracking and scientific analysis (Wang, 2013), according to the various measures of agricultural science and technology poverty alleviation. The mechanism of action, simulating the progress and speed of poverty alleviation work, assessing the effect of poverty alleviation, and ensuring that precision poverty alleviation is completed on time and in good quality (People.cn, 2014).

It is necessary to take the initiative to seize the important historical opportunities of "mass entrepreneurship and innovation", support the construction of industrial integration innovation demonstration bases in poverty-stricken areas in Hebei (Gao & Yu, 2016); attract enterprises, universities, and scientific research institutions to participate in various ways (Zhao, 2016); actively take advantage of the "Internet +" development of express trains; take the public creation, crowdsourcing, public support, crowdfunding, etc. (Zhou, 2015:96–97). It is also necessary to form a good situation of user innovation, open innovation, mass innovation, and collaborative innovation. Additionally, it is vital to vigorously support the innovative demonstration of deep processing technology of agricultural products, extend the agricultural industrial chain, strengthen the integration of the first and second industries. Moreover, there should be a strong focus on supporting the development of rural e-commerce, broaden the circulation of agricultural products, sales channels, transform the mode of agricultural production and management, and strengthen the agricultural, industrial and high-end service industries along with innovation and integration (Gu, 2017: 48).

To curb the poor, the only way to cure the ignorance is to give full play to the wisdom and talents of agricultural researchers and technology extension personnel, and to forge a scientific and extension service team rooted in poverty-stricken areas, close to the poor, which understands the development's needs (Zhao, 2013), and is willing to serve and contribute to the poverty-stricken areas of Hebei. The function of the "self-intellectual hematopoiesis" and the "transfusion of blood" into "hematopoiesis" can completely change the backward appearance of poverty-stricken areas (Gao, 2017: 11).

Strengthening the implementation of the "rain dew plan", strengthening the subsidies for the children of poor families to receive secondary vocational education, higher vocational education, more than 1 year of labor preparation training, and further increasing the batch, number of people and time of training (Xiong, 2013) could help address the issue of poverty. Actively cultivating leaders in industrial development in in Hebei Province, organizing training for entrepreneurial skills and knowledge of industry leaders, and demonstrating the role of the first rich and the role of radiation could also be used. Finally, making full use of "Internet + education", and vigorously promoting a variety of training modes such as agricultural science and technology online consultation, real-time service, and distance education could be used to help the problem of poverty-stricken areas in Hebei Province (Wan & Shi, 2007: 135–136).

Conclusion

The policy of poverty alleviation in agricultural science and technology is inseparable from the fact that researchers are deeply involved in poverty (Yang, 2015). Scientific research must actively serve poor areas, and researchers must take the initiative to approach the poor. In view of the difficulties and needs of resources, environment and technology in poverty-stricken areas in Hebei Province, provincial research institutes should further strengthen cooperation with poverty-stricken areas, "communicate friends" and "pairing pairs" to achieve one-on-one assistance (Liu, 2017). The service group and the science and technology commissioner system could increase talent support and intellectual services for the poor areas in the region (Liu, 2016: 19–21).

Based on implementing the central requirements for the establishment of a village-based task force (group), according to the agricultural ecological conditions, industrial characteristics, production scale, regional layout and poverty alleviation needs of poverty-stricken areas in Hebei, acceleration of the reform of grassroots agricultural technology extension system could further improve the area. Grassroots agricultural technical service teams in poverty-stricken areas ensure that every poor village can receive effective agricultural technology services (Yang et al., 2009: 233–235); give full play to the advantages of "Internet + agricultural technology promotion" (Wan & Shi, 2007: 135–136), carry out agricultural science and technology promotion and application services in multiple forms and multiple channels, and improve the rate of technology households and the rate of arrival.

In order to promote Hebei's innovative agricultural science and technology and common poverty alleviation, several constructive suggestions are proposed, which is conducive to further promoting the integration of Hebei Province and surrounding cities and has important practical significance for promoting the coordinated management of Beijing-Tianjin-Hebei and agricultural poverty alleviation. It is also in line with the core idea of people-oriented approach and is of great significance to the comprehensive construction of a richer society in Beijing, Tianjin and Hebei.

References

Bi, Y. X. (2009). *Animal epidemic prevention and quarantine technology*. Chemical Industry Press.

Bo, Z. Z. (2011). *Research on the demand for agricultural science and technology promotion talents from the perspective of modern agriculture*. Unpublished PhD thesis. Huazhong Agricultural University.

Chen, G. F. (2011). *Data mining and precision agriculture intelligent decision system*. Science Press.

Chen, S. (2016a). Accelerate the adjustment of agricultural structure and promote the development of modern agriculture in poverty-stricken areas – Taking Xingtai City, Hebei Province as an example. *Modern Rural Science and Technology, 5*(16), 6–8.

Chen, Y. B. (2016b). *Numerical simulation of regional source analysis of typical atmospheric pollutants in the Beijing-Tianjin-Hebei region*. [D] Chinese Academy of Environmental Sciences.

Chen, L. (2017). How do farmers and herdsmen's professional cooperatives play a role in precision poverty alleviation. *Shanxi Agricultural Economics, 9*, 43–43.

Chen, C., & Zhao, N. N. (2007). The impact of traffic environment change on rural economic development: A case study of Yichang, Hubei Province. *Agricultural Modernization Research, 28*(3), 298–302.

China Central People's Government. (2017). *Statistics* [Online] available on:http://www.gov.cn. 12 July 2018.

China Geological Survey. (n.d.) [Online] http://www.cgs.gov.cn. Accessed 15 July 2018.

Dai, Z. M., Li, W. D., Ma, S., & Yang, J. Y. (2003). Strengthening the ideological and political work of agricultural institutions in the new era. *Agricultural Science and Technology Management, 22*(4), 48–50.

Deng, Y. Z., Zhang, B. H. Y., Wang, L. Y., & Wang, Z. (2011). Application of internet of things Technology in safety production management and monitoring of agricultural products. *Hebei Agricultural Sciences, 15*(7), 106–106.

Duan, B. Y. (2016). China's rural poverty alleviation development: Recalling and looking forward. *Agricultural Economics Issues, 11*, 6–11.

Fan, X. J. (2010). *Basic experience of poverty alleviation and development with Chinese characteristics* (Vol. 23, pp. 48–49).

Fan, Z. Y. (2014). Deeply understand the important meaning of poverty alleviation development. *Party Construction Research, 4*, 17–18.

Feng, B. W. (2011). Research on the status quo and development countermeasures of agricultural infrastructure construction in poor areas of Northern Province. *Industry and Technology Forum, 6*, 22–23.

Gao, S. Y. (2017). Precise poverty alleviation is increasing the self-hematopoietic function in poor areas. *New Countryside: Heilongjiang, 27*, 11–11.

Gao, Y. Q., & Yu, J. X. (2016). Analysis of the strategy of innovation and entrepreneurship education in Hebei Province under the background of coordinated development of Beijing, Tianjin and Hebei. *Management Manager, 9*(29), 6–9.

Gong, M. G., & Wang, X. Z. (2012). Food access status and its influencing factors of rural residents in poverty-stricken areas of China. *Jianghan Forum, 8*, 41–45.

Gu, X. Y. (2008). *Research on the operation mechanism of agricultural science and technology promotion in China* [D]. Hunan Agricultural University.

Guo, N., & Ye, J. G. (2017). Agricultural science and technology innovation to promote the path of rural precision poverty alleviation. *China Soft Science Academic, 3*(15), 11–15.

Hammond, D. (2015). *Heat treatment for insect control: Developments and applications* (1st ed.). Woodhead Publishing.

Han, B. (2016). Challenges and countermeasures for soil fertilizer technology extension work. *Agriculture and Technology, 36*(8), 138–138.

Han, W., Bi, Z., Lou, W. L., Kang, P. S., & Zhang, X. H. (2013). Research on Hebei Province's poverty alleviation mechanism innovation and poverty alleviation countermeasures. *Journal of Hebei University of Economics and Business, 34*(4), 100–103.

Han, Z., Yang, C., & Zhang, Q. Y. (2018). Analysis of the implementation status of precise poverty alleviation policies in poverty-stricken areas. *Agricultural Outlook, 1.*

Hebei Provincial Department of Agriculture. (2014). [Online] http://www.heagri.gov.cn. Accessed 22 July 2018.

Hebei Provincial Department of Land and Resources. (n.d.). [Online] http://www.hebgt.gov.cn. Accessed 25 July 2018.

Hebei Provincial Forestry Department. (2017). [Online] http://www.hebly.gov.cn. Accessed 22 July 2018.

Hu, J. T. (2012). *Report of the 18th National Congress (full text).* [Online] available on: oa.ahxf. gov.cn. 18 July 2018.

Hu, A. G. and Li, C. B. (2012). *New poverty in the new century: Knowledge poverty.* National conditions report.

Huang, J. K. (2013). Deepen the reform of agricultural science and technology system and improve the ability of agricultural science and technology innovation. *Agricultural Economy and Management, 2*, 5–8.

Hui, L. Y. (2012). Hui Liangyu stressed at the National Agricultural Science and technology education work conference that strengthening agricultural science and technology innovation, revitalizing and developing agricultural education, and accelerating the modernization of agriculture with Chinese characteristics. *Rural Work Communication, 5*(12), 6–6.

Jin, M. L. (2011). *A preliminary understanding of the basic experience and model of poverty alleviation and development in our province.* In Proceedings of the Guizhou symposium on poverty alleviation and development, pp. 58–65.

Jin, L., & Zhang, L. M. (2014). The effectiveness, problems and suggestions of rural financial poverty alleviation in Hebei Province. *Guizhou Agricultural Sciences, 42*(7), 215–219.

Jin, F., & Zhao, Y. X. (2010). Talking about the application and development of corn harvesting mechanization technology. *Xinjiang Agricultural Mechanization, 5*, 36–38.

Kong, X. Z., & Lou, D. (2012). International comparison of agricultural technology promotion, tense evidence and China's countermeasures [J]. *Reformation, 1*, 12–23.

Lei, K. D., & Zhang, S. J. (2017). Accurate poverty alleviation index – The total power of agricultural machinery based on BP neural network SAS analysis and prediction. *Agricultural Product Processing, 6*, 74–76.

Li, Y. H. (2009). The construction of American agricultural technology innovation system and its enlightenment to China [J]. *World Agriculture, 4*, 18–20.

Li, H. L. (2014). The poverty alleviation logic and public governance of Farmers' professional cooperation organizations[J]. *Guizhou Social Sciences, 07*, 133–137.

Li, D. Q. (2016a). E-commerce poverty alleviation under the "Internet +" strategy: Bottlenecks, advantages, and orientation – Based on the reality of rural e-commerce poverty alleviation. *Contemporary Economy, 12*, 27–28.

Li, J. A. (2016b). Suggestions for speeding up the promotion of rural poverty alleviation work. *New Agriculture, 5*, 44–47.

Li, Y. X. (2017). Accurate poverty alleviation, file peers – Promote the people's livelihood with the concept of "innovation, coordination, green, openness, sharing". *Guangdong Archives, 4.*

Li, F. M., Kadambot, H. M. S., Neil, C. T., Ou, Y. Z. Y., & Xiong, Y. C. (2011). Sustainability of agro-ecosystems in arid regions under climate change. *Acta Ecologica Sinica, 31*(9), 1–2.

Li, H., Xu, X. H., & Wang, X. G. (2015). Research on the status quo, problems and countermeasures of edible fungus technical standards in China. *China Edible Fungi, 34*(3), 1–6.

Li, G. F., Xu, G. C., Qiu, M. M., & Shi, Y. J. (2016). The dynamic changes and countermeasures of the development of "one village, one product" in the suburbs of Beijing. *Journal of Agricultural Science, 6*(6), 61–66.

Liao, B. H., Li, Y. J., Jia, J. W., Chai, Y. P., & Chen, Z. W. (2013). The role of rural informatization in promoting poverty alleviation in Hebei Province. *Hebei Agricultural Sciences, 6*, 98–100.

Lin, P., Ma, Y. H., Wang, Q., & Wang, J. (2017). Progress in research and application of agricultural big data technology and resources. *Agricultural Science & Technology, 18*(5), 907–913.

Liu, J. (2009). The history, experience and trend of China's rural poverty alleviation development [J]. *Theory & Science, 08*, 55–58.

Liu, H. Y. (2012). *Problems in the development of poverty alleviation in rural areas of our country and research on the research [D].* The University of Datong Jiaotong University is the Main School of Ma Kesi.

Liu, Y. F. (2015). Full implementation of the precise poverty alleviation strategy and resolutely fight poverty alleviation. *China's Poverty Alleviation, 21.*

Liu, X. M. (2016). Poverty alleviation must focus on talent training in poverty-stricken areas. *Agricultural Development and Finance, 7*, 19–21.

Liu, S. (2017). *The countermeasures of education precision poverty alleviation in Luanping County, Hebei Province.* Hebei University.

Liu, D. M., & Guo, Q. (2013). China's rural science and technology policy: Review, evaluation and prospects [J]. *Agricultural Economic Issues, 01*, 43–48.

Long, X. Q. (2016). On the ethical significance of rural poverty alleviation and development [J]. *Journal of Higher Education, Southwestern Normal University, 01*, 1–4.

Lv, Y. G. (2008). *Resource industry system changes and sustainable economic development.* Geological Publishing.

Lv, J. J., Xiong, Y. H., & Shen, Y. J. (2017). Promoting accuracy with fairness: The key to identification and assistance for rural poor targets. *Decisions and Information, 4*, 59–67.

Ministry of Agriculture and Rural Affairs of the People's Republic of China. (2017). [Online] http://www.moa.gov.cn. Accessed 22 July 2018.

Niu, G. Y., Yu, H. Y., & Zhao, G. Q. (2017). On the selection of the key points of science and technology poverty alleviation and development in the straits of Liupanshan in Ningxia [J]. *China Science and Technology Forum, 08*, 110–115.

Shi, L. Q., Dong, L. D., Jiao, Y. G., Guo, J. H., Chen, L. X., & Yue, X. L. (2013). Efficient planting mode and key supporting technologies for greenhouse vegetables in different ecological types in Hebei Province. *China Science and Technology Achievements, 14*, 79–80.

Sun, X. Y. (2011). Problems and solutions in the development of conservation tillage. *Agricultural Development and Equipment, 4*, 16–17.

Sun, X. G. (2017). The role of agricultural big data in agricultural economic management. *Agricultural Engineering Technology, 37*(2), 72–73.

Sun, D. L. (2018). Innovative agricultural monitoring and early warning technology services modern agricultural construction. *Rural Science Experiments, 1*, 62–62.

Tang, X. B. (2000). Thoughts on the development and utilization of biological resources and sustainable economic development in poverty-stricken areas. *Journal of Hechi University, 2*, 5–8.

The People Government of Hebei Province. (2018) [Online] http://www.hebei.gov.cn. Accessed 25 July 2018.

Tu, T. M., Tu, J. Y., & Du, F. Z. (2011). *Agricultural products e-commerce.* Hubei Science and Technology Press.

Wan, Q. T., & Shi, D. M. (2007). Network-based agricultural information service model exploration. *Shandong Agricultural Science, 4*, 135–136.

Wang, X. L. (2012). *Poverty measurement: Theory and methods.* Social Sciences Academic Press.

Wang, L. (2013). *Design and implementation of agricultural environment dynamic monitoring and evaluation management information system based on WebGIS* [D]. Jiangxi Agricultural University.

Wang, J. H. (2015). Application technology of rapeseed mechanized planting agricultural machinery. *Agricultural Development and Equipment, 8.*

Wang, L. (2016). Accelerate the development of modern agriculture with "internet + agriculture". *Basic Agricultural Technology Promotion, 7.*

Wang, J. G., & Wang, K. L. (2014). Discussion on the construction of integrated information platform for county-level power supply enterprises. *Science and Technology Communication, 10.*

Wu, Y. (2002). *Authority and order in the change of village governance [D].* Central China Normal University.

Xiong, X. Y. (2013). Research on the current situation of education poverty alleviation and existing problems. *Education, 31.*

Xu, W. S. (2009). *Key technologies and applications of agricultural information intelligence analysis.* In National symposium on agricultural information analysis theory and methods.

Yan, B. L. (2017). Promotion and application of agricultural machinery. *Times Agricultural Machinery, 44*(8), 32–32.

Yang, J. W. (2011). Practice and thinking on improving the self-development ability of poverty-stricken areas. *Contemporary Rural Finance and Economics, 9*, 26–27.

Yang, B. B. (2015). *Aiming at agricultural leading industries in poverty-stricken areas [D].* Hebei Agricultural University.

Yang, J. (2017). Current status and countermeasures of modern agricultural industrialization in Jiangsu Province. *Modern Agricultural Science and Technology, 3*, 254–256.

Yang, J. K., & Gao, G. D. (2011). New understanding and promotion of water-saving sprinkler irrigation and drip irrigation in landscaping projects. *China Science and Technology Expo, 23*, 98–98.

Yang, Z. N., Chen, X., Zhang, S. Y., & Tao, P. J. (2009). Countermeasures and recommendations for accelerating the reform of grassroots agricultural technology extension system. *Guizhou Agricultural Sciences, 37*(10), 233–235.

Yu, M. J. (2012). American agricultural science and technology promotion experience and China's innovation – Taking the practice of science and technology commissioner of Zhejiang agriculture and forestry university as an example [J]. *World Agriculture, 3*, 17–21.

Yuan, L. (2009). *Research on the construction of modern agricultural industrial system in Hefei City [D].* Anhui Agricultural University.

Zen, Z. H., Wang, K. W., & Tan, J. (2010). Thoughts and countermeasures for innovating China's agricultural science and technology service system [J]. *Journal of Agricultural University of Hebei: Agriculture and Forestry Education Edition, 3*, 428–431.

Zhang, Y. (2014). *Beijing-Tianjin-Hebei coordinated development [EB/OL], how to do financial enterprises.* Xinhuanet.

Zhang, H. S. (2015). 'Practical experience and demonstration of Dafang County's implementation of poverty alleviation and development'. *Bijie Daily,* 24 August 2.

Zhang, X. R. (2016). Analysis and suggestions on the status quo of precision poverty alleviation: Taking Shangzhuang Village, Nanchuan Township, Zhenyuan County as an example. *Agricultural Science and Technology and Information, 26,* 24–25.

Zhang, Y. L., & Xu, C. H. (2014). Measures to strengthen the operation and management of rural financial poverty alleviation funds in Hebei Province. *Rural Economy and Technology, 8.*

Zhang, S. J., Lu, Z., & Deng, X. (2011). *Evaluation and suggestion of China's agricultural product e-commerce platform construction.* Rural Economy.

Zhao, C. J. (2010). Reflections on the future development of precision agriculture in China. *Agricultural Network Information, 4,* 5–8.

Zhao, B. N. (2013a). *Research on anti-poverty in poverty-stricken areas in Baoding City.* [D], Hebei university.

Zhao, B. X. (2013b). *Research on the efficiency of scientific and technological resource allocation in national agricultural research institutions* [D]. Chinese Academy of Agricultural Sciences.

Zhao, S. H. (2016). Analysis of the effectiveness and countermeasures of the special work of cultural workers in the poverty-stricken areas in Hebei Province – Taking the mass culture field of Hebei Province as an example. *Popular Literature and Art, 9.*

Zhao, C. L. (2017). The impact of Beijing-Tianjin-Hebei integration on Hebei's economic structure. *Times Finance, 15.*

Zhi, M., & Guo, J. (2014). Analysis of the impact of agricultural resources on agricultural economic growth. *Southern Agriculture, 21,* 68–69.

Zhou, S. H. (2015). Planning management must address the shared concept of crowdsourcing, crowdfunding, and innovation. *Urban Planning, 39*(12), 96–97.

Zhuang, T. H., Yu, C. Y., & Liu, R. Y. (2013). Research on the status quo of agricultural technology extension and its influencing factors in ethnic poverty-stricken areas of Southwest China – Based on the survey of 1739 farmers in four southwest provinces [J]. *Science & Technology Progress and Policy, 09,* 37–40.

Chapter 8
Chinese Wine Industry During COVID-19: A Study of the Changyu Wine Company

Bhabani Shankar Nayak and Jiapeng Li

Introduction

The wine industry in China has developed rapidly and occupied an important position in the domestic and foreign wine markets. China is the fifth largest consumer of wine in the world. However, under the impact of COVID-19, the competition to secure a limited market share in the domestic wine market has become increasingly fierce and the previous marketing strategies of the Changyu Wine Company can no longer adapt to the changing consumer environment. In addition, the sales of imported and domestic wine continued the 'double decline' trend in 2018 and some wine production and operation enterprises encountered difficulties.

As a century-long enterprise of China's wine industry, it is imperative for the Changyu Wine Company to consider new marketing strategies. It analyses of the current situation of the Changyu Wine Company to determine the problems of the current marketing strategy during the COVID-19 pandemic. With the influence of 'zero tariff' and the appreciation of the renminbi, imported wines have eroded the Chinese market substantially (Tang, 2009). However, under the impact of COVID-19, the competition to secure a limited market share in the domestic wine market has become increasingly fierce and the previous marketing strategies of the Changyu Wine Company can no longer adapt to the changing consumer environment. The situation of the wine market has changed and the Changyu Wine Company need to deal with the challenges during the COVID-19. The chapter looks at the Changyu Wine Company as an example to identify the impact of COVID-19 on the Changyu

B. S. Nayak (✉)
Business School for the Creative Industries, University for the Creative Arts, Epsom, UK
e-mail: Bhabani.nayak@uca.ac.uk

J. Li
Adam Smith Business School, University of Glasgow, Glasgow, UK

Wine Company. It looks at the role of state in developing the market and marketing strategies by the Chinese Wine industry during the COVID-19.

Marketing can be through cultural engagement. This approach introduced the new situation of Chinese marketing strategies. When Guo (2004) first proposed the establishment of a wine market, one of the initial issues was the information symmetry. In addition to information symmetry between consumers and producers, information symmetry between producers and distributors should also be achieved. Li proposed that brand effect is indispensable to make the wine market larger and stronger and simultaneously combining the wine culture with an extensive history, providing emphasis on the positive role of wine culture in the prosperity of the market. The more the brand effect increases, the more people will be willing to purchase the wine. From this perspective, the final terminal of wine marketing should not be the shops and restaurants on the street, but family consumption (Jin, 2004). The potential of family consumption is infinite. Once a wine consumption group based on the family is formed, the economic benefits will be considerable. Yang believed that the core of the enterprise's development strategy was marketing, which should be rationally distributed to target consumer groups, namely those carefully divided according to different ages, occupations, backgrounds and incomes.

Wine marketing channels should not only be popular ready-to-drink and retail, but also be niche channels for frequent consumers of wine. If companies wish to expand the wine market, they should expand the high-end market and increase the high-end production line. For example, companies should establish a specific supply and marketing channel for the high-end golf baseand the wine which the companies provide should be made by a specialised production base. Zhang proposed a new mode of marketing and promotion for wine, namely, the use of virtual reality technology and other modern technologies for publicity, which provide a beneficial idea for people to purchase during the epidemic.

Marketing of high-end wine could be further improved through concept and word-of-mouth marketing. From this method, the enterprise tailors the corresponding concept according to the product then builds the selling aspect, proceeds with the business activity and the sponsorship, thus obtaining popularity. For example, advertisements provided by sponsors will be played in a loop half a minute before the countdown of the Annual Spring Festival Gala of CCTV to increase the audience's attentiveness to the brand. An analysis of the current market structure of wine can creatively propose marketing methods to improve the quality of wine and promote it through mass media such as internet new media. By analysing consumer preferences and clarifying specific characteristics of the target market, tourism products can be positioned more accurately, precise publicity and promotion can be carried out for the consumer groups of the target marketand wine publicity can be formulated. The influence and mechanism of self-construal on consumers' preference for polarising products have an impact on wine consumption (Wu, 2020).

Moreover, the ambidextrous innovation of the wine brand in the resource endowment of community members can make the company more creative (Ma et al., 2020).

However, there is no study that focuses on the market strategies of wine companies during the COVID-19 pandemic. The market has changed because of COVID-19 and changes have to be taken in the Chinese wine industry. Only by changing marketing strategies according to the current epidemic situation can wine sales increase to ensure that the Chinese wine market will be prosperous in the future.

The Marketing Environment of the Changyu Wine Company

The Changyu Wine Company was founded in 1892 by Bishi Zhang, a famous patriotic overseas Chinese leader, with a history of 126 year (Jin, 2004). The Changyu Wine Company has an extensive history of wine production and sales as the primary business. In 1997, the Changyu Wine Company issued B shares. In 2000, 3 years later, A shares were also listed successfully. The Changyu Wine Company has gradually developed into a state-owned enterprise (SOE) and become an unshakable wine brand in China.

The Changyu Wine Company has focused on producing wine from beginning to endand every bottle of wine on store shelves has endured a number of steps to finally appear (Tian, 2003). The company in the north of the country's low hills and foothills has a vast area of vineyards, accumulating to nearly 300,000 kilometres. A substantial number of planting parks provide sufficient raw materials for the production of the Changyu Wine Company, simultaneously providing sufficient capacity to meet the considerable wine consumption demands in the domestic and foreign markets. In addition, the Changyu Wine Company is also the first enterprise to mechanise the production of wine and its complete facilities have significantly improved the production efficiency of wine (Tang, 2009). The company adopts the mode of acquiring wineries and foreign wineries have encompassed more than 10 regions all over the world, further opening the foreign wine market. These steps have gradually made the Changyu Wine Company the leading and largest wine company in Asia.

The Changyu Wine Company adopts an incentive mechanism in which both the management and employees hold shares, with the management holding shares directly and the employees holding shares indirectly, which is a major change after the restructuring of state-owned enterprises. In addition, the Changyu Wine Company set up the Changyu International Wine Research and Development Centre in Yantai Development Zone to continuously expand production capacity and gradually upgrade the industrial chain. The Changyu Wine Company has experienced researchers who are integral to new wine innovation. At present, the Changyu wine categories have 13 different types of wine, which are divided into high and low grade, health and foreign wines. The Changyu Wine Company constantly develops new products, but also attaches great importance to intellectual property rights, Cabernet and Magic lion products as important representatives.

The Changyu Wine Company, after experiencing obstacles and challenges in the wine industry and with 'industrial development' as the goal, has developed rapidly.

It has set up numerous branches across the world and as wine has a stable level of market cooperation, Chinese wine distributed globally has accrued a considerable number of sales. In 2019, due to the reduction of Chinese economic growth and the COVID-19 pandemic, the domestic wine market was extremely competitive. The sales of imported and domestic wine continued the trend of 'double decline' in 2018 and some wine production and operation enterprises encountered severe difficulties (Liu & Murphy, 2007). Confronting numerous unfavourable factors, the company referred to the market as the centre, adhering to the 'focus on high-end, focusing on high quality, focus on the big item of the development strategy' in order to cultivate consumers to increase sales, 'the marketing concept is not shaken, efforts to promote product sales, has obtained the good effect, the annual business income is 5.03101 billion yuan, achieved falling by 2.16% from a year earlier. The profit attributable to shareholders of the parent company was 1129.74 million yuan, an increase of 8.35% over the previous year. The Changyu Wine Company operates income in 2019 accounted for 34.68% of Chinese wine'.

Chinese Wine and the External Environment

Since the 2000s, the tertiary industry has been developing vigorously and the income of Chinese residents has also increased. People gradually began to pay more attention to improving the quality of life in addition to the necessities of life. Thus, wine became an indispensable part of recreational activities and those factors have driven the wine industry to grow in size. Although the external marketing environment cannot directly affect the enterprise, it has a subtle indirect effect on the development of the company. Therefore, if the Changyu Wine Company wants to emphasise its most suitable marketing strategy during the COVID-19 pandemic and in the future, it needs to have a comprehensive understanding of the wine industry situation. PEST analysis is necessary for this situation. In view of the extensive history of wine, the social and cultural environment is also an important factor in the wine industry.

Wine and the State in China

China has promulgated a number of regulations to stabilise the wine market. For example, 'The Technical Specification for Wine Making in China' defines each type of wine in detail, meticulously dividing the brewing process for each wine and describing the problems that may arise in the fermentation process sequentially (Xu, 2005). 'The Measures for the Administration of Alcohol Circulation' regulates the process of alcohol circulation and requires alcohol managers to conduct alcohol sales in accordance with content requirements. If they violate the regulations, they will be investigated for criminal responsibility. These regulations have greatly restricted the behaviour of inefficient wine producers and played an immeasurable role in maintaining a fair and safe wine market.

The development momentum of the wine industry in China grows rapidly and the rise of private brands in the domestic market has been essentially realised. Since 2005, the country has introduced corresponding policies for imported wine, one of which is to reduce the tariff of imported wine (Tian, 2003). This has led to a steady influx of imported wine into the Chinese market. In addition to the tariff, the wine market in China has been affected by the severe economic situation. Since the 2009 financial crisis, the appreciation of RMB made some consumers earn less income and people attempted to make money more valuable, instead of spending it on the wine consumption. Due to the large population of consumers, Shanghai and Beijing have the largest total wine consumption, occupying a very important market position in the overall market of 20 cities, with a market share of 16% and 13% respectively. The combined market share of Shanghai, Beijing, Tianjin, Wuhan and Shenyang has exceeded half of the total. It can be seen that these regional market changes will affect the overall change to a large extent.

In general, the Chinese current economic environment for the development of the Chinese wine industry has not only opportunities, but also challenges (Li, 2017). Although there is no clear sub-market in the whole market, it is necessary to observe more positive aspects from the economic factors, the most important of which is that the Changyu Wine Company should attach importance to the choice of its own marketing strategy.

China has the largest population in the world and a large population also connotes a potentially substantial consumer market. Not only that, the living habits of Chinese residents have also undergone tremendous changes. This also promoted the development of the wine industry (Liu & Murphy, 2007). From one perspective, the current pace of social life is extremely rapid, therefore, everyone has to continue progressing with the advancing tide of society, whether they can maintain the pace or not. This considerable competitive pressure makes various people decide to drink a small bottle of wine to relieve the insecurity and troubles in life. In contrast, due to the abundance of material possessions at present, people have gradually started to pursue a higher spiritual level, which is a better quality of life. As such, wine is a small commodity that can improve the happiness index. Moreover, with the integration of Chinese and international society, consumer groups are constantly pursuing western grapes which are different from Chinese grapes. This phenomenon makes wine become an indispensable commodity in western restaurants. This also greatly promotes the increase of wine consumption demand.

At present, the new scientific and technological revolution is emerging in the world. Science and technology are developing with each passing day. The growth of production and management relies more and more on scientific and technological progress. It is worth noting that the development of high and new technologies has promoted the industrial structure to be cutting-edge, flexible and service-oriented, which requires marketing managers to pay more attention to cutting-edge technologies, attach importance to software development, strengthen the service for users, and adapt to the requirements of the economic era. In December 2017, China set up the Chinese Wine Industry Technology Research Institute in Yinchuan. The internal researchers of the institute are primarily responsible for the cultivation of drought- and cold-resistant grape varieties and the production of new wine products to provide technical support for the development of the domestic wine industry. The institute of technology also has a close association with the domestic institutions of higher learning in China such as the Beijing University of Industry and Commerce. Moreover, the institute also has notable cooperation with various experts in the fields, such as Baoguo Sun, who is an academician of the Chinese academy of engineering. The Leader of the Chinese Academy of Wine Technology is also an expert from the Institute of Botany of the Chinese Academy of Sciences (Wu, 2020).

The wine industry has an extensive history. Grape planting began as early as 10,000 years agoand the earliest record of the appearance of grapes in China can be traced back to the Shang dynasty in the early seventeenth century BC. At that time, grapes were only eaten as fresh and ready-to-eat fruit. In addition to being used as fruit and wine-making materials, grapes are also part of religious rituals in some regions, such as Greece. Some scholars even blame the decline of the once-mighty Roman Empire on the degradation caused by the Romans' use of wine. There are essentially four uses for grapes, namely eating the fresh fruit raw, making fermented wine, drying them as raisins and squeezing the grape juice. The most widespread is fermentative winemaking, as such, the wine industry flourishes both abroad and at home.

Chinese Wine and Barriers to Entry

The primary barriers to enter into the wine market are as follows. Firstly, the sales channel barrier. At present, the Changyu Wine Company produced wine for the primary domestic market. However, in addition to the wine market, there are other domestic and imported wines. As Changyu company has a prominent grape planting base and winery in China, raw materials would not be the current barrier of the Changyu Wine Company. In order to ensure that the Changyu Wine Company occupies the domestic market, it must strictly control the quality of the wine and design to meet the preferences of different consumer groups (Guo & Zhao, 2018). The second is the brand barrier. Consumers are more attentive to the brand. Occasionally, the power of the brand far outweighs the appeal of low prices. As the wine industry is in the development period, the concentration of the industry is increasing progressively. After several decades, it has gradually established a positive image of its brand in the hearts of consumers. However, maintaining the company's brand image is not straightforward as it requires not only time investment, but also a substantial expenditure of money. The third aspect is the barrier between product quality and research development level. Firstly, people currently pursue a higher quality of life. A substantial number of people have higher requirements in terms of wine than in the last century. Therefore, consumers will pay more attention to the quality of the wine they taste (Brochado & Oliveira, 2018). This has further augmented the wine industry and raised standards. Secondly, grapes are an exceedingly diverse product and the process of making high-quality wine is extremely complex. This requires enterprises to constantly improve their research and development capabilities to ensure that wine technology is of an optimum standard.

Threat of Substitutes to Chinese Wine

Wine is not a simple generic drink. It is based on a particular presence on a particular occasion. However, in the wine industry, the threat of similar wine alternatives is substantial. These alternatives exist in every wine business. At present, the Chinese wine industry has entered into exceptionally rapid. Therefore, each company should function independently and focus on the growth level of the industry. If their product growth is lower than the industry average, they will lose their market share and may be expelled from the wine industry.

Buyers are predominantly distributors (in fact, most of them are also terminal stores) with few end users. As such, relying on distributors increases customers' bargaining power. In addition, due to intensified market competition, wine is primarily a buyer's market, which increases buyers' bargaining power virtually. Meanwhile, as manufacturers have to attach importance to large stores in important terminal channels (relative to the factory of the buyer) because of the special business association, location has highlighted the increasingly important role. Therefore, the bargaining power becomes stronger and terms of trade are stricter. Although some stores are operated by dealers, undoubtedly, it increases the difficulty of the dealers and costs, reducing dealer profits.

The bargaining power of consumers in the wine industry is determined by three aspects. Firstly, it depends on the brand influence of the products which they would like to purchase and the competitiveness of the products themselves (Li, 2017). Secondly, it depends on how competitive the wine industry is in this market. Thirdly, it depends on the number of products consumers can buy. The Changyu Wine Company is predominantly engaged in wine series. The brewing technology is relatively advanced and they are featured with healthy functionality, higher consumer acceptance and weaker buyer bargaining power (Wu, 2020). However, with the rapid development of the future wine market, the market competition becomes increasingly fierce and the subsequent rise and increase of companies entering the country will provide more opportunities for distributors and buyers to choose between various companies. If this occurs, the competitive brands of the Changyu Wine Company will potentially provide more choices for distributors and consumers and the bargaining power of the Changyu Wine Company will decline to improve the bargaining power of consumers.

In terms of the Changyu Wine Company, the bargaining power of suppliers is in a disadvantageous position. This is because it has various wineries and planting sites upstream, which indicates that the Changyu Wine Company has sufficient raw materials. Therefore, the Changyu Wine Company has adequate and reliable supply channels and therefore, does not depend excessively on a few suppliers, which indicates that the bargaining power of the Changyu Wine Company is strong.

According to the product category of the Changyu Wine Company, the competitors of wine, health and foreign wines are different. The Changyu Wine Company encounters competition from domestic wine companies such as Great Wall, Veyron and Dynasty, as well as imported wines. A single domestic wine company is not comparable to the Changyu Wine Company. However, a significant number of small and medium-sized companies assembled together can pose a competitive threat to the company. For example, small and medium-sized enterprises mobilised together to share infrastructure, resources, technology and even labour to produce, develop, sell and conduct wine research. They share resources to others which aims to enhance market share. Imported wine is also closely observing the Chinese market. The Changyu Wine Company and imported wine companies have similar segment markets and fierce competition, which is a huge challenge for the Changyu Wine Company.

The Changyu Wine Company

The Changyu Wine Company has multiple strengths and weaknesses, as well as opportunities and threats within the context of Chinese wine industry development. It is essential to develop the Changyu Wine Company's own advantages, whilst avoiding its own shortcomings and then avoiding potential dangers by developing more suitable marketing strategies for the Changyu Wine Company.

Firstly, the production base and raw material supply are adequate. Through the purchase of grape growing areas, the Changyu Wine Company owns a vast area of vineyards in the north of China, with an amount of nearly 300,000 kilometres. These vineyards share the same characteristics, namely fertile and nutritious land, adequate water for irrigation, suitable weather and climate for grape growth. A large number of planting parks provide sufficient raw materials for the production of the Changyu Wine Company, which occupy a permanent position in the upstream of the industrial chain. It does not only meet the demand of domestic consumers for wine, but also has sufficient capacity to meet the substantial consumption of wine in the foreign market. In addition, the Changyu Wine Company has proceeded to enter the global market and adopts the mode of acquiring wineries abroad (La Porta & Migheli, 2019). Foreign wineries encompass more than 10 regions in the worldand local conditions can directly provide raw materials for grape brewing.

Secondly, the Changyu Wine Company has the product quality advantages. The Changyu Wine Company attaches great importance to the management of product quality and strictly follows the requirements of various national management systems and standards for the special requirements of customers. The Changyu Wine Company treats every bottle of wine equally regardless of its range (high, low or mid-range), using the highest standards of technology in the industry. Moreover, it has equipped its independent laboratory with advanced technology and contemporary testing equipment. In 2015, the Changyu Wine Company established the Changyu International Wine R&D and manufacturing centre in expanding capacity and extending the industrial chain to improve the product quality of wines in Yantai (Guo & Zhao, 2018).

In addition, sales channel advantages are indispensable to the Changyu Wine Company. The Changyu Wine Company has two sales channels with different characteristics at home and abroad. In China, the Changyu Wine Company adopts a three-level marketing system for sales. As such, the headquarters will first delegate the instructions to the branch company and the branch company receiving the instructions will summarise the requirements and then delegate the instructions to the sales office. The sales office which receives the specific requirements will deliver the goods to the distributors in accordance with the specified amountand the distributors will transfer the goods to the wholesalers who will then transfer the goods to the retailers (Oczkowski & Doucouliagos, 2015). In foreign countries, the Changyu Wine Company not only conducts sales activities through agents, but also through foreign wineries as a sales transitand they have a long-term supply agreement as a guarantee.

Moreover, the Changyu Wine Company has the management advantages. At the culmination of 2017, the Changyu Wine Company experienced an important management adjustment. At the beginning of 2018, Hongjiang Zhou became the new Chairman of the Changyu Wine Company. As Zhou commenced his career in human resources at the Changyu Wine Company, management was straightforward for him. Moreover, Zhou had a strong market sensitivity for the wine market (Guo & Zhao, 2018). He further refined the market development model and implemented unprecedented marketing ideas. The layout plan of the wine market he proposed was implemented after constant adjustment according to the unique conditions of relevant, specific problems.

The Changyu Wine Company has created a significant number of enemies. When the Changyu Wine Company first registered with Cabernet's trademark, it discovered that a number of other wine companies were also similarly registering with the same trademark. As Cabernet is the name of a particular dry red wine of the Changyu Wine Company, Cabernet has been used as a trade name as early as the 1930s. However, with the exception of the Changyu Wine Company, a number of other wine companies considered Cabernet to be the name of a fruitand a trademark battle began, which lasted for nearly 6 years and culminated with official ownership given to the Changyu Wine Company. However, this victory made the Changyu Wine Company isolated from other enterprises in the wine market and some small enterprises even gathered to fight the Changyu Wine Company through enterprises, which still continues (Wu, 2020). Thus, the Changyu Wine Company was once isolated in the domestic market.

Besides, the Changyu Wine Company is lack of overseas management talents. The Changyu Wine Company has experienced management in China, but in the overseas market, most of the personnel dispatched by the company were skilled personnel without foreign experience. Although the company had been prepared for a series of possible management problems, with regards to the actual problems, how to appropriately manage the customs and different cultures is a problem for overseas managers. The Changyu Wine Company is still lacking in terms of the training of staff for foreign positions.

The development of the Changyu Wine Company in the international market is far from sufficient. This is primarily due to the fact that the wine is made of imported and domestic products. In contrast to each popular international wine, a domestic wine company has a different brewing process and research techniques which has a profound impact on the product (Guo & Zhao, 2018). As such, Chinese wine may not be fully appreciated in the overseas market. In summary, the popularity of the Changyu Wine Company in the overseas market development is not high.

First, consumers' pursuit of a quality life is significant. The previous section has analysed the political, economic, social and technological state of the wine industry. Through this analysis, it can be observed that China's wine market has entered the launching stage (Zhao et al., 2019). Ultimately, since the 2010s, China's economy has made a qualitative leap, which drives people to pursue better and increasingly high-quality life and consumers have certain economic strength to incorporate a certain amount of high-quality consumption for their lives (Brochado & Oliveira, 2018). Moreover, as social pressure increases, adults release pressure by drinking premium wine. It is worth noting that a moderate consumption of wine is also beneficial to human health This is a great opportunity not only for the Changyu Wine Company, but also for other wine operators.

In addition, it is necessary to analysis the considerable potential in foreign markets. In the contemporary market situation, the Changyu Wine Company needs to be more attentive to expanding its sales scope (La Porta & Migheli, 2019). At present, the Changyu Wine Company sells products primarily for the domestic market. However, in foreign markets, despite whether they are developed or developing countries, the Changyu Wine Company has little involvement. However, this aspect of the market consumption capacity is extremely substantial. Amongst the countries that the Changyu Wine Company does not cover is Italy, a largely mature and well-developed market. Meanwhile, there are still some cities and regions where the local wine market is still in an imperfect stageand consumers have little demand for wine. However, these potential markets will gradually become available with the rapid popularity of wine. This is a great opportunity for the Changyu Wine Company to rapidly expand its scale and establish a global brand.

The first threat is the popularity of the imported wine. China's population ranks the first in the world, which makes the country's wine market capacity considerable and the market prospect is extremely substantial. With regards to the higher economic efficiency, producers from all over the world have been attentive to China and imported wine is also closely observing the Chinese market. If the Changyu Wine Company and imported wine companies disperse into similar markets there will be fierce competition. A notable number of imported wines have entered the Chinese market, undoubtedly instigating surprise from domestic wine enterprises.

The second threat is the low tariff policy. Since 2005, China has introduced relevant policies for imported wines, one of which is to reduce the import tariff on wines entering China. This has led to a steady influx of imported wine into the

Chinese market. By 2012, Australia, Chile and New Zealand were 'tariff-free,' indicating that producers in those countries could enter wine into the domestic market at an extremely low price without having to pay any additional tax (Guo & Zhao, 2018). As the price of imported wine is proportional to the tariff, when the tariff is reduced to zero, the price decreases accordinglyand the final price gradually becomes the same as the price of domestic wine, or even lower. The original price advantage of domestic wine gradually disappeared under the influence of the import tariff reduction.

The third threat is the Economic fluctuation and RMB appreciation. Since the 2009 financial crisis, the economic crisis led to the decrease of the consumer spending power, prompting consumers to search for high-quality yet cheap wine. International wine companies took advantage of this opportunity and imported wine invaded the domestic market. In comparison to before and after 2009, the imported wine in relation to the proportion of the total domestic wine consumption increased each year. It is worth acknowledging that the appreciation of RMB since the 2010s made the price of imported wine lower and also made the export of domestic wine encounter unprecedented pressure.

According to the aforementioned analysis of the advantages, disadvantages, opportunities and threats of the Changyu Wine Company, the following conclusions state that in view of the promising development prospect of the wine industry and the unique characteristics of the Changyu Wine Company, its advantages outweigh the disadvantages and opportunities outweigh the threats. Thus, the Changyu Wine Company has great potential for future development.

Limits of the Marketing Strategies of the Changyu Wine Company

For many years, the Changyu Wine Company has remained faithful toits original business model in its marketing strategy, implementing the office system and operating by unified personnel appointed by enterprises with investment (Li, 2017). The policy is rigid, unable to keep up with the rapidly changing market dynamics, the incentive mechanism is backward and the enthusiasm of business personnel is lacking. Furthermore, information flow transmission link is complex and feedback speed is slow with low efficiency and high cost, leading to the loss of part of the market. In order to expand its customer base and increase the Changyu Wine Company's profits, only by determining the current problems faced by the company can the situation be improved. Accordingly, it is imperative to devise a set of marketing strategies suitable for the Changyu Wine Company.

The Changyu Wine Company mainly produces wine, champagne, brandy and health wine. Of these four categories, wine is the largest, accounting for 78% of the company's total wine production, brandy for 20% and the other two combined for 2%. Such a large proportion not only reflects the basic role of wine products for the

Changyu Wine Company, but also that the other three types of wine did not fully follow the rhythm of wine. For example, the Changyu Wine Company is likened to a sports field. All kinds of alcohol products are athletes. Wine products are running in a vigorous manner, while brandy and other products are running at a slow pace, which obviously separates them from the pack (Liu & Murphy, 2007). Therefore, it can be concluded that the current product structure does not form an echelon that can promote the coordination of various wine products.

Since 2005, China has introduced relevant policies for imported wines, one of which is to reduce the import tariff on wines entering the country (Han, 2010). This has led to a steady influx of imported wine into the Chinese market. By 2012, Australia, Chile and New Zealand were 'tariff-free', meaning producers in these countries could import wine into the Chinese market at a low price without having to pay any additional taxes (Guo & Zhao, 2018). Since the price of imported wine is proportional to the tariff, when the tariff is reduced to zero, the price decreases accordinglyand the final price gradually becomes the same as the price of domestic wine, or even lower (Wu, 2020). Consequently, the original price advantage of the wine produced by the Changyu Wine Company has gradually been eradicated owing to the reduction of the import tariff on imported wine. As a result, the demand for high-quality wine has increasedand more consumers are turning to imported wine with higher price performance compared to the Changyu Wine Company products which are not as good as the previous price performance (La Porta & Migheli, 2019).

The target consumers of the Changyu Wine Company are mainly concentrated in certain income groups, a consumer groups on the basis of the basic in middle-income and higher income crowd marketing (Tang, 2009). These two groups have high income people, for instance, the group of successful people with a broad consumer market for young consumers less involved. Newly growing young consumer groups are willing to try new things and have higher requirements in terms of quality of life (Li, 2017). The Changyu Wine Company may lose a large number of profit and market share if it only concentrates on the middle-income and higher income crowd.

The promotion of the Changyu Wine Company and its products in overseas markets is inadequate. This is mainly due to the wine itself is made of imported and domestic. In contrast to the overseas each big wine, domestic wine company in the brewing process and research techniques compared with the other brands of wine enterprises abroad, which is clearly by the impact (Wu, 2020). These factors make wine in China the rest of the people do not have overseas brand superiority to makes the Changyu Wine Company a global brand. From the perspective of overseas market development, its popularity is not high. The setup of alcoholic products is not echeloned, the price advantage of domestic wine decreases, the concentrated positioning of target consumer groups and the limited promotion efforts in overseas markets are the shortcomings of the Changyu Wine Company since the outbreak of COVID-19. These four factors severely restrict the development and profitability of the Changyu Wine Company.

Future of the Changyu Wine Company

The product is the first and most important element in marketing. When formulating the marketing mix strategy, enterprises should first consider what kind of products to develop to meet the needs of the target market. This question will be answered in a comprehensive and systematic manner through the study of product strategy, which requires coordinated decisions on product mix, product lines, branding, packaging and labelling. When a firm is poised to launch a new product, when it is about to launch a product in a new way, or when it is bidding competitively, it must set an appropriate price for its product. In order to effectively carry out marketing initiatives and promote the increase of sales revenue and profits, the basic price has to be revised. Price is an extremely sensitive and difficult-to-control factor in the marketing mix. It is intrinsically linked to the acceptance of the market to the product, affects the market demand and the profits of the enterprise and encompasses the interests of producers, operators, consumers and other aspects. Therefore, price strategy is an integral part of marketing mix strategy.

Under the conditions of the modern market economy, there are differences between producers and consumers in terms of time, place, quantity, variety, information, product valuation and ownership (Brochado & Oliveira, 2018). Only through certain marketing channels can the products produced by enterprises be supplied to the majority of consumers or users at an appropriate price, time and place, so as to overcome the differences between producers and consumers, meet the needs of the market and achieve the marketing objectives of enterprises.

Successful marketing initiatives not only require companies to set appropriate prices and choose appropriate distribution channels to provide satisfactory products to the market, but also effective ways to promote sales.

For the current products of the Changyu Wine Company, optimising the structure and establishing a reasonable product gradient is an important strategy to maintain market competitiveness (Oczkowski & Doucouliagos, 2015). For the optimisation of product structure, it is necessary to start with the raw materials to ensure sufficient raw materials to produce the wine. As the Changyu Wine Company in the current market demand is increasingly robust, capacity for sales is crucial. The grape is the raw material for the survival of wine companies. When they have greater capacity, then in the wine market can straighten their backs. With the Changyu Wine Company, analyses the core products of Cabernet, because this kind of core product is unique to the Changyu Wine Company (Li, 2017). The basic formula of the current wine market is an increasingly strong demand for Cabernet, if the production of the key raw material is reduced, it will have an inestimable impact on the wine market. The Changyu Wine Company needs to continuously improve the infrastructure of the planting base and use the winery to introduce planting technology and planting talents to ensure the steady supply of raw materials for its wine (Wu, 2020). By improving product quality and providing high-quality after-sales services, the added value of products can be enhanced so that consumers have a comprehensive and correct understanding of products, thereby increasing product competitiveness and market share.

In the contemporary wine market, most wines use similar packaging and have a similar taste, which at first glance means there is little difference. In this scenario, determining how to increase the additional effect of the product must be considered by the Changyu Wine Company. Innovation is certainly a good way to distinguish the brand from other wine products. By enhancing the added value of products, the technical content of wine can be increased, whilst a unique corporate image can be fostered to appeal to consumers. For example, with regards to its well-known product, Cabernet, the company can establish a dry red laboratory to improve the quality of wine and study the brewing process to increase the added value of the product. In terms of product portfolio, the Changyu Wine Company should increase the depth of its product portfolio, integrate high-end products with health benefits on the basis of the original product portfolio, increase the profit of the company and enhance the market competitiveness of Changyu wine by increasing the sales volume of high value-added products (La Porta & Migheli, 2019).

The Changyu Wine Company should increase the depth of the product portfolio, integrate high-end products with health care functions on the basis of the original product portfolio, increase the profit of the enterprise and enhance the market competitiveness by expanding the sales volume of high value-added products. In order to meet the needs of consumers with low purchasing power, the Changyu Wine Company should produce appropriate products, occupy the market to the maximum extent, develop new products and improve market share by taking advantage of its brand and geographical advantages.

In terms of new product development, the Changyu Wine Company should focus on developing new products which have great market potential. The Changyu Wine Company uses mature product profit to support the most extensive application prospect in the largest market potential and the development of new products and sales, for the new product after mature, recycling high profits feedback of new products in recession of the old products, product life cycle to keep the competitiveness of the enterprise for a long time and growth potential (Wu, 2020). In this respect, the company's new product research and development should focus on high-grade healthy edible oil, seize the opportunity, stabilize and improve the product's market share and the reputation of the enterprise brand.

The Changyu Wine Company also needs to adopt some other appropriate distribution strategies for different products. For example, the newly developed varieties can be appropriately adopted exclusive distribution strategy. Exclusive distribution strategy means that the manufacturer only chooses one middleman in a certain region to promote its products (Vrontis & Paliwoda, 2008). Usually, the two parties negotiate and sign an exclusive distribution contract, stipulating that the distributor shall not handle the products of competitors in the same industry to control the business operation of the distributor, arouse its enthusiasm and occupy the market. To adopt the exclusive distribution strategy is to choose a distributor with the best credit and the strongest strength as the exclusive agent among the original distributors, so as to better achieve the sales targets of the Changyu Wine Company. On the one hand, it can maximize the enthusiasm of distributors and urge them to try their best to do a good job of new products. On the other hand, it can avoid malicious competition between distributors, protect the life cycle of new products and ensure the profit margin of new products.

At present, wines on the market are mostly priced according to the year of production, with relatively recent wines given a lower price and older wines priced higher. However, this simplistic and crude approach to consumers only makes the vintage a byword for price and ignores the quality which matters most (Oczkowski & Doucouliagos, 2015).

The Changyu Wine Company should take advantage of its existing comprehensive information network management system, timely through the sales network of business personnel at various levels, information professionals in various areas, various market types, quantity, price, market and competitor information carries on the detailed investigation, collection, analysis, feedbackand form a quick feedback information system, for different regions, different varieties of price changes according to the market to adjust in timeand formulate the corresponding price policy, to ensure that seize the market changes, to ensure the consolidation and expansion of the market, realising the maximisation of profits.

The Changyu Wine Company could also divide the prices based on the level, with different levels corresponding to different price gradients. This according to level classification, the wine is completely determined by the quality, price of old wine not good quality, but good quality wine is high price, or by Cabernet wine, for example, Cabernet wine into optimisation and selected, the collection, master four levels, to some extent, these four levels can make consumers understand gradually, for wine, quality is much more important than the year of production. In addition, the head office and branch sales managers and sales department managers should directly take charge of the management of sales expenses to control and manage the sales expenses according to the requirements. It is necessary to introduce competition and incentive mechanism into the daily sales work which can give full play to the enthusiasm of marketing personnel and improve the economic efficiency of enterprises.

The Changyu Wine Company pricing is mainly composed of four systems. The first system is carried out in accordance with the wholesale channel pricing of wholesale pricing system. The second type of system is through the channels of the hotel, namely, the hotel restaurants supply special wine price system. The third system is through business channels, namely, for residents of daily household purchase large business super price system. Finally, the fourth system is sold in the neighbourhood convenience store price system of the ubiquitous convenience stores. These four systems overlap each otherand issues frequently arise in the actual process. Conflicts between different channels become increasingly fierceand the market price is often unstable (Vrontis & Paliwoda, 2008).

The Changyu Wine Company should identify these four systems, focus on finding out the coincidence points and reset the prices accordingly. The next step is to reduce the price system from the original four to two systems, namely, the hotel and the market price system. In doing so, not only can the company reduce the contradictions between various channels, but it can also let consumers know the price. For the Changyu Wine Company, it can also avoid selling at low prices and maintain the interests of dealers and enterprises. The Changyu Wine Company also needs to adopt some new appropriate distribution channels.

It is important to increase personnel promotion efforts. In personnel sales activities, sales personnel, sales objects, nd sales products are three basic elements. Zhangyu Co., Ltd. in this aspect of the specific strategy should be to divide the domestic market into a number of regions, the implementation of regional salesman system, in different regions, provinces, cities are dispatched a number of salesmen, strengthen the monitoring of the regional market, seize market opportunities, actively promote enterprise productsand implement sales incentive strategy (Song & Xu, 2007). Personnel marketing can properly provide certain services to customers, which, on the one hand, can increase the reputation of the company, establish its own brand, build a loyal customer base to lay a good foundationand on the other hand, can save the cost of re-service expenses. The specific measures in service are as follows: be responsible according to the region, the salesman carry out tracking service to the whole process of the business happeningand establish the idea of enhancing the service to improve the product competitiveness. Formulate sales staff service convention within the enterprise, strengthen the quality inquiry of sold products and negotiate to solve the problems raised by dealers as soon as possible.

Market segmentation refers to the enterprise through market research, according to the different needs and wants of consumers for products, different purchasing behaviour and habits of the overall market for a certain product divided into several children require different market classification processes, including any sub-markets are a similar desires and needs of customers and different son market customer needs and desires of the same products have obvious differences. The heterogeneity of customer demand is the inherent basis of market segmentation (La Porta & Migheli, 2019). Due to the wide distribution of the Changyu consumers, particularly the diverse and ever-changing customer needs, the desires and purchasing behaviours are which leads to the difference in customer needs satisfaction.

Facing the current target market, the Changyu Wine Company only loosely divides the target group according to different income levels. However, this division is too simplistic. Instead, one can further break down the market by dividing variables. With regards to the variable of gender, one can divide the wine market into two parts, namely, the male and female market. If it is divided according to geographical factors, it can be divided into the domestic and international market, which can also be further divided based on region. The domestic market is divided according to small and medium-sized cities, towns and rural areasand the international market is divided into developing countries, Europe and the US and other developed countries. With regards to different purchase purposes, it can be divided into three markets, namely, ordinary consumption, holiday gifts and hospitality. Again, it can be broken down by taste, alcohol and similar characteristics.

With the rapid development of information technology, the traditional operating mode of enterprises has been impacted dramatically. At present, due to the emergence of e-commerce, online marketing, with its unique advantages, is fully expected to replace the traditional marketing mode. Online marketing can be free from geographical and time and space restrictions, is more convenient to obtain informationand to query and receive a quick decision. It can break regional and national boundaries, offering convenient and fast international trade (Wu, 2020). The realisation of online banking payment systems provides more convenient conditions and guarantees for online marketing, saves manpower and reduces risks. (Moreover, the use of e-commerce for online marketing can motivate enterprises to establish and improve their logistics system, with the help of the network, the formation of production, supply, sales, service in one operating system, improve the service. Therefore, the company should make full use of technology, promote enterprise marketing work and improve enterprise competitiveness.

By applying segmentation to these variables, the company can discover the potential market that has not been found before. The Changyu Wine Company can gradually develop its potential market using this methodand it is believed that the benefits in terms of profits of these new markets will be considerable.

One of the key steps for the Changyu Wine Company to expand its target market is to let consumers know that such a wine company exists in the market. In order to increase the presence of the Changyu Wine Company in the wine market, it can promote and publicise itself using contemporary mass media. The last thing the Changyu Wine Company need in this technological age is social software. Various apps within the social software can help the Changyu Wine Company increase its brand awareness.

The Changyu Wine Company can use the Sina Weibo and Tencent micro blog platforms to register official micro blogs on such software and share publicity content. The Changyu Wine Company can attract consumers' attention by uploading videos and photographs of the winemaking process on Weibo and interact with numerous Weibo users through the comments feature. In doing so, it will help the company to get closer to consumers through the internet, acquire more information and better understand consumers' demand for wine. In addition, it is necessary to let more people know about the Changyu Wine Company by forwarding the lucky draw (Tian, 2003). WeChat circle of friends is also a good platform. The Changyu Wine Company can occasionally send benefits on the public account and publicise it by forwarding it to the circle of friends and collecting likes, thereby achieving the purpose of expanding the target market.

The Changyu Wine Company has a long history, dating back to 1892, which is referred to as 'one hundred years Changyu'. Changyu culture is an important spiritual support for the development of the Changyu Wine Company. However, Changyu culture in the past has been inherited with the axle of history till now and many people have gradually forgotten it (Oczkowski & Doucouliagos, 2015). Brand effect can be created by making use of Changyu's profound cultural accumulation to imprint Changyu's wine making with historical marks, which plays an invaluable role in further shaping the brand image of the Changyu Wine Company.

Wine culture is a part of enterprise culture, 'Liquan Spring' is Dr. Sun Yat-sen's heartfelt admiration of the Changyu Wine Company. In their work, every Changyu employee strives to practice the Changyu enterprise spirit of 'patriotism, dedication, quality and striving for excellence'. The Changyu Wine Culture Museum, which was rebuilt in 2000, promotes Changyu's unique wine culture by showcasing its winemaking tools and historical photographs from the last century to consumers with narrators. Changyu winery, which is distributed all over the country, has also become the spreading place of Changyu culture in the production process of high-grade wine, which adds a great deal of colour to the brand culture label of Changyu.

The Changyu Wine Company for wine brand construction has a long history. It is simple to propose the brand-building strategy, yet there are numerous problems in the actual process of applying it. It is a long and arduous project to persist in practice. If the Changyu Wine Company wants to develop its wine market at home and abroad, it must persist in implementing the brand-building strategy.

When the Changyu Wine Company builds its brand, it uses the 'world vision' programme in the global marketing. Through the integration of resources, the Changyu Wine Company makes the acquisition of major wineries and then sets up global distributio. Meanwhile, the Changyu Wine Company focuses on the high-end, high-quality, big item 'strategy, infrastructure, brewing technology and research personnel unified integration. Moreover, it plays the coordination effect on the overseas companies which aims to continue to increase awareness of the Changyu brand overseas to open the door for the company's products in international markets. By optimising and improving the product mix, establishing a system of reasonable prices, expanding the scope of the target market and creating the Changyu brand effect, it can help to deal with the market changes, consolidate and expand its market to achieve the maximum profits for the company. These methods can meet the needs of consumers to the maximum extent, maximise the role of the product so as to enhance its added value and improve the market competitiveness of the product during the COVID-19 pandemic.

Conclusion

Marketing strategy is the key element in enterprise operations. A suitable marketing strategy is the fundamental requirement for enterprise consolidation and development. Low price, high-quality, fast delivery, flexible management and outstanding service are not only the fundamental demands of distributors and consumers, but also the basic guarantee that enterprises should make for their sustained development. A robust marketing operation system is the cornerstone for an enterprise to build a quality brand. Therefore, enterprises should always prioritise marketing, which is not only the true essence of market-oriented enterprise management, but also the key to the survival and development of a company (Vrontis & Paliwoda, 2008).

Due to the COVID-19 pandemic, the trend of wine market consumption of the Changyu Wine Company over the next few years has been forecasted and analysed. Although consumption is increasing, the trend of total supply exceeding demand in the wine industry is predicted to occur either in 2020 or 2021. Under the situation of unchanged market area, small consumption elasticity, limited consumption increases and plummeting production capacity, the Changyu Wine Company will undoubtedly face greater market pressure. Therefore, it is necessary to segment the market, reorganise its market statusand invest limited resources according to different target markets and specific products.

In this chapter, a systematic study of the current status of China's domestic wine and development trend has been conducted, based on the analysis of characteristics and development trend of the wine market, in an effort to construct the market development frame of the Changyu Wine Company. Meanwhile, by adopting modern marketing and enterprise strategic management theory, combined with the current situation and development trend of the domestic wine industry, macro environment, industry environment, resources and environment factors, such as internal to the organisation carried out in-depth analysis and research, through the market segmentation and market demand forecast, the company can determine its enterprise target market.

Marketing strategy can only be described as an important part of enterprise management, enterprise management success or failure of many such as operating logistics system, financial support and human resource configuration and other supporting factors, the present study only on the enterprise market marketing strategy research, hope to help to the Changyu Wine Company, for the other links affecting the development of enterprises require further in-depth study in the future.

References

Brochado, A., & Oliveira, F. (2018). Brand equity in the Portuguese vinho verde "green wine" market. *International Journal of Wine Business Research, 30*(1), 2–18.

Guo, F. (2004). Brand positioning in marketing strategy. *China Circulation Economy, 18*(4), 49–53.

Guo, H., & Zhao, Z. (2018). Research on business model innovation of Yonghui supermarket based on new retail. *Shanghai Management Science, 40*(5), 66–70.

Han, B. (2010). New thinking of solving channeling goods. *Marketing Cases, 24*(2), 41–44.

Jin, W. (2004). The forecast of wine market in China. *SINO-Overseas Grapevine and Wine, 4*(1), 69–74.

La Porta, V., & Migheli, M. (2019). Grapes grow better in the backyard: The effect of organic growth strategies on Italian wineries' profits. *International Journal of Wine Business Research, 31*(2), 243–259.

Li, X. (2017). Macroeconomic determinants of wine prices. *International Journal of Wine Business Research, 29*(3), 234–250.

Liu, F., & Murphy, J. (2007). A qualitative study of Chinese wine consumption and purchasing: Implications for Australian wines. *International Journal of Wine Business Research, 19*(2), 98–113.

Ma, W., Liu, Q., Zhao, Y., & Zheng, J. (2020). Ambidextrous innovation of brand community members' resource endowment. *Journal of Shandong University (Natural Science), 55*(1), 77–85.

Oczkowski, E., & Doucouliagos, H. (2015). Wine prices and quality ratings: A meta-regression analysis. *American Journal of Agricultural Economics, 29*(1), 103–121.

Song, J., & Xu, L. (2007). Discussion on the current situation and development of China's wine industry. *Special Economic Zone, 216*(1), 203–204.

Tang, W. (2009). New direction of wine marketing. *Enterprise Technology and Development, 32* (1), 36–37.

Tian, J. (2003). Research report on China's mainstream consumer market. *Sales and Marketing, 15* (1), 94–94.

Vrontis, D., & Paliwoda, S. (2008). Building the brand in the Cyprus wine industry. *Journal of Brand Management, 16*(3), 145–159.

Wu, L. (2020). The influence and mechanism of self-construal on consumers' preference for polarizing products. *Advances in Psychological Science, 28*(4), 535–548.

Xu, X. (2005). Analysis on marketing innovation strategy of small and medium-sized enterprises. *Enterprise Economics, 14*(2), 66–69.

Zhao, S., Ma, S., Yu, R., Ding, G., Zhang, Y., & Zhao, L. (2019). Evaluation of ecosystem service value of the grape industry at the eastern foot of Helan Mountain, Ningxia, China. *Chinese Journal of Applied Ecology, 30*(3), 979–985.

Chapter 9
Postscript on the Future of China as a Bankable State

Bhabani Shankar Nayak

The rise of China is not only a hope for the Asian people but also inspires working class people all over the world. It instils hopes that there is an alternative to predatory capitalism of the west. The Chinese Communist Party (CCP) played a major role in transforming China as a major world power while uplifting many Chinese from poverty, hunger and homelessness. The Chinese state capitalism or socialism with Chinese character under the leadership of CCP has managed its economy, politics and culture in a progressive manner. The Chinese achievements are potential alternatives to western capitalism. However, there are many issues that is confronting China today that limits the working-class politics. There is falling ideological appeal of the CCP among Chinese youth due to its top down approach. There is growing disillusionment among the CCP members because of the growing gap between theory and ideological practice among the top leadership within the CCP hierarchy. There is huge growth of economic inequality among Chinese population. The growing gap between rich and poor shows the failures of the CCP in developing egalitarian economic policies. The gap between rural and urban China is another concern that CCP ignores in practice. Many of these problems are self-inflicted by the arrogance and dominance of the CCP. It is making the same blunders that USSR made and collapsed. These self-inflicted harms are avoidable for the sake of China, Chinese people in particular and working-class people across the globe.

The internal issues of discontent in Tibet, Hong Kong, Taiwan and fear among the Uighur Muslims reflect democratic distrusts between Chinese government, party and people living within China. It demands democratisation politics and decentralisation governance within the democratic traditions of communist ideology. The CCP led Chinese government has failed to overcome the trust deficit within different regions and provinces in China. The trust deficit of China is accelerated by its

B. S. Nayak (✉)
Business School for the Creative Industries, University for the Creative Arts, Epsom, UK
e-mail: Bhabani.nayak@uca.ac.uk

aggressive postures in its neighbourhood foreign policy. China and India are two civilizational postcolonial states. These two countries share more than 3440 km (2100 miles) long border and have overlapping claims. These two nuclear armed countries can solve their border disputes with debates, discussions and diplomacy. The military confrontation between two diminishes their role both in regional and global forums. It sends wrong signals to regional and world peace. Both the countries need to focus on their own economic development and cooperate with each other for human welfare. China, Nepal and Pakistan are all weather friends. This is how neighbours should be in relationships but there is distrust of Beijing in Kathmandu and Islamabad. Vietnam, Philippines, Sri Lanka and east Asian countries are also good friends with China but scepticisms are growing in these countries because of the highhandedness of Beijing. There is local resistance against Chinese investment and Chinese takeover of their natural and strategic resources. Similar trends are visible in African continent against neo-colonial modes of Chinese investments. The Chinese aggressive postures diminish the good will for China in different regions.

The ruling elites need to understand that these issues are serious liabilities in long run. The sustainability of CCP and the rise of China depends on the good will it generates among people within its effective foreign policy praxis in dealing with neighbours and other friendly nations. The CCP can solve all these issues with a clear, coherent and democratic approach by developing uninterrupted trust between China and other neighbouring countries. It can solve its internal disputes and discontents with an open, honest, progressive and democratic manner. It needs political resolve that can further strengthen China within and outside its territory. But the Chinese aggressive behaviours diminish China and all its potentials. China is making the same mistakes as Soviet Russia has made, which led to its disintegration. It was a major loss to the working-class people of the world. Similarly, the failures of China will further weaken the working-class politics in the world. In this context, the CCP led China need to take responsibility and initiative for peace and development and transform itself within changing requirements of time.

The organisational, ideological and structural transformation of the CCP, Chinese state and government depends on various factors. These factors are local, regional, national and international. The understandings of these factors are central to the initiation of reform processes. The CCP's dominance and monopoly over Chinese politics and state needs serious reflection by which CCP can accommodate different political, cultural, social and intellectual voices within and outside China. The China is no more solely an agrarian economy. There are different sectors emerged in China during the post 1985 reform period. The Chinese party state need to develop capabilities to engage with different professional classes and negotiate with their requirements. It would be political suicide to ignore the new class formations in China. The CCP, Chinese state and government can manage all these challenges and uncertainties if it engages with it in an open and democratic manner. The Chinese communists have nothing to hide but need to reform the way it functions.

China is a part of the global capitalist production and distribution networks. China is using these networks for its own national interests. But the national interests should not be the only criteria for a communist party state to determine its future course of actions in geopolitics. The national interests are not free from the interests of Chinese people and their Asian neighbours. If the CCP looks at its national interest only, it would be very difficult to sustain the Chinese model of economic growth and development. There is growing local resistance movements against special economic zones, industrial and technological parks due to the perilous working conditions and precarity of Chinese workers. In this way, China faces these uphill tasks and challenges during these uncertain times. The Chinese story can survive if Chinese ruling classes can transform themselves by reflecting on their aggressive, neoliberal governance within the country, and poor public relations management, and bullying behaviour with neighbouring and friendly countries.

The western imperialism is taking advantage of Chinese mistakes. The Washington is on an overdrive to reverse the conditions for a multipolar and democratic world order. The salvo of US imperialism is threatening world peace by reviving its anti-Asian imperialist projects through regional and global anti-China formations. In this age of neo-imperialism, there is no competition among imperial powers for dominance. The collaborations have replaced competition among erstwhile imperialist and colonial powers to defeat Chinese achievements. From the Quad to Democracy (D)-10 are imperialist designs against Asia in general and China in particular. The central idea is to contain and destroy the Chinese model of economic development by fuelling regional wars and conflicts between India and China. It is against the peace and prosperity in Asia. It is against regional and world peace.

From NATO, Quad to D-10 – the troika of imperialism in all its reincarnations follows its old maxim outlined by Hastings Ismay in 1949 – to "keep the Soviet Union out, the Americans in, and the Germans down." In 2020, the maxim is to check the rise of peace and prosperity in Asia by fuelling conflict between Beijing and New Delhi. The conflicts and wars in Asia will accelerate economic growth in America and Europe through accelerated defence trade. The future of bankable state in China depends on maintaining a revolutionary path free from capitalist Westphalian states shaped by military industrial complex.

The capitalist states like UK and USA have abandoned their constitutional responsibilities to protect citizens from the COVID-19 pandemic. The pestilence led lockdown impels to rethink, reflect and reject the Eurocentric ideological narratives of 'Westphalian nation-states'; capitalist in letter and spirit. It is also the time to rewrite the ideological narratives and dominance of theso-called success stories of western states and their universalising tendencies of capitalism as only alternatives. In reality, capitalist states like; USA has not only failed to face the pandemic, the USDA under the Trump administration is making all efforts to strip away nutrition benefits from more than a million Americans who depend completely on food stamps. The United Kingdom under Boris Johnson led conservative government has failed to provide basic safety nets to frontline workers. The government is planning to further weaken the working class by freezing the wages, and removing triple lock system on pensions to fund the debt and cover the deficit due to Coronavirus crisis. This is morally indefensible but Malthusian capitalist state in

UK lacks moral compass. The capitalist states in France, Italy and Spain have also failed to protect their citizens during this pandemic. These Westphalian states were formed to consolidate capitalism during mid seventeenth century but they failed miserably to face the challenges of public health crisis during 2020 Coronavirus pandemic. The failure shows the limits of the capitalist states and fallacies of failed state as a narrative. The countries like China was successful because of its swift, scientific and collective response to the crisis. But this is unacceptable to the advocates of failed state thesis. It is impossible for western capitalist state to acknowledge the rise of China by following a different economic and political path, which can be an alternative with all its limitations and challenges.

The democratic deficit, neoliberal authoritarianism and rise of reactionary right-wing politics is a global phenomenon and China is not insulated from it. Local and national contexts are important in search of alternatives. Therefore, it is imperative for China to sustain and expand its progressive achievement and further develop pluriversal praxis to face challenges of today.

The first step is to dismantle the structures of Westphalian capitalist state system and all its affiliated supranational and international organisations. This is only possible by creating solidarity of all grassroot movements for alternative democracy for peace, environment, development and prosperity as inalienable citizenship rights. It is important to have continuous solidarity of struggles to develop conditions for non-discriminatory and pluriversal and inalienable rights based on progressive and scientific thoughts.

The second step is to develop conditions where local communities can control and manage their local resources based on their needs and desires with egalitarian distributive mechanisms.

The third step is to develop local, national and international struggles against all conflicts, wars and industries affiliated with it including nuclear weapons. Defence industry creates wars to expand its profits.

The fourth one is continuous struggle against all forms of authoritarianism and all forms of discrimination in every sphere of life.

The fifth one is about creating a decentralised, democratic, progressive and egalitarian state where individual rights and right to self-determination is inalienable.